CHICAGO LAWYERS

It is characteristic of a democracy to open wide the gates of a profession to "the average man," and then later to attack the entire profession, a part of which has thus been rendered incompetent and dangerous to the public welfare. Having first insured the utter mediocrity of judges and lawyers, it is only human nature to turn and rend them for not being extraordinary and exceptional.

—ARTHUR CORBIN,
presidential address to the
Association of American Law Schools, 1921

"The Bar" is in this country an almost meaningless conglomeration. What we have is lawyers, by their tens of thousands—individual lawyers without unity of tradition, character, background, or objective; as single persons, many of them powerful; as a guild, inert beyond easy understanding.

—KARL LLEWELLYN,
in *Annals of the American Academy*, 1933

The one generalization that it may be safe to make about lawyers— except, of course, for the statistically incontrovertible one that this country has quite a few more of them than it has any need for—is that the profession includes a large number of serious eaters.

—CALVIN TRILLIN,
in *The New Yorker*, 1977

CHICAGO LAWYERS

The Social Structure of the Bar

REVISED EDITION

JOHN P. HEINZ

AND

EDWARD O. LAUMANN

NORTHWESTERN UNIVERSITY PRESS · EVANSTON, ILLINOIS

AMERICAN BAR FOUNDATION · CHICAGO

Northwestern University Press
Evanston, Illinois 60208-4210

ISBN: 0-8101-1189-6

Library of Congress Cataloging-in-Publication Data

Heinz, John P., 1936–
    Chicago lawyers : the social structure of the bar / by John P.
Heinz and Edward O. Laumann. — Rev. ed.
        p.   cm.
    Includes bibliographical references and index.
    ISBN 0-8101-1189-6 (pbk. : acid-free paper)
    1. Lawyers—Illinois—Chicago—Social conditions. I. Laumann,
Edward O. II. Title.
KF297.H42   1994
340'.115'0977311—dc20   94-21561
                                                                  CIP

The paper used in this publication meets the minimum
requirements of the American National Standard for Information
Sciences—Permanence of Paper for Printed Library Materials,
ANSI Z39.48-1984.

To Anne,

& to Anne,

i.e., 2 (Anne).

Contents

Contents

Contents

List of Tables

List of Figures

List of Figures

Preface to the Revised Edition

Before it was broken apart by the antitrust laws, American Telephone and Telegraph was said to be the largest law firm in the world. That is, it employed more lawyers than any other organization. Even in its reduced form, it now has 433 lawyers, including 50 abroad. This counts only the lawyers who are full-time employees of AT&T—it does not include the very considerable number who work in law firms and are retained to handle cases for the corporation. But AT&T is far from the largest employer of lawyers now. Baker & McKenzie, a law firm headquartered in Chicago, has 1664 lawyers (538 partners and 1126 associates) located in 50 offices worldwide. The State's Attorney in Chicago employs more than 800 lawyers, all in one county. In organizations of that size, it is difficult for individual lawyers to capture much attention. The important decisions about their work are made pursuant to bureaucratic rules, through standardized procedures. The state's attorney himself does not try cases. He is a politician who appears on television, makes some policy decisions, and supervises the administration of the office, more or less. It is the *organization* that practices law.

James S. Coleman has argued that "individuals in society, natural persons, show a general and continual loss of power to corporate actors."[1] That is, organizations are becoming more powerful, individuals less. Though Coleman had in mind a much longer historical frame, we may even be able to perceive such a change in the legal profession. The powerhouse lawyers of the recent past—names such as Lloyd Cutler and Clark Clifford—are becoming anachronisms. Of course, there is never any lack of lawyers who hold public office, but which of them today has the enduring personal influence of a Dean Acheson or a John Foster Dulles? The powerful individual lawyer is now, with rare exceptions, a romantic myth. Most lawyers function as anonymous cogs within various forms of bureaucratic machinery. *People* magazine does not devote much ink to lawyers—unless they are members of the Kennedy family, and then the attention does not focus on the portion of their activities that was intended to be public.

But to say that very few lawyers possess personal power, as individuals, is not to say that they are unimportant in sum. Taken together, they play a very large part in determining the outcomes of some of the decisions that are most consequential. They control the machinery that enforces order, structures economic transactions, finances the government through taxation, transfers real property, dissolves marriages, allocates the custody of children, provides compensation for injuries, and punishes wrongdoers.

The quotation from Karl Llewellyn that appears on the flyleaf asserts that many lawyers are powerful as "single persons," but that their "guilds" (i.e., the bar associations) are "inert beyond easy understanding." This statement was published sixty years ago. While it may still be true that the bar associations are not notably influential, the observation about individual lawyers should be revised: today, it would be more accurate to say that many lawyers are powerful as organizational actors, but that as single persons they are usually fungible.

For quite some time now, commentators have been noting (and usually decrying) the fact that large law firms were in the process of being transformed into "businesses." This must be one of the longer processes on record.[2] The same 1933 article by Karl Llewellyn observed that corporation lawyers tend to develop "a business point of view," even toward the way in which they do their own work.[3] If that was true in 1933, it is true in spades today. In recent years, law firms have greatly accelerated their adoption of business methods: they have expanded into new territories by opening branch offices, they have sought to develop "brand-name" identification, they have displayed their wares to potential clients in presentations that are referred to in the trade as "dog-and-pony shows" or "beauty contests" and have extolled the skills of their lawyers in lavishly illustrated brochures, they have increased the pressure on lawyers to work longer hours (or, at least, to make sure that the clients pay for more hours), and they have adopted compensation schemes that reward lawyers who bring new business into the firm. These last points are sometimes referred to in colorful language: "In this firm, you eat what you kill."

Still, it would be a mistake to overstate the extent to which the practice of law is confined to large organizations. Many lawyers pursue their craft in smaller settings. Nationally, a considerable percentage of all lawyers work without partners, in their own "law offices." (These lawyers are commonly referred to as "solo practitioners.") In 1948, about 61 percent of all lawyers in the United States were in solo practice, but by 1970 this had declined to 37 percent.[4] The percentage of such lawyers is lower in big cities; in the sample of Chicago lawyers analyzed in this book, 21 percent were solo practitioners. Another quarter of these Chicago lawyers practiced in firms with fewer than ten lawyers. A pioneering piece of research by Jerome Carlin documented in detail the social fact that lawyers who practice alone are usually not movers and shakers; indeed, they scramble to make a living.[5] This is also true of most lawyers who work in small firms.

This book seeks to identify the types of lawyers who practice in these different settings. It analyzes the factors that influence whether a distinct kind of lawyer, with particular background and educational characteristics, tends to work in a setting that serves distinct types of clients, rather than in some other setting, serving other clients. Are lawyers' career choices determined by their personal preferences, or is there an identifiable social structure that appears to influence the allocation of lawyers to the various kinds of legal work, based on categorical characteristics of the lawyers? If there is a systematic structure of the bar, what might be the relationship between the nature of that structure and the delivery of legal services to various kinds of potential clients? Are some types of law practice markedly more prestigious than others? If so, what determines the structure of that prestige? Is it the amount of money that the lawyers earn, or the intellectual complexity of the tasks that confront them, or the social characteristics of the clients that they serve?

Historically, the gap between the earnings of the highest paid and the lowest paid practitioners is larger in the legal profession than in any of the other professions.[6] In this regard, at least, doctors are only in second place. In 1990, profits per partner at the 100 largest law firms averaged $424,000.[7] By contrast, starting salary in small law firms in 1986 averaged $23,500.[8] The median starting salary for government lawyers, including public defenders, was $30,000 in 1991; for lawyers in public interest jobs, the median was $25,500.[9] The financial rewards of law practice, then, vary considerably depending upon the nature of one's clientele. *The New Yorker* recently reported that a partner in Cravath, Swaine & Moore, a major Wall Street firm, was making $2,500,000 per year at the time of his death in 1992 at the age of 55.[10]

The boom in the economy during the mid-1980s, coupled with the Reagan administration's distaste for the antitrust laws, fueled an unprecedented spate of buying and selling of corporate enterprises. Fortunes were made quickly as businesses were acquired with money obtained through the sale of speculative, high-interest "junk bonds," and large portions of the assets were then often sold in pieces ("spun off") to get the cash needed to pay off the bonds. Sometimes, no doubt, these consolidations and redistributions actually enhanced business efficiency. They also made many investment bankers, and many lawyers, very rich.

Lawyers who handled these transactions described themselves as "doing deals."[11] The specialized language that was spoken in large law firms during the 1980s has already become a bit quaint. Corporate lawyers in those days talked about "LBOs" (leveraged buy-outs), the "poison pill"[12] (a legal device that protected a corporation against takeovers by making the stock less valuable in the event that the corporation was acquired), and "M and A" work (mergers and acquisitions). (The proper pronunciation of this last term was "M 'n A," as in "Surf 'n Sirloin" or "Burger 'n Suds.") When the recession of the early 1990s ended the rush to buy, as the growth of debt outstripped the growth of the economy, the legal work to which these terms were applied became less plentiful. The M and A departments of large law firms waned, but the bankruptcy and litigation departments waxed.

The principal difference between today's Chicago lawyers and those of the mid-1970s is that there are twice as many of them now. In 1970, the U.S. Census counted 13,400 lawyers in Chicago;[13] in 1992, the official registration list of Illinois lawyers included 34,180 in Cook County,[14] of whom about 5000 worked in the suburbs.[15] The other big difference is that a large number of the new lawyers are women. The recent entry of women into the bar shows up dramatically in the age distribution within the profession. At last count, about 58 percent of the male lawyers in Illinois were less than 45 years old; of the women, 89 percent were.[16] Though women began to enter law schools in substantial numbers in the early 1970s, by 1974–75 those who had entered practice in Chicago still constituted only about four percent of the bar. The 777 randomly selected lawyers who were interviewed in our research included only 30 women. The picture would be much different now. The best estimate is that 23 percent of Illinois lawyers today are women.[17] Nationally, in 1970 only 2.8 percent of the nation's lawyers were women. By 1988, this percentage had more than quintupled—to 16.1 percent—but it was still far from the percentage of women among law school graduates, which was near 40 percent.[18] This considerable change in the gender composition of the bar may well have substantial effects on the career patterns of lawyers generally.

The increase in the size of the bar over the past twenty years has not resulted in a lessening of the bar's social exclusivity, however. The new recruits have come from relatively privileged backgrounds, similar to those of the older lawyers. The women who have entered the legal profession are from the same sorts of upper-middle-class families as are the men. The percentage of racial minorities in the bar has increased modestly, but this is largely attributable to an increase in the percentage of Asians. The percentage of African Americans has increased much more slowly.[19]

It is by no means clear, however, that the women and the minorities have entered the same kinds of practice as have the white males. At the national level, reports indicate that women and some minorities are more likely to take jobs in government or in not-for-profit organizations.[20] But when women enter private practice, they are even more likely than men to go into the largest law firms.[21] Robert Nelson has speculated that women "may find larger, bureaucratic law firms a more congenial environment in some respects." "Larger firms tend to have other women lawyers, and formalized recruitment and evaluation processes may give women a measure of procedural protection."[22] Blacks and Hispanics are more likely to take public interest jobs, but the job choices (or opportunities) of Asians are very similar to those of whites.[23]

The kinds of practice options that are available to lawyers today are somewhat different than they were during the 1970s. Opportunities to enter "public interest" law jobs are probably even more limited now than they were then—few additional such positions were created during the 1980s, in spite of the large number of new lawyers entering the bar, and the existing positions were already filled by lawyers who had graduated from law school in the 1960s or 1970s. In real dollars (i.e., adjusting for inflation), government appropriations for legal services to the poor declined by a third during the 1980s.[24] Thus, not many of the new lawyers could make a living doing such work, even if they were inclined to want to do so. Some small part of the decline in the number of solo practitioners may be attributable to the creation of new franchised law firms, such as Hyatt Legal Services and Jacoby & Myers, which serve the same market. These firms employ lawyers at low wages and provide standardized wills, divorces, and similar services to working-class and lower-middle-class clients recruited largely through television advertising.[25] The firms were made possible by two U.S. Supreme Court decisions in the 1970s that abolished the bar's restrictions on advertising[26] and on fee cutting.[27]

While there have been some changes in the manner of organization of the delivery of legal services, therefore, the principal changes since the 1970s have been changes in scale. The markets for legal services that are provided at a profit have become much larger, and most of the contexts in which lawyers practice have expanded correspondingly.

Although the market for services to individuals grows with the growth of the population, the demand for such services is relatively inelastic. People do not purchase wills or divorces impulsively, and would probably not buy a lot more of them even if they became cheaper.[28] But the market for service to businesses is much more volatile, much more sensitive to variations in the level of business activity, and more subject to changes in the nature of the particular business transactions. When the commercial real estate market declined in the late 1980s and early 1990s, lawyers who specialized in serving real estate developers suffered.

But the general market for business law has grown substantially (more than the market for services to individuals[29]). A part of the reason for this is that the national economy has shifted from manufacturing to services. In 1960, manufacturing provided half of the gross domestic product and services accounted for 38 percent. By 1991, these percentages had reversed (53 percent services, 39 percent manufacturing).[30] Moreover, more of the corporations have become multinational and more of the transactions span national boundaries.[31] Robert Nelson has observed: "As economic exchange shifts from domestic manufacturing to global financial transactions, it increases demand for corporate lawyers. There are more deals to put together."[32]

Some would argue that the American public has become remarkably more litigious in recent years, and indeed that we have experienced a "litigation explosion," but this is a highly controversial proposition, at best. Marc Galanter argues that the conclusions about litigation rates have been based on inadequate data:

The information base was thin and spotty; theories were put forward without serious examination of whether they fit the facts; values and preconceptions were left unarticulated. Portentous pronouncements were made by established dignitaries and published in learned journals. Could one imagine public health specialists or poultry breeders conjuring up epidemics and cures with such cavalier disregard of the incompleteness of the data and the untested nature of the theory?[33]

While we still do not know as much about the legal profession as we should, several important studies have been completed in the years since this book was first published. Three of these grew out of the Chicago research and were written by scholars who worked on this project at one point or another: Terence Halliday's *Beyond Monopoly: Lawyers, State Crises and Professional Empowerment*[34] and Michael Powell's *From Patrician to Professional Elite*[35] are studies of bar associations and the politics of the organized bar more generally. Halliday's work deals with the Chicago Bar Association, and Powell's book is a study of the Association of the Bar of the City of New York. Robert Nelson's *Partners with Power*[36] is a systematic analysis of four large law firms in Chicago and examines the role of the large law firm as a social institution.

Scholars who were not affiliated with our project have also made very significant new contributions. Richard Abel's *American Lawyers*[37] is a comprehensive synthesis of and commentary on the growing literature on that subject. With Philip Lewis, Abel also edited a series of three volumes of comparative scholarship, analyzing the legal professions of several countries.[38] Donald Landon replicated portions of our interview design in a study of Missouri lawyers. His book, *Country Lawyers: The Impact of Context on Professional Practice*[39] compares our Chicago findings to a sample of lawyers from a medium-sized city in Missouri (Springfield) and to lawyers from truly small towns. *Tournament of Lawyers*, by Marc Galanter and Thomas Palay, is an economic analysis of the patterns of growth of the largest law firms.[40] *Lawyers' Ideals/Lawyers' Practices*, edited by Robert Nelson, David Trubek, and Rayman Solomon, is a collection of essays on the struggle between the ideals of professionalism and the demands of commercialism.[41] Each of these books makes an important contribution to our knowledge about the legal profession, and we recommend them to the reader. In addition to the book-length studies mentioned here, much significant new research on lawyers has been published in the scholarly journals in recent years, but that list would go on for several pages.

We argue in this book that the social structure of the Chicago bar in the 1970s was divided into two broad sectors or "hemispheres," one serving individuals and the small businesses owned by individuals, and one serving corporations and other large organizations. Given the rapid and extensive growth in the size of the bar, however, and the great influx of women, we might question whether the structure remains the same today. The patterns of differentiation within the profession may have become more complex, but we doubt that the bar is likely to have become more unified or coherent. Increasing specialization in the practice of law might drive the two sectors farther apart, or it might divide each of them into several smaller clusters. Since the cohesiveness of a social group often depends upon the size and homogeneity of the group, the Chicago bar today may well be even less cohesive than it was in the mid-1970s.

*   *   *

The research on which this book is based was sponsored by the American Bar Foundation and the Russell Sage Foundation, and was supported in part by a grant from the National Science Foundation. The original edition includes four pages of acknowledgments, thanking scores of people who made important contributions to the research and to the preparation of the manuscript. While we are no less grateful to those people today, the publisher of this edition was eager to reduce the length and cost of the book, and thus make it more accessible. We will not repeat the acknowledgments, therefore. In the original edition, we also noted that there was no point in trying to excuse our colleagues from their responsibility for this work. But they seem to have managed to live with it for several years now, and we suppose that they may be able to continue to bear the burden.

Preface to the Original Edition

There is, it is true, a dusty quality about the law. One thinks of dusty law books and even of dusty lawyers. And lawyers often make use of the tactical dust storm, designed to obfuscate. But there is also a modicum of genuine drama in the story of the legal profession. The law, after all, deals with the clash of powerful interests; it is thought to have great impact on social policy and on the course of the economy; it stages battles of courtroom advocates that are spiced with eloquence, humor, surprise, cunning, and, occasionally, intelligence; it features struggles for control of vast wealth; and it poses timeless issues of liberty, life, and death. We are having none of that. If this book succeeds at nothing else, it manages admirably to resist the urge to exploit the drama of the American legal profession. Sociological research on lawyers has not often been so resolute, so unbending.

Many of the social scientists who have studied the bar have, in fact, yielded to the natural fascination of the extreme case. The extreme is likely to be conspicuous, and it often includes a disproportionate share of the profession's inherent drama, which promises to sustain the interest of the scholar who labors on the research and, perhaps (though this is less likely), of the other scholars who are obliged to read it. Even leaving aside such titillating journalistic accounts as *The Superlawyers*, therefore, studies of the legal profession have tended to concentrate on the poles of the profession's prestige hierarchy—on Wall Street lawyers,[1] at the top, or on criminal lawyers,[2] personal injury lawyers,[3] or solo practitioners,[4] at the bottom. The profession's center has not inspired a rich literature, and little information is available on the bar's overall social structure. Jack Ladinsky's study of Detroit lawyers covered all types and specialties, and it contributed substantially to our understanding, but the amount and kinds of data available to Ladinsky were quite limited.[5] Dietrich Rueschemeyer's commentary on lawyers in Germany and in the United States has a broader, comparative viewpoint and includes useful theoretical propositions, but it presents no original data on American lawyers.[6] This study attempts to supply original data by systematically describing and analyzing the social structure of the legal profession in a major city.

Identifying the audience to which the study was to be addressed was difficult, but in the end the choices we made were clear. This book has not been written for lawyers. Lawyers will find that they already know all of this or, to the extent that they do not, that our data are clearly wrong. Lawyers, therefore, read this at their own risk. Neither was this written for sociologists. Why should anyone write for sociologists when sociologists do not write for anyone? And the "educated laity" already has far more reading assignments than it can possibly manage; we could not in good conscience set out to burden it further. Having concluded that it would be either inappropriate, foolhardy, or tiresome to attempt to address any of these potential audiences for the book, we opted for appealing to the one, true audience of all academics—ourselves.

But there remains the question of how we happened to develop such peculiar tastes. Why, with our separate disciplinary training and allegiances, do we not offend each other? In part, of course, we do. But, to a far greater extent, we find that we please one another. This may merely be an example of the genius of the American political instinct— if Heinz expresses enthusiasm for the work of Laumann and Laumann praises the work of Heinz, it feeds both egos and serves their mutual interest in finishing the business. It has been a happy collaboration.

Chapter 1

THE SCOPE AND NATURE

OF THE STUDY

It has been apparent for some time that the simple view of the bar as a single, unified profession no longer fits the facts. First of all, lawyers, of course, are not merely lawyers. They are advisors to businesses and are entrepreneurs themselves; they are politicians, lobbyists, and judges or potential judges; they are real estate and insurance agents, claims adjustors, facilitators of zoning variances, scholars, and rich lie-abouts. But even those roles that are usually thought of as lawyer's work, more narrowly defined, display considerable variety.

The division of labor has proceeded in the law as it has in most other fields of endeavor, and a number of distinct types of lawyers are now clearly identifiable. A form of the old general practitioner survives in small towns and in some city neighborhoods, but these are a minority of the profession—in 1970, about 62 percent of American lawyers lived in cities of over 100,000 population,[1] and relatively few of these city lawyers probably served primarily a neighborhood clientele.[2] In large cities like Chicago, the differences among the several sorts of lawyers are dramatic. The lawyer who commutes to Brussels and Tokyo and who spends his time negotiating the rights to distribute Colonel Sanders throughout the world will have little in common with the lawyer who haunts the corridors of the criminal courts hoping that a bailiff will, in return for a consideration, commend his services to some poor wretch charged with a barroom assault. Both of those private practitioners will differ from the government-employed lawyers who prosecute criminal cases or who practice public international law in the employ of the State Department—as, indeed, the two sorts of government-employed lawyers differ from one another. And all of those types will be distinguishable from the partner of the large law firm who devotes his days to advising corporations on the probable tax consequences of alternative real estate acquisition strategies, who in turn will differ from another sort of tax lawyer, the sort who fills out individual income tax forms as April 15 approaches. Then there are the patent lawyers, many of whom prepared for law school not with the traditional liberal arts, prelaw courses but with training in engineering or some other scientific discipline and who may spend much of their time analyzing mechanical drawings; and the divorce lawyers, who may choose to process their cases quickly or to become family counselors or semiprofessional psychotherapists; and the personal injury plaintiffs' lawyers, who devote their ingenuity to devising dramatic ways of making clear to juries what it means to lose a limb; and the personal injury defense lawyers, who are retained by insurance companies to make the same juries understand that insurance rates will go up if they allow themselves to be overwhelmed by emotion; and the civil rights lawyers, whose long hair flies behind them as they stride into battle for the public good. One could posit a great many legal professions, perhaps dozens, and to some degree there are perceptible distinctions among all of these types of lawyers.

But how significant are these differences? Does the differentiation of the lawyers' roles have important implications for the nature of the profession or for the broader society, or is a lawyer still basically a lawyer, drawing upon a tradition and an arcane body of knowledge shared in common by all or most members of the profession whatever the varying applications of their shared principles and skills to different sorts of problems? Are available professional personnel assigned to particular tasks by idiosyncratic personal predilections and by factors such as proximity, or are lawyers selected for different roles by orderly social processes or by standard criteria that have social meaning and consequences? And what is the significance in sheer quantitative terms of each of these types of legal work? That is, how large are each of these subdivisions of the bar? Are some so small as to be inconsequential in any consideration of the general characteristics of the profession, while the volume of work and the numbers of lawyers engaged in other areas of practice have overwhelming weight in determining the overall social structure of the bar? And are all of these types of work clearly distinct from one another, or does the same lawyer perform several of the roles, doing one sort of work one day or week and another the next? Interesting as the differentiation of lawyers' roles may be, however, those questions are of less consequence than the issue of whether the different roles are organized into some sort of hierarchy reflecting or determining the allocation of status, power, economic rewards, or whatever is valued. The analyses presented in this book, therefore, consider the relationship between the division of labor and the structure of social inequality in the legal profession. Mere social differentiation need not imply social inequality, of course, though it often does.

The question of whether differentiated social positions (in this case, the different lawyers' jobs) get systematically different amounts of what there is to get,[3] and, if so, how and why, has been a matter of primary concern to generations of social theorists. One school, including such scholars as Kingsley Davis, Wilbert Moore,[4] and Talcott Parsons,[5] has emphasized the functional utility of inequality in the maintenance of social systems. Another major school, including theorists such as Ralf Dahrendorf[6] and Karl Marx, has stressed the disintegrative or conflict-producing tendencies of social inequality. Though the explanations of the link between social differentiation and social inequality offered by these two schools differ markedly, we believe that both perspectives are useful and we do not find it necessary to reject the insights of one in order to benefit from the other. We draw upon both schools, for example, in our analyses of the manner in which social differentiation is converted into inequality in the distrubtion of rewards, privileges, and social honor or deference. From the functionalist school we adopt the suggestion that the social values embraced by the members of a community will influence their evaluations of the importance of the various roles of lawyers and that they will thus reward the roles differentially and will come to assign high esteem to some and to hold others in lower regard. If the community member attaches special importance to the protection of individual rights and liberties, such as freedom of speech, he will be likely to evaluate relatively highly the lawyers who are perceived as serving such goals; if he especially values economic enterprise and the production of goods and services, he will hold in regard the lawyers who are thought to advance those ends. But we also use, in our analyses, an alternative or complementary view of the process through which social differentiation is converted into patterned social inequality, a view that derives from the so-called conflict school. Those theorists stress the differences in the amounts of power possessed by the incumbents of the several social roles, and they argue accordingly that these power differences permit some social positions to exact greater rewards for their contributions. Thus, lawyers whose advice is sought by powerful corporation executives and whose decisions therefore have far-reaching ramifications in the society at large might secure more reward for their effort than would lawyers who advise the poor and dispossessed.

The first objective of this book, then, is to analyze the nature and extent of social differentiation among Chicago lawyers and to attempt to identify its generative mechanisms. The second is to evaluate the means by which this differentiation is converted into inequality in the distribution within the legal profession of income, organizational resources, access to leadership positions, and honor or deference.

The third and final large theme of the book is an examination of the kinds and degree of social bonds among the various sorts of Chicago lawyers. That is, given the differentiation and inequality within the bar, does the legal profession constitute a true community of common fate or collective goals, or does it consist merely of a disaggregated array of individuals and activities? Does the bar possess mechanisms for achieving social integration of the profession or for sustaining an overarching consciousness of kind among lawyers in spite of their differentiation and inequalities, or do the different types of lawyers live separate lives, seldom coming into contact and adopting conflicting stances on matters of public policy affecting the profession, on basic social values, or on issues of professional ethics? Do the patterns of association among lawyers follow the lines of some intraprofessional logic, or do they correspond to categories that have salience in the broader social world—for example, categories such as political affiliation or ethnoreligious identification? That is, is the bar (or even some portion of it) a primary reference group for most lawyers, or do they seek and find their principal identities in extraprofessional roles? Are common positions on basic social and political issues (especially those that are of particular relevance to the law) widely shared throughout the profession? Does the organized bar speak for all or most members of the profession? Do political activities or other sorts of community work serve as a meeting ground for lawyers and thus as a means of integrating the profession, or do they merely provide competing foci, alternative and conflicting causes that serve to divide the profession?

If systematic strata exist within the profession, to what extent do individual lawyers manage to transcend those barriers? These issues of collective identity and of the social bases of joint activity are exceedingly complex, and it is very difficult to marshall evidence that addresses them directly.[7] Nonetheless, we believe that we have some evidence to offer on these points.

In analyzing the nature of interpersonal association and the structure of joint political activity within the Chicago bar, we use techniques that had been previously employed in community power studies to analyze the roles of various sorts of elites and several cities and towns.[8] Thus, in a sense, we conceive of Chicago lawyers as a community[9] with its own set of elites and its own criteria for inclusion in such categories, its own lines of cleavage that define constituencies, its mechanisms of social integration, and its sets of divisive issues and of personal loyalties and enmities that will tend to produce dissensus. To say that it is treated as a community does not, therefore, imply that the bar is monolithic any more than students of the power structure of cities assume that those communities are undifferentiated, but it does imply that there is some discernible boundary between that set of social actors and others surrounding them in their environment. We are not prepared to offer evidence that there is any such boundary. Indeed, we regard the point as problematic. The assumption of the existence of a community is merely that—an assumption that provides a starting point for the research but that may, itself, be drawn into question by the findings.

In all, we aim to provide a reasonably comprehensive analysis of the social structure of Chicago's bar and, insofar as possible, of the processes that determine that structure.

The Data Set

The data presented in the book are drawn from personal interviews with 777 Chicago lawyers, randomly selected from among the full range and variety of the city bar. The information gathered includes the nature of the respondents' legal practice and clients, their personal background characteristics, their attitudes on major political and legal issues, and their memberships and participation in various professional, civic, and social organizations. The interviews were conducted in the spring and summer of 1975 by our own staff, averaged sixty-six minutes in length, and were almost always conducted at the respondent's place of work during business hours.

The population universe included all lawyers with office addresses within the city limits of Chicago, as listed in either *Sullivan's Law Directory for the State of Illinois, 1974–75,* or *Martindale-Hubbell Law Directory, 1974.* We used two directories to increase the coverage and to avoid biases of individual directories. (This procedure would not, of course, eliminate biases that the directories may share.) We then drew a true random sample from these lists.[10] Our 777 completed interviews represent 82.1 percent of our original target sample. Only 8.4 percent of our potential respondents explicitly refused to grant an interview; we missed the remaining 9.5 percent because of scheduling problems, time constraints, the subject's illness, and the like. An examination of the known characteristics of those lawyers we failed to include, for whatever reasons, suggests that we may slightly underenumerate lawyers who are not members of the Chicago Bar Association and lawyers engaged in solo practice, especially those who maintain only accommodation addresses in the city.[11] This underenumeration, however, is small enough that for most purposes we can treat the completed sample as representative of the defined population.[12] We turn, then, to a presentation of some of the basic characteristics of that sample.

Some Characteristics of Chicago Lawyers

Figure 1.1 is a presentation of the frequencies with which certain characteristics occurred in our sample of Chicago lawyers. For those who prefer words to pictures, however, we will summarize these distributions briefly, noting features that require explanation or warrant emphasis.

The lawyers in our sample are overwhelmingly white and male. The respondents include 747 whites (97.1 percent of the sample), 21 African Americans (2.7 percent), and 1 Asian American (0.1 percent).[13] (All percentages given have been adjusted to exclude the instances of missing information. Because of rounding error, however, the percentages for the individual categories do not always total exactly 100 percent.) Note that this random slice of the bar includes no Hispanics and no Native Americans. Only 30 respondents, or 3.9 percent of the sample, are women. The number of women enrolled in law schools had increased dramatically in the few years preceding our survey,[14] but that recent trend had not then been in progress long enough to have much impact on the traditional male dominance of the Chicago bar. Another of the heralded changes in legal education in the decade before the survey was the increased effort at many law schools to recruit students from minority groups,[15] but our findings indicate that the rise of affirmative action also had not had much effect on the racial composition of the bar. Though both the women and the blacks in our sample tend to be somewhat younger than the average respondent, suggesting that both of the developments were beginning to be felt, we do not have sufficient numbers of either to have much confidence in our estimates of the characteristics of those groups in the general population of Chicago lawyers.

Roughly equal numbers of our respondents—just more or just less than 30 percent—fall into each of three age ranges: under 35, 35 to 45, and 46 to 65. Fewer than 10 percent of the lawyers were over 65.

We asked our respondents for two different political affiliations, local and national, because the Democratic party in Chicago was then divided into rather distinct factions. At the time of our survey, Mayor Richard J. Daley was still alive. Often referred to as the last of the old-style city political bosses, Daley was also chairman of the Cook County Democratic Central Committee. Respondents who told us that they were "Regular Democrats," in local terms, can be assumed to have been more or less loyal to Mayor Daley's political organization, customarily referred to as the "Regular Democratic Organization."[16] The term "Independent Democrats" refers to an even looser conglomeration that was generally more liberal and reformist. It was a coalition of these independent Democrats, sympathetic to the presidential candidacy of Senator George McGovern, that unseated the Daley delegation to the 1972 Democratic National Convention. Of those who are "independents" with respect to Chicago political preference, 72 percent also labeled themselves "independent" with respect to their national preference. The respondents in the "not applicable" category under "Chicago political preference" prefer the Republican party nationally in disproportionate numbers. Most of these respondents live in the suburbs (though they have offices in the city) and probably declined to express a Chicago political preference because of their lack of concern with or involvement in Chicago politics. It is interesting to note that a profession that is often thought to be conservative and establishmentarian includes so few Republicans and so many independent Democrats (in local terms) or independents (in national terms). These results may be attributable to the fact that our survey was conducted not long after the Watergate revelations, within a year of the resignation of President Nixon. They may also reflect the generally debilitated state of the Republican party within the city of Chicago.

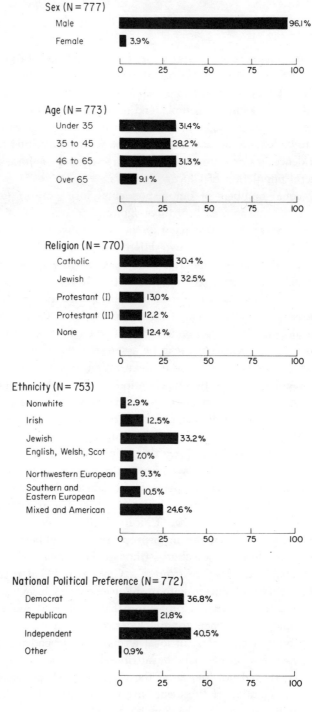

FIGURE 1.1
Selected Characteristics of Chicago Lawyers

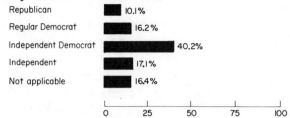

Chicago Political Preference (N = 773)

Republican	10.1%
Regular Democrat	16.2%
Independent Democrat	40.2%
Independent	17.1%
Not applicable	16.4%

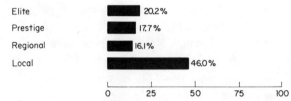

Law School (N = 768)

Elite	20.2%
Prestige	17.7%
Regional	16.1%
Local	46.0%

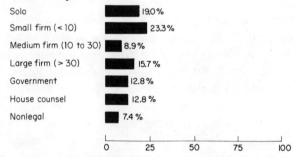

Practice Setting (N = 772)

Solo	19.0%
Small firm (< 10)	23.3%
Medium firm (10 to 30)	8.9%
Large firm (> 30)	15.7%
Government	12.8%
House counsel	12.8%
Nonlegal	7.4%

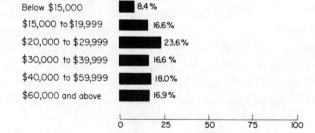

Law Practice Income (N = 724)

Below $15,000	8.4%
$15,000 to $19,999	16.6%
$20,000 to $29,999	23.6%
$30,000 to $39,999	16.6%
$40,000 to $59,999	18.0%
$60,000 and above	16.9%

Our respondents were asked a series of questions about their religious and ethnic identifications. Those who said they were Jewish, in response to either set of questions, are included in that category under both the "religion" and the "ethnicity" headings in figure 1.1. That is, ethnic Jews have been included in the Jewish religion category, and vice versa.[17] The Protestant denominations have been divided into two groups that are often distinguished in the sociological literature.[18] The denominations in the first group (type I) tend to include disproportionate numbers of persons of higher socioeconomic status, from older immigrant stock— most numerous in this category are Presbyterians, Episcopalians, and Congregationalists.[19] The largest number in the second group (type II) are Lutherans, Methodists, Baptists, and Protestants who did not express any denominational preference. Respondents included in the final line of the "ethnicity" category are those who were of mixed national origin, being unable to choose any nationality as predominant in their ancestry, or who told us that they were "just American."

We found that nearly half of our sample of Chicago lawyers had attended one of four local law schools—Chicago Kent, DePaul, Loyola, and John Marshall—located in the central city. Other law schools are grouped here in categories that are intended to reflect general repute or prestige. Though all such categorizations are to some extent arbitrary, and though all are also certain to be distasteful to some, it is necessary to combine the schools for purposes of analysis because of the small numbers of respondents attending most of the schools. We believe that our categories reflect the general standing of the schools at least as well as any alternative scheme. Only six schools are included in our "elite" category: Chicago, Columbia, Harvard, Michigan, Stanford, and Yale. These six schools ranked at the top of the ratings by law school deans reported by Peter Blau and Rebecca Margulies in 1974–75.[20] The lowest ranking of these schools, Stanford, was rated as among the top five law schools in the country by 45 of the 104 deans responding to the survey; the next highest school received only 19 such ratings. Though other ratings of law schools have appeared since the Blau and Margulies report, they are quite consistent with the use of these categories.[21] The largest number of graduates of these elite schools in our sample are from the University of Chicago and, next, Harvard. Among the schools included in our "prestige" category, graduates of Northwestern are by far the most numerous, while the University of Illinois predominates in the regional grouping. Other schools represented in the prestige category are Georgetown, Wisconsin, and Virginia, together with one graduate of the University of Pennsylvania and one from New York University. The "regional" category includes the remaining law schools of the Big Ten Conference universities and those of Notre Dame and George Washington.[22]

The distribution of our respondents across the various practice settings, which is only one of many possible ways to categorize general types of law practice, reflects the long-term reduction in the proportion of solo practitioners among the bar and the continuing growth in the numbers of both corporate house counsel and government-employed lawyers.[23] These phenomena—the decline of the individual, general practitioner who serves a variety of clients, and the great increase in the full-time employment of lawyers by a single client, usually either a corporation or a government agency—are probably the most significant changes in the nature of law practice in this century.[24] Many of the lawyers who would formerly have gone into solo practice undoubtedly contribute to the size of the small firm category here. And, though our findings reflect the often-remarked growth during the twentieth century of large law firms,[25] It is important to note that only about a sixth of all Chicago lawyers worked in firms with more than thirty practitioners. The respondents in the "nonlegal" category were not presently engaged in the practice of law on a regular basis.[26]

Finally, we asked all of our respondents to indicate the amount of the income that they received from law practice. As might be expected, a larger number of our respondents refused to answer that question than any other in the interview. Of the 777 lawyers interviewed, 724 did respond, but we have no way of assessing whether there is systematic bias in the failure to respond and few ways of evaluating the validity or truthfulness of the answers that we received. Some may have exaggerated their incomes as a form of boasting, while others may have understated theirs through modesty or from fear of the Internal Revenue Service. (Though our interviewers did not much resemble IRS agents, some respondents might have thought it desirable for their responses to be consistent with their tax returns.) And we cannot be certain that either possible bias in their answers is not systematically related to other variables in the respondents' background or practice characteristics. Therefore, we report these findings with more than the usual degree of caution. Nonetheless, our findings appear to be generally consistent with such other data as are available on lawyers' incomes.[27] That more than half of our respondents reported income from law practice alone of $30,000 or more per year indicates that the lawyers were earning far more than the average Chicagoan in 1975.[28]

The Profession: Context

The social differentiation within the bar that this book seeks to analyze has occurred despite official endorsement of a holistic conception of the profession. Unlike the medical profession, which formally recognizes and certifies many specialties, the legal profession embraces the myth of the omnicompetent practitioner. Until recently, the profession's ethical rules forbade lawyers to represent themselves as specialists except in three small, abstruse fields: patents, trademarks, and admiralty.[29] In the last decade or two, some states have begun to certify legal specialists in a few fields, but these initial steps in the formal recognition of specialization have been halting and tentative, being formally labeled "experimental."[30] Illinois still has not adopted any scheme of specialty certification.[31] Moreover, certain legal institutions buttress the resistance to specialization. The bar examinations, for example, require some minimal level of competence in all of the major, traditional fields of law as a condition of entry into the profession. And yet, in spite of the continuing vitality of the myth of omnicompetence, the inexorable advance of the division of labor within the legal profession has been too obvious to ignore. More than sixty years ago, Karl Llewellyn said of the "modern metropolitan bar": "Most of its best brains, most of its inevitable leaders, have moved masswise out of court work, out of a general practice akin to that of the family doctor, into highly paid specialization in the service of large corporations."[32] While specialization was occurring at the individual level, however, a process of integration was taking place in the organizational contexts within which the law is practiced. Industrialization, the rise of large corporations, and the consequent growth of government regulation of economic enterprise have for at least a century steadily increased the consolidation of law practice into larger and larger firms. Though two-thirds of the lawyers in private practice at the end of World War II were individual entrepreneurs, or solo practitioners, the solos had declined to half of the private practitioners by 1970, and the trend was even more pronounced in large cities.[33] Moreover, the number of private practitioners of all sorts, including lawyers in firms, declined from 89 percent of the bar in 1940 to 73 percent in 1970 as a result of large increases in the numbers of salaried lawyers employed by corporations as "house counsel" or by the various levels of government.[34] There is reason to believe that these trends have continued since 1970 (see figure 1.1).

These developments have taken place in the context of a rapid increase in the overall size of the profession. In recent decades the estimated number of lawyers in the nation has increased steadily; there were about 220,000 in 1951, 285,000 in 1960, 355,000 in 1970, well in excess of 400,000 in 1975, and in 1980 the estimate was slightly more or slightly fewer than 500,000 American lawyers.[35] Though the population of the country also grew during this period, the number of Americans per lawyer declined from 696 persons per lawyer in 1951 to 572 per lawyer in 1970, and 440 in 1979.[36] In 1970, there were about 14,000 lawyers with offices in the city of Chicago, the population analyzed in this book.[37] Though it is very difficult and perhaps misleading to compare numbers of lawyers across national boundaries because of great differences in the roles included within the category "lawyers," as well as because of imprecision in the collection of such data, the best estimates are that in the mid-1970s the number of lawyers per unit of population in the United States was twice that of Canada and England, about seven times that of France and the Netherlands, and about fourteen times that of Japan.[38]

The expansion of the legal profession in the United States and the simultaneous decline of the solo practitioner has meant that the social roles of lawyers have also changed. C. Wright Mills's characterization of the nineteenth-century advocate may be compared to what we know about the modern urban lawyer:

> Before the ascendancy of the large corporation, skill and eloquence in advocacy selected nineteenth-century leaders of the bar; reputations and wealth were created and maintained in the courts, of which the lawyer was an officer. He was an agent of the law, handling the general interests of society, as fixed and allowed in the law; his day's tasks were as varied as human activity and experience itself. An opinion leader, a man whose recommendations to the community counted, who handled obligations and rights of intimate family and life problems, the liberty and property of all who had them, the lawyer personally pointed out the course of the law and counseled his client against the pitfalls of illegality. Deferred to by his client, he carefully displayed the dignity he claimed to embody. Rewarded for apparent honesty, carrying an ethical halo, held to be fit material for high statesmanship, the lawyer upheld public service and was professionally above business motives.[39]

Though Mills's picture is probably exaggerated or idealized, it does seem likely that the prespecialized lawyer dealt with a greater range of human problems—all of the problems, save those of health and of the soul, that were of greatest consequence to the individual. They dealt with, in Mills's phrase, "the liberty and property of all who had them." The modern lawyer, by contrast, encounters a smaller range of problems, and those are unlikely to be the intimate problems of an individual or a family. Apart from financial woes, relatively few lawyers now confront human suffering in the course of their work. While it is hard to believe that the nineteenth-century bar can have been so pure (or, indeed, so "professional") it is plausible that the modern, specialized lawyer may be less involved with the community than was the old general practitioner. In part, this may simply be a concomitant of urbanization, a difference between the ethos of the big city and of the small town. But the same result might also follow from the process of specialization. From whichever cause, then, and notwithstanding the obvious continuing prominence of lawyers in politics,[40] the urban lawyer is now probably more likely to be a technician and less likely to be the gentleman advocate who maintains both professional and social distance from the client, less likely to play the role of the sage, quasi-judicial figure who personally resolves disputes within families, within church congregations, or between the Lions and the Elks. In spite of this change in the social roles of most lawyers, however, we believe that the roles of modern, specialized lawyers remain important.

Talcott Parsons and some generally like-minded theorists, including Joseph Ben-David and William J. Goode, have argued that the growth of the professions is one of the most salient features of modern industrial societies.[41] In the introduction to his final book, a retrospective on over forty years of scholarly work, Parsons commented:

> [T]he penetration of the professional complex beyond the more academic parts of the university into many branches of the organization of society . . . may be regarded as an important aspect of a principal structural change in modern society. . . . The central process has been the emergence of . . . the "cognitive complex" into a new position of structural salience in Western societies, in part superseding the previous position of the economy. For this reason (among others) a predominantly economic interpretation of the course of development of modern societies is unacceptable to me.[42]

The occupations included by these theorists within the "professions" were lines of work that emphasized involvement with the "cognitive complex"—that is, in a sense, the emphasis was on the "learned" in the term "learned profession." The professions thus were seen as rising to prominence naturally or almost inevitably because they were functional to the needs of complex, urbanized, modern societies.

Though even the scholars who are counted as adherents of this functionalist view of the professions differ on the specific list of attributes that are said to distinguish the professions from other occupations, most would agree on the primacy of the professional's possession of a body of arcane knowledge, acquired only after an extended period of specialized training, and they also tend to agree on other general characteristics of the professions, including some or all of the following: professionals enjoy an unusual degree of independence or autonomy vis-à-vis their clients in work decisions (this autonomy is said to occur because the knowledge professionals possess is not shared by the clients); professionals are generally accorded elevated social standing or prestige, and tend to be compensated accordingly; the professions manifest devotion to public service rather than to narrow self-interest; and, associated with this emphasis on duty, the professions inculcate in their members special standards of ethical conduct, which are far more specific and exacting than are the common norms of the society.

There is, however, an opposing view. The lines of division of opinion correspond generally to the split between the functionalist and the conflict schools of thought, to which we have already referred. The functionalists believe that it is possible to identify sets of characteristics that distinguish the professions from other occupations—the characteristics that serve their functions. The conflict or "power" theorists, on the other hand, contend that no set of traits that account for the social standing of the professions has been or can be defined. This view has been succinctly put by Magali Larson in her influential book, *The Rise of Professionalism:*

> [T]he professional phenomenon does not have clear boundaries. Either its dimensions are devoid of a clear empirical referent, or its attributes are so concrete that occupational groups trying to upgrade their status can copy them with relative ease. For instance, it is often emphasized that professional training must be prolonged, specialized, and have a theoretical base. Yet, as Eliot Freidson ironically points out, it is never stated *how* long; *how* theoretical, or *how* specialized training must be in order to qualify, since all formal training "takes some time," is "somewhat specialized," and involves some attempt at generalization. The service orientation is even more problematic: it is, undoubtedly, part of the ideology and one of the prescriptive norms which organized professions explicitly avow. Yet the implicit assumption that the behavior of individual professionals is more ethical, as a norm, than that

of individuals in lesser occupations has seldom, if ever, been tested by empirical evidence. . . .

The most common ideal-type of profession combines heterogeneous elements and links them by implicit though untested propositions such as the proposition that prestige and autonomy flow "naturally" from the cognitive and normative bases of professional work.[43]

The conflict theorists thus argue that the status of an occupation as a profession is not determined by its possession of some identifiable set of objective characteristics but rather that such status is politically determined—that the claim of professional status is a claim of entitlement to legitimacy or a form of power, asserted by many occupational groups with more or less success depending upon the extent to which they can mobilize various sorts of resources.

Quite apart from the obvious divergence in ideological preconceptions, some of the difference in these two perspectives may be accounted for by methodological style. The vantage point of the functionalists is typically quite remote from workaday professional practice, stressing instead the macrostructural features of the society, very abstractly conceived, and focusing on the sweep of major institutional changes over lengthy historical periods. Detail is obviously lost at such a distance. The conflict view has more often arisen in the context of close-up studies of rank-and-file practitioners making their daily livings. This approach was originally identified with the fieldwork of the "Chicago School" of sociology, particularly with the work of Everett Hughes[44] and his students, including Eliot Freidson[45] and Jerome Carlin.[46] Carlin's classic book, *Lawyers on Their Own*, which is based on interviews with Chicago solo practitioners, gives the flavor of the daily scramble to hustle clients and to make ends meet, and it notes the conflict between these lawyers and the more prestigious practitioners in the large corporate law firms who were seen as dominating the organized bar. Questioning the self-satisfied pretentions of the elite and instead adopting the viewpoint of lowly "outsiders" is a hallmark of the Chicago School's approach to the study of the occupations of urban America. More recently, the conflict-oriented writings on the legal profession have adopted an explicitly Marxian approach.[47]

Works that attempt some theoretical synthesis or historical analysis of the nature of the legal profession have in fact been more numerous than have efforts to collect primary data on the social organization of the bar.[48] With the exception of Ladinsky's pioneering work on social stratification among Detroit lawyers[49] and Carlin's Chicago study, most of the primary research on the bar in the last two or three decades has focused either on a specific problem or policy area or on lawyers in a limited type of practice. Among the former, noteworthy examples include Carlin's subsequent research on the ethical conduct of New York private practitioners,[50] Douglas Rosenthal's work on the relationship between lawyer and client,[51] Stewart Macaulay's study of lawyers' handling of consumer law matters in Wisconsin,[52] Richard Watson and Rondal Downing's book on the roles of Missouri lawyers in judicial selection,[53] and Frances Zemans and Victor Rosenblum's work on legal education.[54] Among the studies of lawyers in particular specialties, we would note Erwin Smigel's early and excellent study, *The Wall Street Lawyer*,[55] Hubert O'Gorman's work on divorce lawyers,[56] Arthur Wood's book on criminal lawyers,[57] and the national survey of legal services lawyers conducted by a group of scholars at the University of Wisconsin.[58] Valuable as all of these major pieces of research are for what they tell us about their specific areas of concern, they give us only an incomplete picture of the overall social structure of the legal profession in any geographic area. This book attempts to provide some of the missing detail for one major city and to fill in some of the gaps in the analysis.

Is Chicago Typical?

The importance of ethnicity in our analyses of Chicago lawyers could reflect general characteristics of the legal profession, at least as the bar is constituted in large cities, or it could be peculiar to Chicago. In his classic essay on Chicago's social system, A. J. Liebling, the Henry Mayhew of American urban sociology, commented on the city's ethnic segregation:

> Communication between the residents of the different wards is further limited by the pronounced tendency of immigrant groups in Chicago to coagulate geographically. In Chicago, a man known as a Pole or Norwegian may not have been in Poland or Norway, or of parents born there. If even only his grandparents were so born, he refers to himself as a Pole or a Norwegian if he wants to sell coffins or groceries or life insurance to others like himself. A national identification is absolutely essential if he wishes to enter politics. A Chicago party ticket is an international patchwork, like Europe after the Treaty of Versailles. Most of the members of the Chicago national blocs, however, think of Europe as it was cut up by the Congress of Vienna. The

great waves of immigration that carried them or their forefathers to their jobs in this country ended with the beginning of the first World War. . . . The national blocs are as entirely cut off from Europe as they are from the rest of America—or from the next ward. And the division between the Negro wards and the white is even more drastic.[59]

On the other hand, much the same was true of other large American cities in the early 1950s, when Liebling's ethnography was published.[60] The salience of religious background in the patterns of stratification among Detroit and New York lawyers, documented by Ladinsky[61] and Carlin,[62] respectively, are generally consistent with our own observations. If we were to replicate our study in other major American cities that vary along a social stability dimension—with, perhaps, Boston, Philadelphia, Baltimore, and St. Louis near one end of the continuum and Houston, Phoenix, Atlanta, and Los Angeles closer to the other— we would expect to find that Chicago lies somewhere between the extremes, particulary with respect to the rigidity of its patterns of social stratification. But that research has not been done.

Until replications have been completed in other cities, we will not be sure of the extent to which Chicago lawyers are typical. We believe, however, that Chicago is an important and interesting case in its own right, and we know of no reason to believe that its bar is unrepresentative in fundamental ways of those in other large American cities with diversified economies.

Chapter 2

THE ORGANIZATION OF

LAWYERS' WORK

Studies of the legal profession have customarily used the individual practitioner as the unit of analysis. This is true both of the analyses of cross-sectional survey information[1] and of the accounts of lawyers at work, whether in large law firms, divorce courts, or solo practice.[2] What could be more natural or commonsensical than to encapsulate lawyers as identifiable persons with interesting biographies? But the assumption that the individual is the proper unit of analysis may lead us to neglect the import of a hard-won sociological insight—that it is not persons as totalities but persons in roles, engaged in regular transactions with other persons performing related social roles, who are the constitutive elements of a social system.[3]

In complex societies, people occupy many social positions simultaneously. If we are to understand the confusing and fluid social reality, rarely demarcated with unambiguous natural markers dividing one field of social activity from another, we must seek to identify those aspects of an actor's social behavior that define membership in a particular social system. This analytic delineation, indicating where one social role ends and another begins, must ultimately be arbitrary, however, both as a theoretical and as an empirical or practical matter. There has long been debate, for example, over the "proper" roles, responsibilities, and privileges of the lawyer with regard to clients, fellow lawyers, the public, and the courts.[4] Even with the relative crystallization in recent decades of the rules of entry into the bar, requiring specialized training and examinations, ambiguities remain about when a person is functioning as a lawyer, as a business or marital advisor, or as a concerned citizen. The lawyer's role is still the product of an ill-defined process of social and self-labeling.

The several lawyers' roles require quite different skills. Many of them require mastery of esoteric or arcane legal knowledge, but others have little to do with formal legal training. Some can be distinguished from other occupational roles—such as real estate agents, bankers, or tax accountants—only with great difficulty, if at all. One of our key conceptual and empirical tasks, then, is to define the nature of these diverse work tasks in a manner that captures the various roles of lawyers. These role positions, and not the individuals who perform them, will be the unit of analysis in the discussion to follow. Since no description of these positions can hope to pay attention to every detail, the identification of the set of roles is a crucial step of empirical abstraction.

Analysis of the social structure of the profession presupposes some description of the extent to which groups of lawyers differ in the tasks they perform, in the functions they serve, in the values they hold, or in other social characteristics. Insofar as they differ in work they perform as a part of what is socially labeled as their professional activity, we may say that they occupy distinct legal roles. The categories of lawyers' work employed in our analysis were, therefore, intended to be a set of these distinct roles, but until we had collected our data we did not know which fields of law were, in fact, socially distinct. Our approach to this dilemma was to begin with categories that consisted of commonly used labels for types of legal work—that is, we accepted for test and examination a set of preexisting, socially defined categories. One goal of our research, then, was to determine the extent to which these categories that are in common use describe roles that are, in fact, distinct. If our analysis should disclose that the social characteristics of two or more fields are substantially identical, we would conclude that, for our purposes, these categories collapse into one, more general role.

Many of the recognized fields of law correspond to bodies of doctrine that are generally regarded as distinct legal subjects and are taught as separate courses in law school—for example, crimes, real estate, commercial transactions, personal injury, tax, labor, corporations, antitrust, and securities. But the practicing bar commonly distinguishes between two sides of many of these doctrinal areas, sides that serve adverse clients—for example, criminal defense versus prosecution, personal injury plaintiff's work versus personal injury defense, and labor law on the union side versus the management side. Other fields divide into parts that, though not necessarily adverse, are nonetheless distinct. Corporate tax planning differs from personal income tax work, real estate development work from home mortgage preparation and title searching, and corporate litigation from a general trial practice that may encompass bits of divorce, commercial, personal injury, or even criminal work. As these examples make clear, lawyers think in terms of categories of work that distinguish, within broader doctrinal areas, fields or subfields defined by the types of clients served.[5]

Thus, the boundaries among the fields of law are not the products of pure intellectual invention. Admiralty and labor law were not created as distinct fields by ratiocination alone. The dividing lines are defined by the needs of types of clients—by the existence of actors who have been subjected to legal regulation or who make or defend claims cognizable at law. The categories of actors dealt with by the various fields of law are, of course, overlapping, and they differ in size or inclusiveness. The criminal law, for example, is addressed to the whole society (in form, at least), while other fields are directed toward much more narrowly defined groups such as the shipowners and charterers who are subject to the admiralty law. Specialized courts or regulatory agencies may be created to deal with these more narrow fields, regulating a strictly delimited constituency—the Federal Communications Commission to regulate broadcasters, for example—and these narrow specialties may then be practiced in a particular institutional setting almost exclusively.

A first step in our analysis, therefore, is to ascertain the extent to which the operational definitions of the customary categories of legal work—which may themselves influence the structure of the profession— are determined by corresponding categories of client types rather than by doctrinal categories or other systematic theory.

The Fields of Law

The allocation among lawyers of the various sorts of tasks that the profession is called upon to perform is an important determinant of the other patterns of social differentiation within the profession and thus of its degree of social integration. In this chapter we analyze three interrelated characteristics of the fields of law. The first deals with the amount, or volume, of effort devoted to each of the fields. What are the relative amounts of lawyers' effort—the work that lawyers do as lawyers—expended in the various fields of law? To answer this question will require us to allocate the effort exhaustively across the fields, which will not be easy. The fields surely differ greatly, however, in the volume of attention they receive from lawyers considered either collectively or as individual practitioners. Some fields, such as eminent domain and admiralty, are relatively small; there is simply little demand for those services. Other fields, such as real estate or tax, command some of the attention of large numbers of lawyers but occupy only a small fraction of their practitioners full-time. Yet other fields, such as patents, have modest numbers of practitioners but command the more or less exclusive attention of many of them. To compute the relative amounts of effort devoted to the fields, therefore, we will need to take into account both the numbers of their practitioners and the varying degrees of exclusivity with which they are practiced.[6]

The second issue to be analyzed is the exclusivity itself—the extent to which the fields differ systematically in the proportions of work time that their practitioners devote to them. The subject matter and technical procedures of patents or labor union work may be so lacking in generalizability or so time-consuming to master that part-timers will be at a severe competitive disadvantage. By contrast, the fundamental doctrines of fields such as real estate will have been acquired by most lawyers in the course of their law school training, and, thus, clients may believe that the work can be done by nearly all lawyers. The latter fields will be dominated by generalists, the former by specialists.[7]

The third characteristic of the organizaton of the fields that we wish to assess is the varying interdependencies among them. Most lawyers are active in at least two fields. Thus, we want to direct attention to the various subgroupings of the fields according to the likelihood of their co-practice by the same persons. Lawyers doing probate work, for example, are likely to do some real estate or personal tax work as well, but they are much less likely to do securities or antitrust work. Conversely, lawyers doing antitrust defense work are more likely to be active in other corporate fields than in fields that serve individuals. Because fields that share many of their personnel are also likely to share work tasks, clientele, and practice contexts, examining the patterns of co-practice may provide insight into the social organization of the legal profession as a whole. In particular, we may identify the major "faults," or cleavage lines, in the profession. These cleavages occur where few, if any, practitioners are found who do work in fields located on opposite sides of the line. The explanation of why these cleavages occur where they do is one of the principal objectives of our analysis.

The first item in our survey presented the respondents with a list of thirty fields of legal work. One of the sources consulted in compiling this list was Carlin's study of solo practitioners in Chicago,[8] which used a list of fourteen specialties. Though some of our categories are identical to Carlin's, many are more narrowly defined, and we added some fields that have emerged only recently (e.g., environmental law).[9] The respondents in the survey were then asked to indicate the percentage of their professional time they devoted to each of the thirty types of work during the past twelve months—less than 5 percent, 5 to 25 percent, 25 to 50 percent, or more than 50 percent.[10] The answers to this question were used to identify the practitoners in each of the various fields. Respondents who reported spending less than 5 percent of their time in a field were not regarded as active in the field. Since there was, unavoidably, some overlap among the categories of work, there is certainly some degree of imprecision in the manner in which our respondents classified their tasks. The defense of a person charged with a crime, for example, might in some cases be classified as "civil liberties" work just as plausibly as "criminal defense."[11] Such imprecision should tend to diminish the clarity of our findings. The findings are, nevertheless, striking.

Distribution of Lawyers' Effort among the Fields of Law

Table 2.1 indicates the total number of practitioners who spent at least 5 percent of their professional time in each of the fields and an *estimate* of the percentage of total legal effort expended by Chicago's metropolitan bar in each of the fields. We have divided the fields into two broad categories, corporate versus personal and small business. These categories are further subdivided into clusters of fields that disproportionately share practitioners, as we demonstrate below when we discuss the interdependencies among fields. While there is nothing especially problematic about the numbers of practitioners, our estimates of legal effort are considerably more conjectural; they rest on assumptions about the data

TABLE 2.1

Number of Practitioners and Estimated Percentage of Total Effort
Expended in Various Fields of Law by Chicago Lawyers

Fields of Law	Cluster N	Number of Practitioners in Field[a]	Estimated Percentage of Total Legal Effort[b]
A. Corporate client sector		541	53
1. Large corporate	242		
Antitrust (defense)		47	2
Business litigation		56	3
Business real estate		80	4
Business tax		51	3
Labor (management)		39	2
Securities		53	2
Cluster total			16
2. Regulatory	110		
Labor (unions)		18	1
Patents		45	4
Public utilities and administrative		52	4
Cluster total			9
3. General corporate	396		
Antitrust (plaintiffs)		24	1
Banking		60	3
Commercial (including consumer)		102	3
General corporate		262	11
Personal injury (defendant)		73	6
Cluster total			24
4. Political	46		
Criminal (prosecution)		20	2
Municipal		30	2
Cluster total			4
B. Personal/small business client sector		421	40
1. Personal business	287		
General litigation		53	2
Personal real estate		153	5
Personal tax		57	3
Probate		195	8
Cluster total			18
2. Personal plight	296		
Civil rights		41	2
Criminal (defense)		91	5
Divorce		153	6
Family		84	3
Personal injury (plaintiffs)		120	6
Cluster total			22
C. General, unspecified legal work	248	248	8
Total		699	101

NOTES: a. The number of practitioners is defined as all the persons who report devoting at least 5 percent of their work to the field.
b. See text and note 12 for explanation.

that reasonable persons might find questionable. We thus offer these results as a first approximation only.

The most critical simplification we have made is to assume that all lawyers' contributions of effort are equal—that is, Lawyer A's work year is assumed to be equivalent in time, efficiency, effectiveness, and intensity to Lawyer B's work year. While that is patently false when comparing specific individuals, it is less troublesome if one thinks of averaging many practitioners so that individual idiosyncrasies tend to cancel one another. But we should worry about whether the amounts of work that lawyers do are systematically related to their fields of practice. One might point, for example, to "undoubted" differences between the intensity of effort that litigators as a group expend in their work compared to the presumably more leisurely pace of attorneys handling probate transactions. With hindsight, we regret that we gathered no information on the number of hours per week put in by different kinds of practitioners—one among several obvious (though surely not foolproof) ways to evaluate the validity of this objection. We know of no study that reports such information. But the magnitude of the differences among the fields in the calculations presented is sufficient that, even allowing for a considerable margin of error, we get some idea of the relative levels of effort devoted to the various fields. Only very substantial and systematic deviations of effort by *fields* would seriously modify the aggregate picture. We caution the reader, however, not to overemphasize the size of particular proportions but instead to focus on the overall structure of relative shares of effort. To extract the maximum information about an individual's allocation of effort across fields, we created an elaborate set of coding rules that took into account both the total number of fields checked and the amount of time reported for each field that was checked.[12]

On the basis of these calculations, we estimate that somewhat more than half (53 percent) of the total effort of Chicago's bar is devoted to the corporate client sector, and a smaller but still substantial proportion (40 percent) is expended on the personal client sector.[13] More than half of the lawyers in Chicago spend some of their time in one or more of the fields in the "general corporate" cluster, and 627 of the 699 practicing lawyers devote at least some fraction of their effort to either the "general corporate" or the "personal business" cluster. On the other hand, these two substantial segments of the profession are largely separate. Only 56 of our respondents devoted as much as 25 percent of their time to a personal business field *and* at least 25 percent to a general corporate field—these overlapping lawyers are fewer than 17 percent of the total number of respondents who practice in those fields at least 25 percent of their time. The relatively small degree of overlap in the practice of these two groups of fields is, perhaps, surprising when we consider that the substance of legal work for personally owned businesses may not be far different from work for small corporations. The separation of the corporate and individual client sectors of practice is explored further in the section of this chapter entitled "Patterns of Co-practice Among Fields of Law."

Level of Specialization in the Fields of Law

Only one field of law commands the exclusive attention of as many as half of its practitioners.[14] That field is criminal prosecution.[15] Of the others, only patents even comes close to this criterion of specialization of effort, with 40 percent of its practitioners doing that work exclusively. Corporate tax comes in a very distant third, with 22 percent of its practitioners reporting full-time activity. All the other fields tend to cluster fairly tightly around the average of 5 to 6 percent full-time practitioners. The median number of fields of practice to which our respondents devoted as much as 5 percent of their time was 2.7. It is important to note this diffusion of individual effort across the fields of law, but a more systematic exploration of the varying effort given to the different fields may prove to be illuminating, both empirically and theoretically.

The data in hand, of course, provide only a somewhat crude indication of the amounts of time that individuals devote to one or another field of law, but they do provide a satisfactory basis for distinguishing among those individuals who spend relatively little time in a field (i.e., 5 to 25 percent of their professional time), those who spend moderate amounts of time (25 to 50 percent), and those who devote the majority or all of their time to the field. Since our analytic purpose is to characterize the differences among the fields of law and not to account for the differences in participation by individual lawyers, the aggregation of these individuals permits us to compare the relative levels of concentration that the fields appear to command from their practitioners.

These variations among the fields are, no doubt, determined by the demand for and supply of the services provided by each of the fields. We may think of the demands as being arrayed on a continuum of generality, breadth, or inclusiveness of client eligibility. At one end of this continuum are the fields serving needs that are likely to arise during the course of the daily affairs of most individual or corporate actors. For example, one would expect most persons of even moderate means, as well as business concerns of whatever size, to engage in the sale or purchase of real property, the preparation of tax returns, the transmission of wealth, the establishment of contractual obligations, and the resolution of the consequences of accidents. The demand for such legal services is large and dispersed throughout society. At the other extreme are fields serving the needs of highly circumscribed and identifiable sets of actors who will often have been made the objects of special legal regulation. Defendants in admiralty claims, inventors and authors, corporate actors subject to special statutory provisions—such as labor unions, corporations offering securities or those with antitrust problems, or manufacturers discharging environmental pollutants—are but a few examples of sources of narrowly defined demands for specialized legal services.

As to the supply side, we can again conceive of a continuum of available professionals capable of meeting these differentiated demands. The standardization of legal training in law schools and the requirement of a standard examination for admission to practice assure that some limited skills are shared by most practitioners, no matter how wanting the level of competence may be. Lawyers are certified as generalists, each being licensed to serve all the legal needs of his or her clientele. Practitioners exposed to the traditional fields of law in their professional training may feel little hesitancy in practicing these if the occasion arises. But other fields require extensive specialized training and experience that is often not acquired in law school. Real estate syndication and much corporate litigation are probably examples of the latter sort of field.

The central thrust of our argument, then, is that generalists and specialists have differing competitive advantages and disadvantages in serving clients, depending on the nature of the supply of the relevant skills and on the nature of the client demands. A specialist must invest substantial amounts of time and effort to master knowledge that has little application to other legal matters. Handling cases outside the specialist's area of expertise is costly because it fails to utilize this investment. On the other hand, because specialists have arcane knowledge readily available, they can handle cases within their areas much more efficiently than can generalists, whose knowledge of the relevant law and procedures is likely to be sketchy or out of date. The generalist can provide service efficiently only if the matters handled are relatively routine and of frequent occurrence. Once a matter begins to pose issues that arise infrequently, the generalist rapidly loses the competitive advantage to the specialist; it then becomes inefficient for the generalist to invest the time to acquire the necessary knowledge.

Clients thus need a mechanism for locating appropriate lawyers, and the specialists need to be put in touch with clients who require esoteric services. The narrower the range of clients demanding such services or the more difficult it is to identify them, the more the specialists come to depend on the existence of reliable means for linking them to their clientele. Specialists usually achieve this link either through connections with a network of other lawyers who will refer cases to them or by securing a position in a large law firm that has a sufficient volume of legal business to permit internal specialization.

The first four columns of table 2.2 are self-explanatory: they provide the total numbers of practitioners in each field (col. [1]) and the percentages of those practitioners who devote each of the categories of time to the field (cols. [2]–[4]). The final column indicates the nature of the practitioners' time allocations. G denotes a *generalist* pattern in which the largest number of practitioners devote only 5 to 25 percent of their time to the field. S denotes the *specialist* pattern, where the modal participation in the field is at the level of more than 50 percent of a practitioner's time. M denotes a *mixed* or *bimodal* pattern—the practitioners devoting only 5 to 25 percent of their time *or* in excess of 50 percent of their time occur much more often than the intermediate category, those spending 25 to 50 percent of their time in the field. (To be designated an M or bimodal distribution, we followed the rule of thumb that each of the two other categories had to be at least 75 percent larger than the intermediate category.) Broadly speaking, we found considerable congruence between our speculations about the demand and supply characteristics of the fields and the empirically observed pattern of time commitment.

Patterns of Co-practice among Fields of Law

As we argued at the beginning of this chapter, at least two hypotheses about the nature of the determinants of the patterns of co-practice of the fields should be considered. First, one could entertain the *hypothesis of cognitively based connectedness*—that there are conceptual affinities in the knowledge and modes of reasoning used by certain fields that may influence the patterns of co-practice. A number of fields have his-

TABLE 2.2
Concentration of Effort in Selected Fields of Law by
Individual Practitioners: Percentage Distribution

Fields of Law	Total No. of Practitioners (1)	Percentage of Practitioners in Each Time Category			Nature of Time Distribution (5)
		5–25 (2)	25–50 (3)	50+ (4)	
A. Corporate client sector					
1. Large corporate					
Antitrust (defense)	47	57	15	28	M
Business litigation	56	45	20	36	M
Business real estate	80	48	16	36	M
Business tax	51	41	20	39	M
Labor (management)	39	44	13	44	M
Securities	53	58	13	28	M
2. Regulatory					
Labor (unions)	18	28	17	56	S
Patents	45	24	7	69	S
Public utilities and administrative	52	44	14	42	M
3. General corporate					
Antitrust (plaintiffs)	24	58	21	21	G
Banking	60	45	33	22	G
Commercial	102	63	26	11	G
General corporate	272	40	33	18	G
Personal injury (defendant)	73	42	19	38	M
4. Political					
Criminal prosecution	20	25	5	70	S
Municipal	30	40	30	30	G
B. Personal client sector					
1. Personal business					
General litigation	53	54	24	21	G
Personal real estate	153	60	24	16	G
Personal tax	57	44	32	25	G
Probate	195	49	34	17	G
2. Personal plight					
Civil rights	41	66	15	20	G
Criminal defense	91	52	12	36	M
Divorce	153	63	24	13	G
Family	84	68	20	12	G
Personal injury (plaintiffs)	120	48	21	31	G

torical and intellectual roots in the English common law tradition (e.g., torts, contracts, real property, and the law of trusts and estates). Other fields are allied because they result from regulatory codes that create a body of administrative procedure and practice, subjecting specific sets of actors to legal control (e.g., regulation of broadcasting, natural gas, railroads, or airlines). Though the human and corporate actors subject to regulation may be diverse, the argument is that the underlying principles of the common law versus the newer administrative law create a systematic distinction among the fields and organize co-practice accordingly. There is an analogous logic of co-specialization in medical practice where the developing theory and empirical knowledge about biology and disease tends to group specialist fields into various clusters.[16] Thus, one finds some surgeons and internists doing specialized work on gastro-intestinal problems, others concerned with cardiac and vascular problems, and still others specializing in neurological disorders.

Second, one could advance the *hypothesis of client-centered organization of legal problems.* This hypothesis would assert that the primary determinant of the lawyer's allocation of time to the various fields of practice is the need to serve the interests of an identifiable set of clients. Thus, the neighborhood lawyer, serving individuals and small businesses, would seek to handle all of the matters that commonly confront his clientele—income tax, home sales, marital problems, automobile accidents, wills, and perhaps even some criminal charges. He would have an incentive to provide "full service" to his clients rather than refer them to another lawyer. The lawyer representing a large corporation, on the other hand, might or might not attempt to serve all of the corporation's legal needs. The corporate lawyer and his client might well find that the client's interests would be better served by the lawyer's specialization in a limited set of tasks requiring arcane knowledge (e.g., tax, labor relations, or public utility rate making). The large law firm that serves corporate clients may, through the specialization of "departments" or of individual lawyers within the firm, seek to achieve something like the full service provided by the neighborhood practitioner—and probably for the same reason.

In evaluating the relative merits of these deceptively simple and straightforward alternative explanations of co-practice, we pursued several strategies that differed in key theoretical and substantive assumptions, but the results converged so strongly that we feel justified in serving brevity by reporting here only one set of results. To identify localized regions or clusters of fields according to the varying probabilities of co-practice, we used a method of analysis that creates successively more and more inclusive clusters of specialties on the basis of their conditional probabilities of co-practice until we reach only one cluster containing all the fields.[17] A specialty is added to a cluster when it has at least a stipulated minimum probability of being linked with all the other fields in that cluster. The investigator can then examine and seek to interpret the resulting nested hierarchy of clusters. Figure 2.1 presents a graphic summary (called a dendrogram). Reading the dendrogram from right to left, the reader can observe where specialties were successively added to particular clusters as the conditional probabilities of co-practice decline in value.

The use of conditional probabilities to link fields occurred to us because of the intuitively obvious substantive interpretation of the measure. At the one extreme, two fields are clearly separated from each other when there is *no* likelihood that work in one field is associated with work in the other. At the other extreme, if there is a 100 percent probability of doing work in one field given that one does some work in the other, it is difficult to imagine maintaining a real distinction between the fields.[18] Choosing cutting points between these two extremes is, of course, not so easy. The choice will depend on the analyst's purpose in differentiating among the fields.

Figure 2.1 reveals that there are five distinct clusters (indicated by roman numerals) that are distinguished by the fact that there is virtually no likelihood of their mutual co-practice. Cluster I includes fields concerned with business transactions, usually involving corporations of substantial size. Using an arbitrary cutoff at .20, this broad cluster can be further subdivided into four subclusters: (a) antitrust and patents; (b) business tax; (c) securities and general corporate; and (d) banking and commercial. These subgroups probably reflect patterns of internal specialization within large law firms and in the offices of house counsel working for corporations. Of these fields, business tax is the least closely connected to any of the others, and it is probably the field that is most likely to be practiced within a separate, specialized department of a large law firm or house counsel's office, or in a specialty firm devoted more or less exclusively to such work.

In Cluster II we find the balance of the corporate law fields. Of these, only business litigation and business real estate join at the .20 level, and these are the two fields within the cluster that are most likely to be found in large law firms, again often in separate departments within those firms. The other fields in the cluster are relatively free-standing specialties that are more often practiced outside the confines of the large, corporate firms and are done instead by government lawyers, house counsel, or smaller specialty firms. The services of litigators and real estate lawyers, like those of tax specialists, are likely to be required at

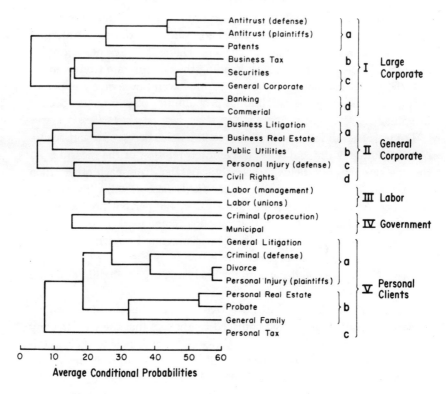

FIGURE 2.1
*Hierarchical Clustering of Joint Activity Using Average Conditional Probabilities,
Diameter Method (5 Percent or More Time in Each Field)*

one time or another by many of the corporate clients of a large law firm, but since these fields cut across nearly the full range of the firm's clients they will be less tightly connected to any particular subset of clients. Cluster III is quite straightforward: it includes both the union and management sides of the practice of labor law. Though lawyers who represent unions seldom also work for management, and vice versa, there is a third side to labor law work that tends to pull these two fields together. Labor law is also practiced by government lawyers and by professional mediators or arbitrators who stand between unions and management. When we asked these lawyers about the fields in which they worked, they responded that they worked in both sides of labor law, thus creating overlap. Cluster IV is, again, quite clear. It consists of the two fields of practice where municipal governments are the primary clients. The final cluster includes all of the fields that are primarily devoted to the service of individual persons and small business. Within this personal client cluster, there are three subdivisions if we use the .20 cutoff criterion. The first includes the fields most characterized by litigation on behalf of persons. The second consists of the fields (other than tax) that are most concerned with personal financial transactions or the transmission of personal wealth. And the third is personal tax, which—like business tax—appears to be a separate specialty that does not have a great affinity for any other field, in particular, but that cuts across fields insofar as they may involve tax issues.

In sum, though there is some clustering of the fields according to their cognitive similarities, the primary structure of co-practice appears to be client centered. That is, co-practice appears to be organized by the demands of distinct groupings of clients who have distinct sets of legal problems and who establish relationships with distinct types of lawyers.

Conclusion

Chicago's lawyers spread their work over a broad range of activities, none of which commands a very large percentage of the total legal effort. Even the two largest fields—general corporate and probate—claim a mere 11 and 8 percent, respectively, of the total (see table 2.1). None of the other twenty-two fields receives more than 6 percent. On the other hand, the numbers of practitioners in both of the largest fields constitute substantial portions of the profession—37 percent of all practicing lawyers characterize at least some of their work as "general corporate." But only a few fields of law receive the undivided attention of as many as 10 percent of their practitioners; only criminal prosecution gets the undivided attention of as many as half of its practitioners.

If we shift from the field of law to the individual lawyer as the unit of analysis, however, we get a somewhat different view of the matter. About 22 percent of our respondents indicated that they practiced in one field exclusively, while another 39 percent devoted more than half of their time to a single field but also did some work in one or more other fields. (This is consistent with the distribution across fields because the time of these lawyers that was not devoted to their fields of specialization and the time of the nonspecialists was spread across a variety of fields.) Thus, from the point of view of the individual lawyer, there is a substantial degree of specialization in the work of most Chicago practitioners. We asked our respondents whether they considered themselves "specialists," and 70 percent replied that they did. (Fewer than three-quarters of these self-labeled specialists, however, devoted as much as half of their practice time to a single field of law.) But the firms in which many of these lawyers work no doubt offer a broader range of services to their clients; one of the principal efficiencies of the large law firm is the division of labor that it makes possible, and one of the main attractions of such firms to the client is the range of service that is available. Though individual lawyers may see their work as specialized, therefore, clients may see a general practice firm and may talk primarily with a senior partner who bridges the firm's departments. And it is important to emphasize that few of the fields are dominated by specialists. Unless the specialists are aggregated into *roles* that have social meaning, their individual patterns of specialization have little consequence. If the fields of law are an adequate set of lawyers' social roles (or, at least, of some such roles), then, the relative lack of specialization in most of the fields is the important social fact.

A majority of the work of Chicago lawyers is devoted to corporate clients (see table 2.1), and the profession's overall preoccupation is with business transactions, transfers of wealth, and the defense of property rights (including work in the personal business fields). Though about 42 percent of all lawyers do spend at least some time in fields concerned with the alleviation of personal "plight" (see cluster B2 in table 2.1), only 22 percent of the total effort is directed to these activities. The personal plight fields rank at the bottom of the profession's prestige hierarchy (see chap. 4), and we find that these fields are heavily dominated by part-timers (see table 2.2). Whether these fields are disvalued because few practitioners devote exclusive attention to them or whether few lawyers specialize in them because of their disvalued standing in the profession is a matter for speculation or further research, but the latter seems more plausible. Practitioners dividing their activities among several fields may well identify more closely with those that enjoy higher social standing among their colleagues and may try to minimize their involvement with the lower status field.

Particular types of clients tend to be afflicted with particular congeries of legal problems, and the lawyer has an incentive to deal with as broad a spectrum of these needs as is consistent with the reasonably efficient provision of service to the client. A law firm that does estate planning for rich clients is likely to handle their real estate transactions as well; a lawyer who settles divorce cases for clients from the lower middle class may also be called on to handle consumer credit problems or even to negotiate a plea to a criminal charge. This does not mean that the majority of Chicago lawyers, those who practice in firms with ten or more lawyers or who are employed by corporations or governments, do not manage to limit their work to a narrow range of fields and to allocate most of their time to one, principal area of practice—as we have seen, they do. But it is our thesis that the scope of that area of practice will be shaped to accommodate their clients' range of needs, broad or narrow.

To what extent, then, do our findings suggest that the patterns in the organization of lawyers' work correspond, in fact, to client type rather than to doctrinal substance or to similarities in the tasks that lawyers perform (e.g., litigation versus office practice)? Some doctrinal areas coincide so closely with one type of client that the lawyers who give more or less exclusive service to those narrow classes of clients (e.g., broadcasters or labor unions) are also likely to be specialized by task type or doctrinal substance. The issue is, therefore, the extent to which lawyers generally tend to deal within broader but mutually exclusive social groupings of clients. We can provide an answer to at least one important question that is relevant to this issue: what fraction of the profession regularly represents both corporations and individuals? Our data show that only about a seventh of all practicing lawyers do a substantial amount of work both for corporate clients and for individuals or small businesses. Of 777 respondents, 699 of whom were actively practicing, 101 devoted at least 25 percent of their professional time to one or more of the fields in the corporate sector *and* at least 25 percent to one or more of the fields in the personal sector.[19] From these data and the patterns of overlap in the practice of the fields (see fig. 2.1), we are inclined to argue that, while the organization of lawyers' work surely reflects affinities of doctrine and of task type, the Chicago bar is even more clearly specialized by type of client. Personal injury work done for plaintiffs (usually individuals) is, for example, quite separate from that done for defendants (usually insurance companies). And the clustering of fields according to the overlaps among them in lawyers' patterns of practice quite clearly shows that corporate law fields tend to group together, regardless of doctrinal substance, as do personal client fields and fields where governments are the primary clients.

The set of fields that we defined at the beginning of this study may, therefore, depend too much on substantive categories. Our findings suggest to us that lawyers' roles are determined less by doctrinal distinctions among tasks and more by social distinctions among clients. Rather than the role of antitrust defense practitioner, the lawyer may occupy the position of counsel to large corporations that have antitrust problems.

Specialization within the legal profession is not so much a division of labor as a division of clientele. Lawyers tend to specialize in the representation of limited, identifiable types of clients and to perform as broad or narrow a range of tasks as their clientele demands.

Chapter 3

SOCIAL DIFFERENTIATION

WITHIN THE PROFESSION

The tendency of lawyers' work to address sets of problems associated with particular types of clients organizes the profession into two broad types of lawyers: those serving corporations and those serving individuals and individuals' small businesses. In this chapter we explore the extent to which differences in the social characteristics of lawyers follow the same lines of cleavage as this division of labor or division of clientele. Do the patterns of social differentiation within the bar correspond to the organization of work? That is, are the different sorts of clients served by different sorts of lawyers?

We begin this analysis by considering some of the mechanisms—beyond the incentive for lawyers to serve a broad range of the needs of their particular clients—that could determine the structure of the relationships among the fields of law. What social processes might tend to make two fields more alike in their social characteristics or, perhaps, to separate other fields, to drive them apart?

The referral system through which lawyers find clients and clients find lawyers is surely one mechanism that creates contacts and ties among the fields. Patent lawyers, for example, may maintain close ties with counsel for corporations that are likely to invent patentable products, and lawyers specializing in commercial litigation may seek connections with office lawyers who represent commercial enterprises. Thus, the common interest of lawyers and clients in the facilitation of their contacts may bring together doctrinally and organizationally differentiated fields of law, but note that these fields will share a concern with the same sort of client. By contrast, other types of lawyers—criminal prosecutors, for example—may not need to seek clients, and this will deprive those fields of one incentive for decreasing their social isolation from professional colleagues in other fields of practice.

Similarly, referral networks among graduates of particular law schools may bind together some fields and separate others. If practitioners of the most elite forms of corporate law attended the same few law schools, while personal injury or criminal lawyers studied at less prestigious, local schools, "old school tie" networks may increase the social distance[1] between these types of practice. This phenomenon is part of a more general tendency toward equal status contact.[2] That is, lawyers in fields that enjoy similar levels of prestige within the profession will be more likely to associate with one another than will lawyers from fields with widely differing prestige.[3]

Obviously, these mechanisms reinforce one another. Practitioners in fields concerned with corporate clients' legal problems may recruit at the same law schools, participate in the same client referral networks, and share similar prestige within the profession. The tendency of all these factors will be the same: to forge relationships among the fields of corporate law practice and to separate them from noncorporate fields.

But characteristics more intrinsic to the practice of the various fields of law may also contribute to the degree of their social differentiation. Similarities in the legal doctrines, statutes, or regulatory schemes dealt with by two fields might, thus, beget a kinship that could increase social proximity, as could their general modes of analysis or the strategic problems they characteristically address. Some fields of law, for example, involve "symbol manipulation" and others "people persuasion." The former category might include preparing securities registration statements or similarly complex, technical documents; divorce, criminal, or personal injury work might fall into the latter category.

There are also some more specific differences in the types of tasks performed. The practitioners in some fields are nearly always in court or preparing for it, while those in other fields are almost exclusively engaged in office practice. And within both litigation and office practice, further fundamental distinctions may be drawn. Within litigation, important distinctions of status and task type exist between state court and federal court litigation and between trial and appellate work. Within office practice, lawyers in some fields primarily advise clients on possible tax or antitrust consequences of alternative courses of action, for example, or on techniques of real estate acquisition, while lawyers in other fields, such as matrimonial law, devote much time and energy to the emotional needs of clients, to personal counseling, or to smoothing ruffled feathers. Practitioners in still other fields characteristically spend their time drafting legal documents such as wills, trust agreements, debentures, or contracts. To the extent that these distinct tasks call for distinct skills, the mobility of lawyers among fields is inhibited. The probability that a lawyer will do a substantial amount of work in two fields of law is, of course, one measure of the social distance between the fields. Once that probability exceeds a certain point, we would say that no social or behavioral distinction exists between the two fields and that any distinction between them is purely conceptual or doctrinal.

For similar reasons, the fields of law that deal with statutory or regulatory codes may be more insular than those that work primarily with older common law. All lawyers learn the basic principles of the common law in law school and, thus, may accept a simple tort or contract case even though they principally attend to some other field. By contrast, lawyers may be less confident of their skills, or less willing to invest the time necessary to acquire them, in fields such as broadcast regulation or labor law, and there may therefore be less tendency to accept the occasional case in that kind of field. Much of the innovation in regulatory law, with the consequent growth of multivolume codes, has occurred at the federal level, spawning entirely new specialties in federal regulatory law. Because these new fields share some common elements or common skills (and also because of the types of clients, the networks among clients and lawyers, and the differences between federal and state procedural rules), the distinction between federal practice and state practice creates social distance among the fields—federal law usually involves larger, corporate clients and enjoys higher prestige within the profession.

Finally, fields of law that process large numbers of individual clients through the state courts will tend to be socially distant from fields that require several years of lawyers' time on each case (antitrust work, for example). But it is exceedingly difficult to separate this difference among the fields from a corresponding socioeconomic difference. High-volume cases and the lawyers who handle them are unlikely to resemble the processing or the processors of "unique" legal problems, but the discovery of a unique issue is likely to be a function of the amount of time that lawyers devote to a case and, thus, of the amount of money that the client spends on lawyers. If the stakes are high, the problems can become very complex; if the client lacks money, problems are likely to be routine. The consequent difference (perceived or real) in the levels of intellectual challenge presented by the varying fields of law may well, then, affect their relative levels of prestige within the profession and thus serve as yet another basis for differentiation among them. This possibility is considered in chapter 4.

These mechanisms of differentiation will probably create divisions within the legal profession in spite of the endorsement by the courts and the organized bar of the myth of the omnicompetent practitioner.[4] In fact, many distinct fields of legal work do exist.

As noted in chapter 2, we asked the respondents to indicate whether they devoted less than 5 percent, 5 to 25 percent, 25 to 50 percent, or more than 50 percent of their professional time to each of the thirty fields of law that we had listed. The respondents who reported that they spent 25 percent or more of their time on a field are the practitioners whose responses were used in computing the characteristics of the fields that are reported here. That is, we derived the attributes of probate law and of its practitioners from the responses of the 100 lawyers who estimated that they devoted at least a quarter of their legal effort to that field. Obviously, this criterion is largely arbitrary and, because our categories unavoidably overlap, our respondents' classifications of their work must be imprecise.[5] If we had set the inclusion level at 50 percent of legal effort, we would have had purer categories—categories less contaminated by the responses of practitioners not strongly committed to or involved with the field—but we would also have lost data and our findings would have been based on smaller numbers. Had we chosen the 5 percent level, we would have been more inclusive, but we would have had a weaker, more contaminated measure of the field's characteristics. At the 25 percent level, of course, the respondents counted in a given field may be even more active or involved in one or two other fields of law, where they will also be counted.[6] This is, then, a conservative measure of the degree of differentiation among the fields of law.

The Degree of Differentiation

Notwithstanding the conservatism of our measure of the differentiation among the fields of law, that differentiation is quite substantial. We analyzed the set of twenty-five fields on forty variables—an even thousand observations—but we will spare the reader here and present our data somewhat more parsimoniously in only two simple tables and one rather more complex figure. The nuance lost by reducing the data is compensated for by the increased comprehensibility of the overall structure. The first table displays the differentiation among selected fields of law on a number of social variables; the second examines the hierarchical structure of that differentiation, on the same variables, across a set of categories that includes all of the fields; and the figure graphically represents the structure of the relationships among the twenty-five fields of law, simultaneously accounting for several kinds of social variation among them.

Table 3.1 presents the findings for six selected fields of law on twenty variables. The variables include characteristics of the fields' clients and of the practitioners' relationships with clients, the tasks performed in the fields, the nature of the social organizations or institutions in which the fields are practiced, the types of law schools attended by the fields' practitioners, and some information about the practitioners' social origins.

Even a cursory inspection of table 3.1 discloses large differences among the fields on many of the variables. Client volume, for example, ranges from a median of 2 in public utilities to 102 for divorce. (A field not presented here, personal injury plantiffs' work, has an even higher client volume: a median of 149 clients represented in the past year.) The percentage of lawyers in each field who are solo practitioners ranges from 0 to 61 percent, and for those who practice in firms with more than thirty lawyers the range is from 0 to 77 percent. (This range of variation occurs among only five fields, excluding criminal prosecution.) Similarly, the percentage of lawyers who attended elite law schools varies from 0 to 45, that for local law schools ranges from 14 to 67, and in the three religion categories 36 to 44 percentage points separate the high and low scores. Thus, the fields are highly differentiated on these important variables. Moreover, we will argue that this striking differentiation is highly ordered, that it is organized in a consistent hierarchy.

The pattern of the differences among the fields on many of the variables seems clear and interpretable. The mean percentage of blue-collar workers among the clients of these six fields varies from 0 to 38, while the mean percentage of income received from major corporate clients—the other side of the socioeconomic scale—ranges from 4 to 61 percent. Disregarding criminal prosecution, where by definition government is

TABLE 3.1
Differentiation among Six Selected Fields of Law

Fields	Number of Practitioners (1)	Clients — Mean % Blue-collar Clients (2)	Clients — Mean % Business Income from Major Corporate Clients (3)	Clients — Mean % Stable Clients (4)	Clients — Median Number of Clients per Year (5)	Median Number of State Court Appearances per Month (6)	Task Type — % High Encroachment on Practice (7)	Task Type — % High Negotiating and Advising (8)	Task Type — % High Professional Expertise (9)	Task Type — % High Specialization of Work (10)	Practice Setting — % Solo Practitioners (11)	Practice Setting — % Firms of More Than 30 Lawyers (12)	Practice Setting — % Corporate House Counsel (13)	Law School — % Attended Elite Law Schools (14)	Law School — % Attended Local Law Schools (15)	Personal Characteristics — % Type I Protestants (16)	Personal Characteristics — % Catholic (17)	Personal Characteristics — % Jewish (18)	Personal Characteristics — % Metropolitan Origin (19)	Mean Age (20)	Prestige Score (21)
Securities	22	0	61	60	26	0	36	23	86	72	0	77	9	45	14	36	9	14	68	39	68
Public utilities	29	3	46	92	2	0	36	54	55	72	10	10	24	24	17	17	21	31	83	45	59
General corporate	135	6	39	72	35	1	35	37	62	30	19	21	16	30	34	13	27	38	73	45	59
Criminal prosecution	15	Government is only client				19	20	18	50	53	All Government employees			0	67	7	53	20	87	39	44
Probate	100	14	22	70	60	5	37	44	49	26	30	13	9	23	44	17	35	22	72	51	58
Divorce	57	38	4	42	102	15	52	57	36	23	61	0	0	11	65	0	26	56	94	45	35
Total Sample	699	13	35	67	35	3	30	40	52	45	21	17	14	20	45	13	30	33	78	44	50

Differentiation among Six Selected Fields of Law

Notes: In the explanations of the column headings, numbers prefixed with "A" indicate the question numbers in the interview schedule.

(1) *Number of Practitioners*: This is the number of respondents who devoted at least 25 percent of their time to a field (table 3.1) or a group of fields (table 3.2). All other entries in the row rest on this sample base, but are reduced by the small numbers of respondents who did not provide the information reported in a given column.

To determine the lawyer's distribution of time across fields, we asked:

A1.   While a lawyer's time is often spread over many different areas of the law, we wish, for comparative purposes, to characterize those areas in which you spent the major part of your time during the last twelve months. [Respondent then was handed a card listing thirty fields of law.] In which of the listed areas have you spent: a. more than 50 percent of your time? b. between 25 percent and 50 percent of your time? c. between 5 percent and 25 percent of your time?

For purposes of analysis, the thirty fields were reduced to twenty-five. Four fields were excluded because of insufficient numbers of practitioners (admiralty, environmental defense, environmental plaintiff, and condemnation). Three areas were redefined to include fields that, by themselves, had insufficient cases (family law was redefined to include general family practice—paying clients; general family practice—poverty level clients, and consumer-buyer law; commercial law was redefined to include consumer-seller law; real estate was redefined to include landlord/tenant). Lawyers who spent time in tax, real estate, and civil litigation were classified as follows: if they derived 80 percent or more of their income from business clients, they were classified as business real estate, business tax, and business litigation; if they derived less than 80 percent from such sources or if this information was missing, they were classified as personal real estate, personal tax, and general litigation.

(2) *Mean Percentage of Blue-collar Clients*: These percentages were derived from answers to the following question:

A5C.   Would you now think about the clients for whom you have handled personal matters in the last twelve months. [Respondent was handed a card listing five occupational categories.] What proportion of your clients fall into the occupational categories . . . ? Professional; Technical; Managerial; Sales and Clerical; Blue Collar Workers; Unemployed; Retired; In-School, Keeping house.

House counsel, government lawyers, and lawyers who spent less than 10 percent of their time on "personal matters" (defined as legal work for persons rather than for businesses) were not asked this question, and we therefore assigned a value of zero for their percentages of blue-collar clients.

(3) *Mean Percentage of Business Income from Major Corporate Clients*: This is the mean percentage of law practice income reported by respondents who indicated that they received 10 percent or more of their income from work for businesses and who then answered the following question:

A5B.   What proportion of your business income would come from the following size business clients?

The categories were major corporations (those with sales over $10,000,000 per year), medium-sized firms, or small businesses (those with sales of less than $250,000 per year). Those who responded that they were employed as corporate house counsel were recorded as deriving 100 percent of their income from major corporate clients. Government-employed lawyers were recorded as deriving no income from major corporate clients.

(4) *Mean Percentage of Stable Clients*: These are the averages of respondents' estimates given in answer to the following question:

A7.   What proportion of your clients have you represented for three years or more?

We did not ask house counsel or government lawyers this question, and we assigned them a value of 100 percent on this variable.

(5) *Median Number of Clients per Year*: This is based on responses to the question:

A4.   During the past twelve months, approximately how many clients have you done some work for—more than just going through a file, or turning over a file to another lawyer?

Again, house counsel and government lawyers were not asked this question; they were assigned a value of 1.

(6) *Median Number of State Court Appearances per Month*: This is the median number of state trial and appellate court appearances per month over the past year, as reported by respondents.

(7)–(10): Respondents were presented with several sets of statements about the nature of their practice, with the following instruction:

TABLE 3.1 (continued)

A9. Different kinds of law require different kinds of professional activities. [Respondent received card listing seven pairs of statements.] Each pair represents polar opposites. Please circle the number which best represents your position in relation to the two opposites. If the situation in your practice is midway between poles, circle code 3; if your situation is at one or the other extreme, circle 1 or 5; if your position leans somewhat to either pole, circle 2 or 4.

The percentages reported in cols. (7)–(10) are based on the two values closest to the specified extreme (that is, either values of 1 or 2, or values of 4 or 5).

(7) *Percentage with High Encroachment on Practice:* This is the percentage who chose the following description of their legal practice: "There are aspects of my professional work which are being encroached upon by other occupations." The opposite was: "No other occupation is engaging in the kinds of legal matters with which I am primarily concerned."

(8) *Percentage with High Negotiating and Advising:* This is the percentage who chose the following description of their practice: "My specialty and type of practice requires skills in negotiating and advising clients, rather than detailed concern with technical skills." The opposite was: "My area demands skills in handling highly technical procedures rather than skills in negotiating and advising clients."

(9) *Percentage with High Professional Expertise:* This is the percentage who chose the following description of their practice: "The type and content of my practice is such that even an educated layman couldn't really understand or prepare the documents." The opposite was: "A para-professional could be trained to handle many of the procedures and documents in my area of the law."

(10) *Percentage with High Specialization of Work:* This is the percentage who chose the following description of their practice: "The area of law in which I work is so highly specialized that it demands I concentrate in just this one area. "The opposite was: "The nature of my legal practice is such that I can handle a range of problems covering quite a number of different areas of legal practice."

(11)–(13): Respondents were asked, in the following question, about the type or form of organization of their law practice:

A3B. Which category best describes [your] job? [Respondents received card with ten types of practice: solo; firm; federal, state, municipal/county or military government; corporate, insurance, banking, or railroad house counsel; or other.]

The four house counsel subcategories are here combined into one category (column [13]). Respondents were then asked: "How many lawyers are in your firm/office now?" Column (12) reports the percentages of respondents in firms with more than thirty lawyers.

(14) *Percentage Attended Elite Law Schools:* This is the percentage who received law degrees from Chicago, Columbia, Harvard, Michigan, Stanford, or Yale. (See chapter 1 for discussion of categories of law schools.)

(15) *Percentage Attended Local Law Schools:* This is the percentage who received law degrees from DePaul, Kent, Loyola, or John Marshall, all located in Chicago. (The other two schools in Chicago—Northwestern and the University of Chicago—were included in the "prestige" and "elite" categories respectively.)

(16)–(18): The general question on religious background was:

A43. Do you have a religious preference? That is, are you either Protestant, Roman Catholic, Jewish, or something else?

We then asked Protestants to specify their denominations and Jews to specify whether they are Orthodox, Conservative, or Reform.

(16) *Percentage of Type 1 Protestants:* This is the percentage who indicated affiliation with the following denominations: Congregational, Presbyterian, Episcopal, and United Church of Christ. (See chapter 1.)

(17) *Percentage of Catholics:* This is the percentage who indicated that they were Roman Catholics.

(18) *Percentage of Jewish Practitioners:* This is the percentage who either expressed a preference for Judaism in response to question A43 or indicated that they were of Jewish origin in response to: "What nationality background do you think of yourself as having—that is, besides being American?"

(19) *Percentage of Metropolitan Origin:* This is the percentage reporting that they had lived during high school in a metropolitan area with a population over 250,000.

(20) *Mean Age:* This is the average age of respondents in the field or group of fields.

(21) *Prestige Score:* Standardized prestige scores of the fields of law were computed, based on the responses of a subsample to the following question:

On the following specialty list, would you please indicate the general prestige of each specialty within the legal profession at large?

These findings are presented and discussed in chapter 4, at table 4.1.

the only client,[7] the rank orders of the fields on these two client type variables are, without deviation, exactly reversed. Many of the other variables reproduce this same rank order to a greater or lesser degree. If we measure the adherence of the other variables to this order by the rather stringent criterion that no more than one field may depart from it and that field may depart by no more than one position in the rank, we find that the following additional variables qualify:

- the volume of clients served by the field; i.e., median number of clients represented during past year
- the percentage of pracitioners who say that their work demands a high degree of professional expertise
- the degree of specialization by practitioners in the field, i.e., percentage of respondents indicating high specialization
- the percentage of lawyers in the field who are solo practitioners
- the rating of the prestige of the field within the legal profession

Several more of the variables, while less strongly associated with this rank order, nonetheless share it to an obvious degree.

If we inspect the intercorrelations among four of the variables included in table 3.1—the percentage of blue-collar clients, client volume, the percentage of solo practitioners, and the percentage of practitioners who attended local law schools—computed across the full set of twenty-five fields, we find that the six correlation coefficients in the matrix range between .63 and .91. Since these are correlations of aggregated data (i.e., they are performed on the averages or composite scores for whole fields rather than for individual respondents), we would expect relatively high coefficients, but these are high by almost any standard. In fact, one of the most vexing problems we confronted in analyzing these data is that the variables are so highly associated with one another, either positively or negatively. That is, the variables have the statistical property of multicollinearity.[8] This makes it difficult, at the least, to distinguish each variable's independent effects, but the point to note here is that a strong, overarching structure appears to organize these variables when they are analyzed at the level of the fields of law. It is less important for our purposes to state precisely each variable's effect on the legal profession's overall social structure than it is to observe their coincidence. The variables reflect interrelated social processes that reinforce one another to produce an impressively persistent and highly coherent structure. We will argue that the types of clients served—the characteristics of the

TABLE 3.2

Differentiation Among Six Groups of Fields of Law and Generalists

Groups	Number of Practitioners (1)	Clients					Task Type					Practice Setting			Law School		Personal Characteristics				
		Mean % Blue-collar Clients (2)	Mean % Business Income from Major Corporate Clients (3)	Mean % Stable Clients (4)	Median Number of Clients per Year (5)	Median Number of State Court Appearances per Month (6)	% High Encroachment on Practice (7)	% High Negotiating and Advising (8)	% High Professional Expertise (9)	% High Specialization of Work (10)	% Solo Practitioners (11)	% Firms of More Than 30 Lawyers (12)	% Corporate House Counsel (13)	% Attended Elite Law Schools (14)	% Attended Local Law Schools (15)	% Type I Protestants (16)	% Catholic (17)	% Jewish (18)	% Metropolitan Origin (19)	Mean Age (20)
Large corporate	151	2	62	69	25	1	30	33	62	53	6	44	24	28	32	15	29	28	72	41
Regulatory	77	6	50	83	20	0	26	40	60	75	12	6	18	19	32	19	23	27	71	45
General corporate	226	6	43	71	33	2	31	35	57	35	15	24	17	27	36	13	31	33	75	44
Political	32	3	11	84	3	9	19	26	55	38	0	3	0	12	59	16	44	25	78	40
Personal business	165	18	18	64	75	6	38	42	43	30	34	12	5	22	47	12	35	29	76	49
Personal plight	171	34	10	49	100	15	34	52	42	36	42	3	2	12	64	4	33	42	92	44
"Generalists"	86	15	41	71	50	5	25	41	49	33	27	13	21	17	52	16	26	35	78	45
TOTAL SAMPLE	699	13	35	67	35	3	30	40	52	45	21	17	14	20	45	13	30	33	78	44

clients and of their use of lawyers—are the primary explanatory variables that organize and control the others, but such proofs as we will be able to offer are necessarily less statistical than sociological.

To facilitate our observation of this structure of differentiation within the profession, we present a second table utilizing data on all twenty-five fields grouped into six hierarchical categories. Table 3.2 is similar in form to table 3.1 and includes the same set of variables, but, rather than report values at the level of individual fields of law, it presents scores for larger groupings of the fields. As table 3.1 indicates, our sample includes relatively few practitioners in many of the fields, and the groupings of fields thus provide larger, more stable numbers for analysis.

Because the groups contain fields that differ substantially, the aggregation of the fields suppresses the degree of differentiation, as compared with that at the level of the individual fields. Nonetheless, the differences among the groups remain quite substantial. Very large ranges still occur on the two variables relating to socioeconomic type of client, client volume, frequency of state court appearances, type of practice organization, and percentage of high-status Protestants among the practitioners. In five more of the variables, the maximum value at least doubles the minimum; these are the "encroachment on practice," "negotiating and advising," and "specialization" variables, and the law school types. Thus, thirteen of the nineteen variables exhibit differences among the groups of at least this magnitude.

Four of the groups of fields are in the corporate sector of the profession; the remaining two are in the sector that primarily represents individuals or small businesses. We intend the groups to comprehend cognate areas of practice. Although we believe that the types of clients primarily define these areas, we have refrained from simply using statistically generated clusters of fields to maximize homogeneity in the client type data. Instead, we took into account conceptual notions about the nature of the fields, including subjective characteristics of the clients and of the substance of the work. The fields are distributed among the groups as indicated below.[9]

The tables also include a "generalists" category—86 respondents who did not devote as much as 25 percent of their time to any one field and thus are included in none of the fields or groups of fields. Seventy-eight more respondents (10 percent of our random sample) were not then practicing law; the tables include only the responses of the 699 practicing lawyers. Many respondents qualify for inclusion in more than one field within the groups used in table 3.2, but in computing group scores we

Corporate Sector	Personal Sector
Large Corporate Group	Personal Business Group
Antitrust (defense)	General litigation
Business litigation	Personal real estate
Business real estate	Personal tax
Business tax	Probate
Labor (management)	
Securities	Personal Plight Group
	Civil rights
Regulatory Group	Criminal (defense)
Labor (unions)	Divorce
Patents	General family practice
Public utilities and	Personal injury (plaintiffs)
administrative law	
General Corporate Group	
Antitrust (plaintiffs)	
Banking	
Commercial	
General corporate	
Personal injury (defense)	
Political Group	
Criminal (prosecution)	
Municipal	

counted each respondent within the group only once. A respondent who devoted at least 25 percent of his or her time to fields in two or more groups, however, was included in the analysis of each of those groups. With the 25 percent time criterion, therefore, a respondent might be included in as many as four fields. In general, this double counting has the effect of understating the degree of differentiation among the fields of law. We discussed overlap among the fields in detail in chapter 2, but we may note here that, of the 699 practicing lawyers, the 86 generalists are included in none of the groups, 390 respondents are counted in only one group, and 190 are in two groups.

The Dimensions of Differentiation

We have noted the magnitude of the differences among the fields of law on several variables and have observed the more obvious patterns of those differences, but it is difficult to grasp the overall structure of the differentiation by pondering numbers in a table. If we consider several kinds of similarities and differences in the fields simultaneously, what will be the resulting structure? In a graphic representation of that structure, will the fields be grouped by type of client or will some other dimension or dimensions appear to determine the structure?

Multidimensional scalogram analysis provides one approach to answering these questions.[10] Figure 3.1 depicts the relationships among the fields of law, representing them as points in two-dimensional space and accounting for their positions on a number of variables. Fields with similar profiles lie in close proximity (i.e., share a region of Euclidean space); those with greater differences on the variables lie at greater distances from one another.[11]

The nine variables used in this analysis are:

1. Business clients (mean percentage of income received from clients that are businesses rather than persons)
2. Stability of practice (mean percentage of clients represented for three years or more)
3. Lawyer referrals (mean percentage of clients obtained through referrals from other lawyers)
4. Freedom in choice of cases (percentage of practitioners indicating wide latitude in selecting clients)
5. Negotiating and advising (percentage of practitioners indicating their work often involves negotiating and advising rather than the use of highly technical procedures)
6. Government employment (percentage of practitioners employed by federal, state, or local government)
7. Local law school (percentage of practitioners who attended any of four local law schools in Chicago)
8. High-status Protestants (percentage of practitioners who state a preference for one of the type I Protestant denominations)
9. Jewish origin (percentage of practitioners who report either Jewish religion or ethnicity)

Three criteria determined the choice of these nine variables. First, to minimize the redundance built into the model, we sought to avoid choosing highly intercorrelated variables. Given the structured nature of the data—and, presumably, of the social system under study—we could have avoided substantial intercorrelations completely, however, only by choosing variables of tangential relevance or doubtful substantive significance.[12] Second, we sought to represent the full range of variables and to avoid overrepresenting any one type. Thus, the nine variables include

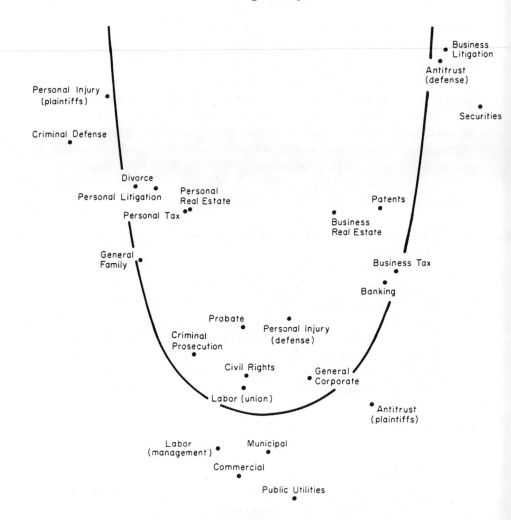

FIGURE 3.1

*Multidimensional Scalogram Analysis of Twenty-five Fields of Law on Nine
Selected Variables*

data on client type, sources of clients, task type, practice setting, school-
ing, and social origins. Finally, and perhaps most importantly, we required that the variables chosen have substantive significance. There is
a persuasive case that each of the variables used might have important
influence on the social distances among the fields. Those arguments have,
in fact, already been summarized at the beginning of this chapter.

As we see from figure 3.1, the relationships among the fields form a
structure that may be interpreted as roughly U-shaped. (The U-shaped

line is not a part of the statistical solution. We have drawn it to aid interpretation.) The fields that serve corporations lie to the right; fields that serve persons lie to the left. Fields that serve either a mixture of the two or special sorts of corporations such as governments or labor unions fall toward the middle.[13] The reader will recall that only one of the nine variables used in the multidimensional scalogram analysis explicitly measures the type of client—though, as we have already noted and argued, some of the other variables correlate with client type.

The vertical dimension of the structure appears to be related to the distinction between litigation and office practice. The fields with higher rates of court appearances tend to be higher in the space. Other general patterns in the structure are perhaps less striking, but they are surely discernible. The median size of the law firm or other practice organization increases as one moves from the upper left counterclockwise around the U. Client volume and the percentage of practitioners who attended a local law school both move in the opposite direction, increasing as one proceeds clockwise around the U. The percentage of stable clients generally increases as one moves toward the bottom of the figure. The most prestigious fields of law are at the upper right of the U and the least prestigious are at the upper left. Prestige, in fact, decreases in a very orderly clockwise fashion; the correlation between our measure of the prestige order of the fields and their order on the U is .9.[14]

The grouping of fields in the figure is similar to the grouping used in table 3.2. A small cluster of high status fields representing the largest corporations lie at the upper right of the U. Generally, the work for larger business corporations appears to be concentrated higher on the right side of the U, and the size of the businesses represented then decreases as one moves down. Moving clockwise, we encounter a group of fields dealing with financial transactions, particularly those regulated by government. Farther clockwise, a more diffuse cluster contains the remainder of the corporate sector. The field of probate law—which, of all the personal client fields, most deals with the transmission of wealth and thus with the wealthier personal clients—is a part of this general cluster but is on its upper left periphery, nearest to the other personal client fields. The remaining fields in our personal business group are included in the next cluster of points in the figure, still moving clockwise. Finally, we find four of the five fields of the personal plight group in the upper left quadrant of the U. The fifth, civil rights, is a special case. Because half of its practitioners are full-time government employees, we could in fact define civil rights work as a governmental function and place the field in the political group of the corporate sector, which is about where it appears in the figure.[15]

Conclusions

These findings suggest that even though the measures used to determine the characteristics of the fields of law (principally, the 25 percent time criterion) generate rather weak or contaminated categories, the variables display a consistent structure based primarily on the nature of the clients served by the fields. Because particular types of clients are often associated with corresponding types of legal issues, however, it is often difficult to determine whether some aspect of the structure of the fields of law is more plausibly attributed to the nature of the clients served or to the knowledge or skills used in the fields. For example, in analyzing the overlap among the fields of law in the allocation of lawyers' time (chaper 2), we found a small, tight cluster consisting of patent law and the two sides of antitrust law. What common attributes of patents and antitrust enhance the likelihood that a lawyer who practices one will also practice the other? Broadly, both fields involve legal doctrines that in some way regulate competition, and they share common origins in English legal history.[16]

But this overlap in the doctrines of the fields corresponds to an overlap in the types of clients served. We may often think of patent lawyers as dealing with an "inventor," and we may also think of inventors as individual entrepreneurs, independent, idiosyncratic, obsessive, and quirky. This is, of course, a romantic, nineteenth-century view of the inventor, fostered by juvenile fiction of the Tom Swift genre. However quirky they may be, most commercially significant inventors are now surely organization men in the research and development departments of major corporations, and most valuable patents are now owned by large corporations or exploited by them under license. As is the case with antitrust specialists, therefore, patent lawyers' principal clients are corporations. The patent lawyers in our sample estimated that they derived an average of 95 percent of their practice income from businesses rather than persons.

Moreover, the historical importance of using patents as a means of monopolizing further exacerbates this confounding of knowledge base and client type. One of the methods used by the classic trusts to monopolize an industry was acquisition of the patents for the key manufacturing processes.[17] The clients who owned the patents became, then, the clients charged with restraint of trade, and the legal issue became whether the scope of the patent-granted monopoly privilege conflicted with the scope of the antitrust laws.[18] Today, litigation brought by the Justice Department, the Federal Trade Commission, and private plaintiffs often charges illegal restrictive practices in the licensing or use of patents. Patent infringement claims are also met with antitrust counterclaims or a defense of misuse of the patent; that is, the defendant in the infringement action charges that the plaintiff used the patent to restrict competition in violation of the antitrust laws or of the policy favoring competition. Thus, both the doctrines and the types of clients served by the two fields merge at some points.

To attempt to distinguish the independent effects of client type and of knowledge base on the structure of the fields would, in such circumstances, be not only difficult but artificial and misleading. We should, instead, appreciate that the two are inextricably entwined and then seek to understand their relationship and how the legal and social systems produced it.

In some areas of the law, however, the adversary system provides a natural control of the two variables. In criminal law, labor law, or personal injury work a rather rigid division separates practitioners serving opposing sides of the cases—with their corresponding, distinct types of clients—while the substance of the law is constant within each area. Therefore, where one doctrinal area of the law contains specialized fields of practice that are dictated by the type of client, we may want to examine the extent to which those fields are socially differentiated. How socially distant is labor law work for unions from the representation of management, criminal prosecution from criminal defense, or plaintiffs' antitrust or personal injury work from defendants'? We may, of course, look at the differences between those pairs of fields on any variables that particularly concern us, but the multidimensional scalogram analysis summarizes the extent of their social distance. Inspecting figure 3.1, we find the two sides of labor law located relatively close together at the base of the U. The other pairs, however, lie quite a bit further apart: criminal prosecution and defense are both on the left side of the figure but they are sufficiently separated to be clearly distinct; similarly, antitrust defense is considerably higher on the right side of the U than is antitrust plaintiffs' work; and personal injury plaintiffs' work reaches the far upper left corner, while personal injury defense falls into the general corporate cluster located near the lower middle of the U.[19] In some cases, therefore, differences in the clients served apparently produce clear social distinctions between the fields even though the fields' knowledge bases are substantially identical.

We would argue, in fact, that the more the clients of two fields differ, the more socially distant the fields will tend to be. Consider, for example, the comparisons just made between these pairs of fields. Though labor unions and the corporations that battle them doubtless differ in many significant ways, both are usually large organizations with substantial assets. The differences between criminal defendants and the government officials whom prosecutors consider their clients are probably greater (though the two kinds of clients do on occasion coincide), and greater yet are the differences between clients of the pairs more widely separated in figure 3.1. The two sides of antitrust work appear to serve distinct sorts of businesses—the defense lawyers serve very large corporations, while the plaintiffs' lawyers serve the individuals and smaller businesses that sue the "trusts." Antitrust defense lawyers report that they derive 77 percent of their practice income, on the average, from major corporations, while an average of only 22 percent of the income of antitrust plaintiffs' lawyers comes from major corporations. Of these pairs of fields, however, the difference in the clients is probably greatest between the two sides of personal injury work. The clients of the personal injury defense lawyers are almost exclusively insurance companies—major corporations with very substantial assets.[20] By contrast, the clients of the plaintiffs' lawyers are usually individuals, and although doubtless drawn from a range of social classes, they are from the lower classes far more often than are the clients of most lawyers.[21]

As was the case with respect to the organization of lawyers' work, therefore, we conclude that the most plausible interpretation of the findings is that the nature of the clients served primarily determines the structure of social differentiation among the fields. This reading of the data raises an issue that we address in the remaining chapters: given the tendency of the profession's structure to respond to interests and demands of clients—that is, of parties external to the profession—how much autonomy does the legal profession enjoy in defining professional roles, in determining which lawyers will perform which services for which clients, and in organizing the delivery of those services?

Chapter 4

HONOR AMONG LAWYERS

The law is a high-status profession, and the desire for elevated professional standing is presumably a part of the motivation that induces persons to enter the occupation. In choosing fields in which to practice, therefore, a lawyer may seek the work that will maximize prestige within the bar.[1] Such prestige might correspond to the differences among the types of clients served, following the division of labor and the patterns of social differentiation among the fields noted earlier. Service to the rich and the powerful might well earn one prestige in many circles (and some of the money and power might rub off as well, probably with no deleterious effect on prestige), while service to the poor and powerless might be less highly regarded. But the conferring of honor or deference is in its nature a process that is highly charged with symbolic content, and it might therefore be influenced less by economic and power considerations and more by norms or values. Learned professions are, after all, said to embrace values that set them apart from ordinary occupations—values that emphasize the importance of intellectual skills and devotion to public service. If this is so, honor and deference might be accorded by the bar to those lawyers' jobs that are most characterized by conformity to these values, and thus prestige within the profession and its consequent impact on the distribution of legal services might be determined by the standards and criteria of the profession itself rather than by the clientele or by other factors external to the profession.

Yet another possibility exists: lawyers might simply try to make money. That is, in selecting among the available work, they may seek to maximize profit.[2] Or there may be some trade-off between prestige and profit, some optimal level of each with respect to the other. The necessity of choosing between profit and prestige will be avoided, however, to the extent that the sorts of work that enjoy greatest prestige within the profession are coincidentally those that are also most highly paid. If high income should bring high prestige, or (no matter how remote the possibility may seem to a professor) if high prestige should command high pay, or if service to the rich and powerful should earn one both honor and riches, such a result would follow. But that may or may not be the case. If the values of the profession do, in fact, emphasize the duty of public service or the desirability of intellectually challenging work, there might not then be a close correspondence between wealth or social power and honor among lawyers.

In their discussion of the theoretical and methodological difficulties of current empirical work on occupational prestige, John Goldthorpe and Keith Hope note that prestige has classically been defined as "a particular form of social power and advantage that is of a symbolic rather than of an economic or political character, and which gives rise to structured relationships of deference, acceptance and derogation."[3] They thus emphasize that prestige judgments are functionally autonomous from the hierarchies of wealth and power—that they are, instead, subjective responses rooted in generally shared value orientations. As they observe, while it is common to speak of a person's possessing "naked power," or wealth through which preferences may be enforced, it is meaningless to speak of a person's "naked prestige" because giving deference to another ultimately requires the complicity of the lower-status person. Goldthorpe and Hope assert that "advantage and power in the form of prestige remain distinctive in that they entirely depend upon the existence of some shared universe of meaning and value among the actors concerned."[4]

Broadly speaking, theories of prestige conferral may be distinguished according to whether they have a macrostructural or a microstructural focus. Some macrostructural theories of prestige generation attempt to account for the patterning of prestige and deference in terms of a functionalist model of society in which the society's members make differing valuations of social activities according to what is usually assumed to be a widely shared value system.[5] Prestige or its opposite, derogation, in this view becomes expressive of the deep-seated feelings about the core symbols or meanings that constitute the very definition of that society's identity and basis of existence. Other macrostructural theorists, following a more conflict-oriented perspective that questions the broad value consensus postulated by the functionalist,[6] tend to regard prestige as a more manipulative or instrumental strategy of those who hold power positions, employed to bolster their domination by eliciting the voluntary compliance of the persons who occupy subordinated positions in the system. Prestige here alludes to its original Latin meaning of creating illusion or bedazzlement. Both the functionalist and conflict perspectives, despite their radical differences in the underlying processes postulated, imply almost identical predictions with regard to which positions will enjoy high or low prestige (although, admittedly, prestige in the conflict perspective tends to be a more precarious phenomenon).

Microstructural perspectives on theories of prestige conferral, on the other hand, direct attention to the social-psychological processes by which individuals come to make their subjective evaluations of the relative standing of various social positions. Concern here is with identifying the various factors an individual takes into account in making such judgments and with how the judgments are affected by information or ignorance about a particular position or by personally held values and social attributes of the judges, such as age, sex, race, class, and so on.[7] Because they are based much more on empirical, quantitative work than are the macrostructural theories, microstructural approaches tend to be descriptively oriented, to be tied to particular techniques of measurement, and to avoid more qualitative interpretations of why certain individual-level variables are more productive than others of relative prestige standing.

In the following analyses we draw on several of these differing perspectives in our efforts to account for the levels of prestige accorded by the respondents to the various fields of practice.

The Prestige Order

A randomly selected, one-in-four subsample of our survey respondents was asked to rate the "general prestige within the legal profession at large" of each of thirty fields of law. The ratings used a five-point scale, ranging from "outstanding" to "poor."[8] The resulting prestige scores of each of the fields, converted to a standard scale (see table 4.1, n. 2), are presented in table 4.1, where the fields are listed in rank order of declining prestige.[9]

The degree of consistency among the respondents in their prestige evaluations, especially with respect to the impact of their own fields of law on their allocations of prestige, is a matter of considerable theoretical

TABLE 4.1

Prestige Ranking of Thirty Fields of Law[1]

Rank Order	Field of Law	Prestige Score[2]	Rank Order	Field of Law	Prestige Score[2]
1.	Securities	68	16.	Labor (unions)	49[b]
2.	Tax	67	17.	Environmental (defendants)	49[c]
3.	Antitrust (defendants)	65	18.	Personal injury (defendants)	48
4.	Patents	61	19.	Environmental (plaintiffs)	47
5.	Antitrust (plaintiffs)	60	20.	Civil rights/civil liberties	46
6.	Banking	59[a]	21.	Criminal (prosecution)	44
7.	Public utilities	59[b]	22.	General family (paying)	42
8.	General corporate	59[c]	23.	Criminal (defense)	41
9.	Probate	58	24.	Consumer (creditor)	40
10.	Municipal	56	25.	Personal injury (plaintiffs)	38[a]
11.	Admiralty	55	26.	Consumer (debtor)	38[b]
12.	Civil litigation	54	27.	Condemnations	37[a]
13.	Labor (management)	53	28.	Landlord-tenant	37[b]
14.	Real estate	51	29.	Divorce	35
15.	Commercial	49[a]	30.	General family (poverty)	34
				TOTAL SAMPLE	50

NOTES: 1. Note that there are some discrepancies between the labels for the fields of law used in table 4.1 and those used in the preceding two chapters. The thirty fields used here are the original list presented to the respondents in the survey. After the data were in hand, we were in a position to create more inclusive fields of practice when there were too few respondents in the more narrowly defined fields to sustain statistical analysis, or to differentiate broadly inclusive fields into more homogeneous subfields. In the latter case, for example, we could distinguish between personal and corporate real estate or between personal and corporate tax work by taking into account other information the respondents gave us about their typical clients. We have, thus, aggregated and disaggregated some of these thirty fields in other analyses.

2. A random subsample (N=224) of our total sample of Chicago lawyers was asked: "On the following specialty list would you please indicate the general prestige of each specialty within the legal profession at large." The respondent rated each specialty on a 5-point scale, from "outstanding" to "poor." We then computed the mean rating for each field. To facilitate comparing the prestige ratings, we calculated a standard score for each field by determining the grand mean of the thirty field means and its standard deviation and then subtracting the grand mean from each field mean and dividing by the standard deviation. To eliminate decimal points and negative numbers, we multiplied the standard score by 100 and added 50 to the result. Thus, 50 represents the average mean prestige rating, with 10 points being the standard deviation. To illustrate: "Securities," the most highly regarded field, is 1.8 standard deviations above the average mean prestige rating, while "General family (poverty)," with its score of 34, is 1.6 standard deviations below the average mean.

a,b,c—Differentiate the prestige scores of fields of law that are tied when rounded to nearest full point.

import. If lawyers active in the fields that rank low in the overall prestige standing invert the order of prestige, or if those in higher-prestige fields inflate the prestige of their own fields, then a key assumption of the analysis—namely, that deferent behavior requires the voluntary complicity of the subordinate participant in the transaction—is cast into serious doubt.

We examined the data in a number of ways to determine the degree of agreement on prestige evaluations and the extent to which the evaluations are affected by the respondents' personal values. For example, lawyers espousing strong civil libertarian and social welfare values might accord prestige to fields serving these values, while lawyers holding strong pro-business values might give high ratings to fields serving business interests and give lower standing to more welfare-oriented fields.

Summarizing these analyses, if we divide the fields into three broad prestige levels—high, middle, and low—we find very substantial agreement between the mean prestige ratings assigned by respondents practicing in each of these three groups of fields and the overall evaluations of the sample as a whole. The rank-order correlations range between .85 and .97. With respect to evaluations of particular fields, however, there are some statistically significant differences. Moreover, there is a discernible pattern in these differences, respondents in low-ranked fields tending to assign higher prestige to such fields and, conversely, those from high-ranked fields assigning disproportionately high prestige scores to high-ranked fields. But the overwhelming tendency is for judges at all prestige levels to concur on the general prestige rank order of the fields, providing evidence that the lower-status lawyers understand the general hierarchy of the fields in the distribution of deference.

As a more concrete illustration of this general tendency, consider the fact that practitioners in the five fields ranked highest in prestige rate the following as the six most prestigious fields (in declining order): securities, antitrust defense, tax, general corporate, banking, and antitrust plaintiffs' work. By comparison, practitioners of the bottom five fields in overall prestige say that the top fields are securities, tax, probate, civil litigation, antitrust defense, and banking. Four fields are thus included in both lists of six. Similarly, practitioners of the five highest-prestige fields assigned the lowest places on the prestige scale to consumer (buyer), landlord-tenant, condemnations, family (poverty), personal injury plaintiffs' work, and divorce (again in declining order), while practitioners in the five lowest-prestige fields chose for those same positions personal injury plaintiffs' work, condemnations, family (poverty), landlord-tenant, consumer (seller), and consumer (buyer). Here they agree on five in each list of six fields. Thus, even raters who practice at the respective extremes of the prestige order display a high degree of similarity in their prestige ratings. Whether they like it or not, practitioners in the lower-status fields know which positions get the prestige, and their recognition of that hierarchy is, in itself, a form of complicity in the existing distribution of deference.

Turning to the characteristics of the prestige order itself, let us initially note some of the most striking general properties of the scores presented in table 4.1. First, the top of the prestige ranking is quite clearly dominated by fields that might be characterized as "big business" law. Of the first eight fields in the rank order, only tax is a type of work that is likely to be done for individual as well as for business clients, and the great predominance of tax work that lawyers do is almost certainly done for businesses or well-to-do individuals. The respondents spending 25 percent or more of their time doing tax work indicated that they derived 38 percent of their income from individuals—somewhat less than average—and that, of these individual clients, 70 percent were in the highest-status (professional, technical, or managerial) category. Not until we reach probate work, ranked ninth in prestige, do we come to a type of legal work that is done exclusively for individuals, and it may be significant to note that it is by its nature concerned with the transmission of wealth.

At the other end of the prestige ranking, we find the sorts of legal work that are characteristically done for individuals—general family practice, divorce, personal injury, consumer, and criminal law. Some of these types of practice may be derogated not only because of the lower socioeconomic status of the clientele but because of the "distasteful" or "unsavory" nature of the work. Divorce work involves emotionally charged, embarrassing personal situations, the clients are often at their worst, and the fate of children often hangs in the balance; personal injury work deals with grisly facts; and criminal work often requires the lawyer to associate with persons who are less than pleasant. Thus, the low prestige of these fields may be seen as analogous to the derogation of refuse collectors, coal miners, and others whose work involves untidy, burdensome tasks.[10]

Toward the middle of the prestige ranking, we find types of work that are done to some degree by large numbers of lawyers (e.g., real estate, civil litigation, and commercial work) and that might, thus, be seen as mediating fields. A type of work done by a great many lawyers, with widely differing characteristics, is unlikely to be regarded as either particularly high or particularly low in prestige. There are also some fields near the middle of the ranking that might be regarded as problematic; they possess ambivalent characteristics and may thus be inconsistently valued. For example, the practice of labor law (both for unions and for management) involves considerable financial stakes, but it also involves association with blue-collar workers or their representatives. Similarly, the lawyers who represent defendants in personal injury cases usually work for high-status clients, since those defendants are typically insurance companies, but their work involves unsavory fact situations.

The nature of the clients represented by the fields thus immediately appears to be an important determinant of field prestige, but this may bear further analysis and some alternative hypotheses might also be considered.

The Structure of Prestige

In attempting to account for the ways in which Chicago lawyers allocated prestige among the fields, we have used two structure-revealing techniques: smallest space analysis and hierarchical clustering. As the first step in our analysis, we computed the product-moment correlations of the respondents' prestige evaluations for every possible pair of fields. A high positive correlation between the scores given any two fields tells us that the respondents tend to see the two as having similar prestige standing in the profession. A negative correlation, on the other hand, tells us that lawyers who evaluate one field as having a high-prestige standing in the profession tend to regard the other as having lower social standing. A lack of correlation (i.e., a coefficient approximately zero in value) indicates no relationship in the evaluations of the fields under consideration.

These correlation coefficients can be treated as estimating the relative proximities of fields with respect to their prestige standings: fields similarly evaluated and thus having comparatively high positive coefficients are more proximate than are fields that are dissimilarly evaluated and that thus have either zero or negative coefficients.[11] These latter fields would appear to be farther apart in the minds of the judges. Note, however, that in comparing these proximities with one another, we do not expect them to order themselves automatically along a single or unidimensional prestige ranking unless prestige is, in fact, a unidimensional variable—

as income, for example, would be. The patterning of the coefficients could indicate the presence of several divergent dimensions or bases underlying the generation of prestige judgments. Thus, our conceptual framework and method of analysis permit prestige to be a multifaceted, subjective phenomenon that need not fit neatly into a single prestige hierarchy.

The structure of the resulting 30-by-30 matrix of correlation coefficients, which contains 435 coefficients, is obviously very difficult to discern by visual inspection of the matrix itself. Fortunately, however, a number of techniques have been developed to facilitate the recovery of the underlying structure of such a matrix. Smallest space analysis[12] was designed to represent such a matrix graphically in the fewest possible dimensions of a Euclidean space. Most readers will be familiar with such representations from their exposure to plane and solid geometry in high school or college.[13] Perhaps an analogy will help to clarify the procedure and its purpose. If we were to perform a smallest space analysis of the mileage chart presenting the distances between all the principal cities of the United States, we would obtain the conventional two-dimensional map of the United States on which the locations of the individual points— representing the cities—are arranged so that they accurately reflect, according to a specified scale, the distances between any given city and every other city. Similarly, the original matrix of correlation coefficients among prestige judgments estimates the relative (i.e., rank-order) distances between each field and all of the others.

Figure 4.1 presents the three-dimensional smallest space solution. It has a coefficient of alienation of .129, indicating a satisfactory fit.[14] In considering how this picture can best be interpreted, we should first emphasize that three dimensions were, in fact, required to achieve an adequate representation of the original matrix of correlations. The one-dimensional solution had a very high coefficient of alienation. This indicates that a representation with only a single dimension, presumably arranging the fields from highest to lowest prestige, would distort the more complex order present in the original data beyond acceptable limits. The respondents thus appear to have rated the fields on the basis of a more complex conception of their similarities and differences with respect to prestige or deference entitlements.[15]

One of the special attractions of smallest space analysis over other data reduction techniques is that we are not limited to using unidimensional ordering principles in interpreting the spatial configurations.[16] It is, for example, quite permissible to look for localized regions in the

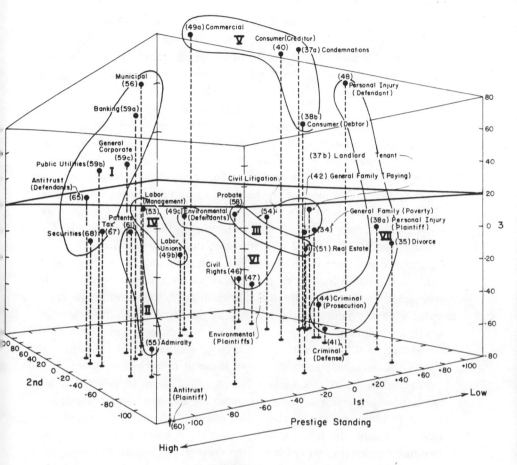

FIGURE 4.1

Three-dimensional Smallest Space Solution for Prestige Judgments of Legal Specialties

space in which the points are relatively homogeneous with respect to some characteristic that distinguishes them from other points in the space. This may be thought of as sector differentiation.[17] Another aspect of the configuration that may be interpretable is the relative distances of the points from the centroid of the solution[18]—that is, points in peripheral locations may differ in systematic ways from more centrally located points.[19]

In interpreting the smallest space solution, it is helpful to be able to give labels to particular regions of the space—that is, to identify clusters of points that seem to have something in common. To accomplish this by criteria more objective than visual impressions, we submitted the original matrix of correlation coefficients to a hierarchical clustering analysis, using the minimum average diameter method that was described in chapter 2. Figure 4.2 presents the dendrogram summarizing the results of this analysis. Reading the dendrogram from left to right, the reader can readily see how fields were successively added to particular clusters as the correlation coefficients linking given fields declined in value.

Inspection of the dendrogram suggests that a minimum value of .20 would provide a meaningful cutoff point for identifying the clusters. For ease of reference, these are listed in table 4.2 (and indicated in figure 4.1 by roman numerals and encircling lines around the relevant points). Note, however, that most of the fields in a given cluster are much more highly correlated with one another than this minimum. The average correlation of the pairs of specialties in the big business cluster (I), for example, is .40. Figure 4.2 also indicates that these seven clusters can be grouped into two mutually exclusive clusters, that is, higher status fields with predominantly corporate clientele versus lower status fields with small business or individual clients. Indeed, this penultimate clustering is finally joined in the last step of the hierarchical clustering (in which all points are put into one all-inclusive cluster) with a negative correlation of −.21, indicating that prestige evaluations of fields in one cluster are negatively correlated with those of fields in the other.

Within Cluster A (see table 4.2) one can discern an internal order from those fields serving establishment, big business, and government clients to those serving relatively less esteemed clients in the corporate world—namely, the labor unions. Similarly, Cluster B appears to be internally ordered from fields serving "respectable" small business and personal clients to those having to do with more varied or less highly valued classes of persons.

The smallest space analysis, presented in figure 4.1, tells essentially the same story as the dendrogram but with the added advantage of showing how the clusters are related to one another. (Remember that the closer two points are in the space, the more highly correlated they are and the more similar are their profiles of correlations with all the other points.) The seven clusters (plus the one nonclusterable field, antitrust plaintiffs' work) all roughly fall on the surface of a sphere. Using the first axis of figure 4.1 as an orientation for examining the spatial arrangement, we can divide the sphere into hemispheres, with the left hemisphere containing Cluster A and the right hemisphere mapping Cluster B. Roughly the upper half of the globe consists entirely of commer-

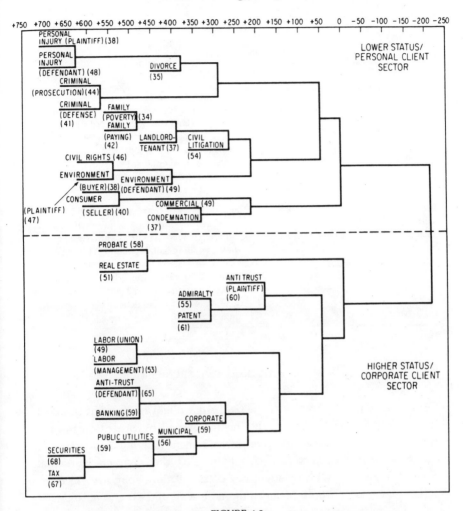

FIGURE 4.2
*Hierarchical Clustering Solution for Correlations among Prestige Ratings of
Fields of Law*

cially oriented fields, whether the clients are major corporations or small
businesses (note how personal injury defendants' work in Cluster VII is
pulled into this region because its clients usually are corporations), while
the lower half of the globe consists of fields serving individual clients.
Thus, these analyses provide additional support for the hypothesis that
client type is the primary determinant of the prestige structure of the
fields, just as it was of the division of labor and of the social differentiation of the fields, but this cannot be the end of our inquiry.

TABLE 4.2

Prestige Clusters Identified by Hierarchical Clustering Analysis of Original Matrix of Correlation Coefficients

	Cluster No.	Cluster Label	Specialties in Cluster (with Standardized Prestige Score)[a]
(A) Higher status/ corporate clientele clusters	I	Big business	Securities (68), tax (67), antitrust (defendants) (65), banking (59a), general corporate (59), public utilities (59b), municipal (56)
	II	Classic specialties	Patents (61), admiralty (55)
	III	Property	Probate (58), real estate (51)
	IV	Labor	Labor (management) (53), labor (union) (49b)
(B) Lower status/ small business/ individual clientele clusters	V	Small business/ commercial	Commercial (49a), consumer (creditor) (40), consumer (debtor) (38b), condemnations (37a)
	VI	Public interest & litigation	Civil litigation (54), environmental (defendant) (49c), environmental (plaintiff) (47), civil rights (46), family (paying) (42), landlord-tenant (37b), family (poverty) (34)
	VII	Personal litigation	Personal injury (defendant) (48), criminal prosecution (44), criminal defense (41), personal injury (plaintiff) (38a), divorce (35)

NOTE: a. Antitrust (plaintiff) (60) was not assigned to any of the above clusters at the criterion specified.

Correlates of Prestige: Imputed Characteristics

Of the many characteristics of the fields that might be thought to affect their prestige, some—such as the income earned by practitioners—are capable of more or less "objective" measurement (leaving aside issues of the reliability or validity of such measures). Other characteristics that may be associated with prestige, however, are more subjective in character, or at least it would be much more difficult and expensive to devise objective measures of them—the degree of "intellectual challenge" presented by the fields, for example. Like prestige, such characteristics are themselves more a matter of repute, but this does not mean that they may not reflect "real" differences among the fields. To assess such characteristics that are less amenable to objective measurement, we have relied upon ratings made by a panel of experts. This panel consisted of fifteen Northwestern University professors in various fields of law and four lawyer-researchers on the staff of the American Bar Foundation. We sought experts who were not active in the practice of law in the hope that this would minimize bias or defensive reactions,[20] and we asked them to rate all thirty fields on five characteristics. The averages of their judgments, converted to the same sort of standardized scores used for the prestige ratings made by the subsample of practitioners, are presented in table 4.3.

All five of these "imputed characteristics" of the fields were hypothesized to have significance for the prestige structure of the types of legal work. The first, intellectual challenge, might be expected to be highly valued within a community that characterizes itself as a learned profession. If, as the question we presented to the raters put it, "the legal doctrines, cases, statutes, and regulations involved in some types of practice are characteristically more difficult, complex, and intellectually challenging than are those in others," then we would expect the fields that are regarded as more demanding to command a higher degree of respect and, thus, of prestige. Similarly, the second imputed characteristic, rapidity of change, was also intended to address a factor that would make the practice of a field more difficult and, therefore, more entitled to respect. If the substantive law involved in an area of practice changes only seldom or slowly, practitioners will not have to work as hard at keeping up with developments in the law, and their practice is likely to become more routine. By contrast, practitioners in a rapidly developing field will have to devote more effort to keeping abreast of the field, they are likely to have more opportunities for creativity in their work, and they may thus be regarded as more deserving of deference. The third imputed characteristic, referred to in table 4.3 as the public service score, was intended to measure the degree to which work in the specialty tends to be done *pro bono publico,* or for altruistic or reformist motives, as opposed to being motivated primarily by a desire for profit. Our hypothesis was, of course, that altruism or dedication to public service might be positively valued and, thus, might enhance the prestige of fields where such motivations are characteristic. The ethical conduct dimension also represents a quite straightforward hypothesis, in some respects similar to the hypothesis concerning altruistic motivation. A reputation for rectitude may be thought to enhance prestige and power,[21] and a field that is thought to have a high incidence of unethical conduct or sharp practice may, conversely, be derogated. Finally, the freedom of action characteristic refers to the degree to which practitioners in the field are free to pursue the courses of action suggested by their own professional judgments, as opposed to being constrained by knowledgeable clients or by organizational superiors who supervise and guide their decisions. Autonomy has often been proposed as one of the characteristics that distinguishes the professions from other occupations.[22] In addition to the value given to independence in society generally and in the other pro-

TABLE 4.3
Imputed Characteristics of Fields of Law Practice

Public Service Field	Intellectual Challenge Score[1]	Rapidity of Change Score[2]	Public Service Score[3]	Ethical Conduct Score[4]	Freedom of Action Score[5]
1. Securities	63	62	44	57	39
2. Tax	67	66	43	55	46
3. Antitrust (defendants)	64	56	40	53	39
4. Patents	56	44	45	62	47
5. Antitrust (plaintiffs)	65	57	46	47	65
6. Banking	47	42	42	58	35
7. Public utilities	55	53	48	56	39
8. General corporate	51	48	44	59	41
9. Probate	45	32	44	57	46
10. Municipal	44	38	45	56	41
11. Admiralty	52	34	42	62	48
12. Civil litigation	52	48	51	45	55
13. Labor (management)	52	53	45	46	38
14. Real estate	45	37	43	48	50
15. Commercial	52	48	46	55	48
16. Labor (unions)	53	53	51	47	42
17. Environmental (defendants)	61	65	47	51	43
18. Personal injury (defendants)	33	42	43	38	46
19. Environmental (plaintiffs)	61	65	72	58	66
20. Civil rights/civil liberties	61	65	77	64	70
21. Criminal (prosecution)	48	56	56	47	53
22. General family (paying)	38	41	52	54	55
23. Criminal (defense)	51	57	57	33	64
24. Consumer (creditor)	50	60	46	43	41
25. Personal injury (plaintiffs)	35	43	43	25	64
26. Consumer (debtor)	52	59	65	50	62
27. Condemnations	35	36	43	39	49
28. Landlord-tenant	43	47	55	41	52
29. Divorce	30	45	50	30	54
30. General family (poverty)	38	51	76	61	64
TOTAL SAMPLE	50	50	50	50	50

NOTES: 1. An expert panel of nineteen persons, composed of Northwestern Law School professors and American Bar Foundation research specialists on the legal profession, answered the following question for the thirty fields: "The legal doctrines, cases, statutes, and regulations involved in some types of practice are characteristically more difficult, complex, and intellectually challenging than are those in others. Would you say that the degree of intellectual challenge presented by the *substance* (as opposed to the strategic considerations) of this type of work is: very great, higher than average, average, lower than average, or very little." The resulting means were standard scored, following the procedure described in table 4.1, note 2. A high score indicates a field that is above average in intellectual challenge.

2. The expert panel was asked: "The substantive law involved in some areas of practice changes more rapidly than it does in others. The practitioner, thus, may find it more difficult to keep up with developments in the former specialties than in the latter. Would you say that the law involved in this type of work: changes very rapidly, changes relatively quickly, changes at a moderate or average pace, changes relatively slowly, or changes very little or seldom." The resulting means were standard scored, following the procedure described in table 4.1, note 2. A high score indicates a field that is above average in rapidity of change.

3. The expert panel was asked: "Some types of legal work are more often done *pro bono publico*, or for altruistic or reformist motives, while other sorts of legal work much more clearly involve a profit motive. Would you say of this type of work that it is: highly money- or profit-oriented, substantially profit-oriented, neither or average, substantially *pro bono*, or mostly *pro bono*." The resulting means were standard scored,

fessions, the legal profession might give special weight to the ideal of the individual advocate fighting lonely, gallant battles, as opposed to the lawyer as bureaucrat, as a small cog in a large machine. Thus, we thought that freedom of action might also enhance the prestige of a field.

Let us now examine in some detail the ways in which each of these characteristics is related to prestige in our findings. In order to focus on the nature of the fields, as well as on the individual characteristics— that is, on the rows as well as on the columns of table 4.3—we have selected five fields for particular attention, though we will not be slavish about following them through all of their characteristics. These five are more or less evenly spaced along the prestige ranking; securities, the highest in prestige; public utilities, which has a moderately high prestige rating; real estate, which ranks near the middle; criminal defense, which has a moderately low rating; and divorce, which is the lowest-prestige specialty for which we have a large enough number of respondents to make generalization sensible. These fields have not been chosen, then, because of any special substantive significance but rather because they represent a range of positions in the prestige order. We will also call attention to other fields that are particularly noteworthy on one or more of the dimensions.

Beginning with the first variable in table 4.3, we find that securities work ranks fourth in degree of intellectual challenge. Its score is exceeded only by those of tax and of antitrust plaintiffs' and defendants' work. Thus, the four highest intellectual challenge scores are all held by fields that rank among the top five in prestige. The consistency of this tendency throughout the ratings is reflected in the fact that the intellectual challenge and prestige scores are correlated at .65.

Securities work is concerned with the regulations governing the dis-

---

following the procedure described in table 4.1, note 2. A high score indicates a field that is above average in public service motivation.

4. The expert panel was asked: "Some types of legal work have a reputation for 'sharp practice' or for a higher incidence of unethical conduct than is common in some other types of legal work. Would you say of this type of work that its reputation for ethical conduct is: very good, above average, average, below average, or poor." The resulting means were standard scored, following the procedure described in table 4.1, note 2. A high score indicates a field that is above average in ethical reputation.

5. The expert panel was asked: "In the practice of some types of law, the practitioner is, to a considerable degree, a 'free agent,' free to pursue whatever strategic course of action his own professional judgment may suggest. By contrast, the freedom of action of a practitioner of some other types of law is more highly constrained by knowledgeable clients or by organizational superiors who supervise and guide his decisions. Would you say that the practice of this type of law is characterized by: a high degree of freedom of action, above average freedom of action, average, below average freedom of action, or little freedom of action." The resulting means were standard scored, following the procedure described in table 4.1, note 2. A high score indicates a field that is above average in freedom of action.

tribution and resale of stocks, bonds, and other securities. The sorts of matters dealt with include the registration of securities being sold by corporations; the disclosure of information by corporations; insider trading; corporate takeover and proxy solicitations; and the regulation of underwriters, broker-dealers, securities exchanges, investment companies, and other entities involved in the securities industry. As such, it deals with a complex set of federal statutes and regulations. It is interesting to note that all four of the fields rated highest in intellectual challenge and all of the top six in the prestige ranking deal predominantly with federal rather than state law and that all of them require their practitioners to deal with federal regulatory boards, commissions, agencies, or departments (as well as, potentially, the federal courts). Thus, involvement with the federal government would appear to enhance prestige. This observation is strengthened by the negative correlation between the prestige of a field and the frequency of appearances by its practitioners in state courts, at $-.68$. (The frequency of appearance in state courts is also correlated at $-.65$ with the intellectual challenge scores of the fields.) At the other end of the scale, we find that divorce is assigned the lowest intellectual challenge score of all the fields. Other fields with notably low scores on this dimension are personal injury work (for both plaintiffs and defendants) and condemnation law (eminent domain), all of which also rank relatively low in the prestige order.

All of the four fields rated highest in intellectual challenge also have rapidity of change scores that are well above average, with the tax field again receiving the highest score. Keeping up with developments in a rapidly changing specialty may make that field more demanding than it would otherwise be, or slow change may make it less so. Probably for this reason, the rapidity of change and intellectual challenge scores are correlated at $.69$. The other high scores on the rapidity of change dimension were assigned to environmental law (plaintiffs and defendants) and to civil liberties work, which have been areas of rapid and substantial change in public policy in recent years. The lowest change scores went to probate and admiralty law, both of which are fields with very long histories and traditions.

On the dimension that dealt with the extent to which work in the fields is motivated by altruism as opposed to a desire for profit (the public service score), we find that securities work received one of the lowest scores, as did the other high-prestige fields. The only fields with lower public service scores were antitrust defense, banking, admiralty, and real estate. Real estate work deals with the transmission of property or with real estate development, both of which pretty clearly involve the profit motive—as do banking law, the defense of companies charged with antitrust violations, and the representation of shipowners or insurers in admiralty cases. Divorce work, by contrast, received one of its higher scores on this dimension—it reached the mean, 50. The personal injury lawyers, however, were not given much credit for altruistic motivation— the field received a score of 43, tied with real estate—while criminal defense work was scored substantially above average. The highest public service scores were assigned to civil liberties work, understandably enough, and to general family practice with poverty-level clients, the field ranked lowest in prestige. More generally, the public service score is negatively correlated with prestige at –.51. If altruistic motivation is highly valued within the legal profession, then the weight given it does not seem to be sufficient to offset the value attached to other factors that influence prestige judgments.[23]

The ethical conduct score behaves very differently than the public service score, and ethical behavior appears, therefore, to be seen as quite separate from altruistic motivation. This would be consistent with the role conception of the lawyer as a "hired gun" who provides professional representation, within the ethical rules, for anyone who is able to afford the fee. Securities work, like most of the high-prestige fields, has an ethical conduct score that is well above average. Though the highest ethical conduct score was assigned to civil liberties work, as was the case with the public service dimension, and one of the highest scores went to general family work for impoverished clients, most of the high ethical conduct scores were assigned to fields that represent big business clients and, particularly, to the more traditional of those fields such as patents and admiralty. The lowest ethics scores were given to fields that represent individuals in the sorts of cases that are characterized as "unsavory"— personal injury plaintiffs' work, divorce, and criminal defense. That is, the circumstances of the cases are thought to be unsavory, by hypothesis, for reasons quite distinct from the unethical conduct of practitioners in the field. There may be a tendency, then, to see work that is "dirty" in one respect as dirty in another, or the labeling process may lead to unethical conduct in work that is already derogated for other reasons.[24] The score of personal injury plaintiffs' work on this dimension, for example, is particularly striking: 25, the lowest score that any of the fields received on any of the dimensions. The image of the "ambulance chaser" is apparently quite vivid. The ethical conduct score is correlated with prestige at .53.

The freedom of action score summarizes the scholars' judgments of the extent to which practitioners in the field are free to pursue their own courses of action, rather than being constrained by clients or superiors. Both securities work and public utilities work, for example, have quite low scores on this dimension. These kinds of work are typically carried out in large organizations, with senior lawyers supervising juniors, and the clients are highly knowledgeable. A large percentage of the lawyers who devote at least a quarter of their time to public utilities work are house counsel in either corporations or governments, and 77 percent of the securities lawyers practice in the largest firms, those with more than thirty lawyers. The practice of securities law is, in fact, reputed to be confined largely to a few major urban centers where the underwriters are located. The only fields with lower freedom of action scores are banking and the management side of the labor law practice, both of which serve very sophisticated clients who are capable of assessing the situation and guiding the lawyers' actions. Thus, the higher-prestige fields serving business clients tend to have low freedom of action scores: consequently, this dimension is correlated negatively with prestige (−.54).

Criminal defense work has a very high freedom of action score. This may reflect not only the large number of solo practitioners among criminal defense lawyers but also the characteristic lack of sophistication and influence of their clients, persons charged with crimes. The only fields with higher freedom of action scores than criminal defense are civil liberties, environmental plaintiffs', and antitrust plaintiffs' work. In the case of civil liberties, the powerlessness of the clients may be one of the factors accounting for the score, but another contributing factor may well be the inherent creativity or lack of legal structure of the field, which permits the civil liberties lawyer great freedom of action in devising the theory and strategy of a case. This explanation may also apply to environmental plaintiffs' work, which is a new and relatively unstructured field.

The other field receiving a high score, antitrust plaintiffs' work, is a very interesting deviant case. That field ranks fifth in prestige and has a freedom of action score of 65—not until we descend to nineteenth position in the prestige order (environmental plaintiffs' work) do we find another freedom of action score in the 60s. The lawyers who represent the plaintiffs in antitrust cases must have all the same knowledge and abilities as do those who represent the large corporations that are the defendants in these cases. In addition, however, the plaintiffs' lawyers have the task of creating novel theories on which to base antitrust treble damage actions—some of these have involved class actions on behalf of large numbers of consumers[25]—and the fact that they search out their clients, rather than being presented with a problem by a client, enhances their freedom of action. The antitrust plaintiffs' lawyers tend to be seen by other lawyers as, in a sense, "traitors to their class." They have the skills of antitrust lawyers, but they make those skills available to the "wrong" sort of client (and profit handsomely by doing so, if they are successful). The profession's view of the antitrust plaintiffs' lawyer as a species of pariah may also be reflected by the field's score on the ethical conduct dimension, which is substantially lower than would be anticipated from its prestige rank.

Correlates of Prestige: Practitioner Characteristics

The literature on "deference entitlements" suggests that several of the differences among the fields that were discussed in chapter 3 might have an impact on prestige. At least four broad categories of characteristics are worthy of examination:

1. Social origins of the practitioners. Persons of higher social origins are expected to gravitate toward more prestigious work, while persons of derogated origins are relegated to the less attractive work tasks. In an important sense, this is a result of a prestige hierarchy rather than a cause, although one would expect a differential distribution according to esteemed and derogated social origins to reinforce perceptions of the prestige differences.
2. Work context and task characteristics. Such variables as the size of the employer organization have implications for predictability and routinization of work flow, for the range and variety of tasks performed, for the dependence of one's goal achievement on the satisfactory performance of others, and so on.
3. Client characteristics. The social evaluation of the relative importance (in power or social status) of the organizations and persons for whom services are being rendered might also affect prestige. Thus, honor or derogation might be acquired by association with the high and the mighty or the lowly and despised.
4. Rewards. There is reason to think that prestige might be affected by the characteristic levels of extrinsic and intrinsic rewards associated with practice in the fields, including direct financial rewards, the quality of working

conditions, and the personal job satisfaction arising from the presence or absence of monotony, excitement, risk taking, or challenge in one's work.

Let us examine a few variables that exemplify each of these categories. In the analyses discussed here, as in those reported in chapter 3, the description of the characteristics of each field and of its practitioners is based on the responses of lawyers who said that they devoted at least 25 percent of their time to the field.[26]

The extent to which the practitioners have their origins in a metropolitan community has a strong negative correlation with the prestige of a field (-.69). That is, lawyers who resided during their high school years in cities with populations in excess of 250,000, or in suburbs of such cities, make up a larger percentage of the practitioners in the lower-prestige fields than in the types of work enjoying higher prestige. Securities work, for example, has a relatively low percentage of practitioners of metropolitan origin. Two of the other top-prestige fields, antitrust defendants' work and patents, have percentages that are significantly below the norm. By contrast, many of the fields with very high percentages have very low prestige—in divorce, criminal defense, and personal injury plaintiffs' work the proportion of practitioners who were raised in cities exceeds 90 percent.

We find, then, a process of selection in the recruitment of practitioners to the various fields that results in a negative correlation between metropolitan origin and the prestige of the fields. Some of this may well be self-selection. Our sample was drawn only from lawyers with offices in the city of Chicago, and persons of rural or small-town origin who have chosen to practice law in such a large city might be expected to be highly motivated for success or "upward mobility." The recruitment of lawyers for the high-prestige fields may also be more wide ranging, resulting in a greater diversity of origin of the practitioners. The large law firms and corporations that employ disproportionate numbers of the lawyers in the high-prestige fields are likely to recruit at the top national law schools and to select students with high academic achievement, regardless of whether the students grew up in the firm's locality. In the lower-prestige fields, by contrast, the lawyers tend to be solo practitioners or to be in smaller firms. The sorts of contacts that are facilitated by the kinship and acquaintance networks of locals may be more important to survival in these fields—that is, the flow of legal work to these lawyers is not so likely to be guaranteed by affiliation with a large, ongoing organization.

The percentage of Jewish practitioners in each field and the percentage of Republicans appear to be almost mirror images of one another. Securities work has a relatively low percentage of Jews and a relatively high percentage of Republicans, which is the general tendency for the higher-prestige fields—though the Republican percentage is more strongly correlated with prestige (.67) than is the Jewish percentage (-.45).[27] Divorce and consumer work both have relatively high percentages of Jewish practitioners and relatively low percentages of Republicans, as is the case with the other lowest-prestige fields.

The meaning of these findings seems straightforward, if unpleasant. Jews are, perhaps, the most derogated of the ethnic groups that are represented in the bar in any substantial numbers,[28] and the Republicans tend to be, conversely, high on deference entitlements such as family wealth and social origins.[29] These factors may bias both the actions of the gatekeepers who limit entry into the high-prestige fields and the perceptions of the prestige of the fields that have high concentrations of the derogated or privileged group. Thus, two complementary tendencies may reinforce one another here. Jews have tended to be excluded from the high-prestige fields and Republicans (or persons with the sort of social origins, family wealth, and connections that Republicans tend to possess in disproportion) to be welcomed in them, leaving the Jews with only the less prestigious work available if they choose to practice law and leaving the Republicans free of the necessity of doing such work. The presence of Republicans in the higher-prestige fields may then serve further to enhance the prestige of those fields by association, and the presence of Jews in the lower–prestige fields may serve further to depreciate the prestige of those fields in the eyes of lawyers who derogate that ethnic group.

A phenomenon that is in some respects similar may be observed in the data on the percentage of practitioners in each of the fields who attended one of six elite American law schools (see chap. 1). Forty-five percent of the securities lawyers had graduated from these schools, while only 11 percent of the divorce practitioners, 8 percent of the personal injury plaintiffs' attorneys, 4 percent of the criminal defense lawyers, and none of the prosecutors had done so. The two sides of antitrust work both have high percentages of elite school graduates, which is consistent with their high prestige and their intellectual challenge scores. Noteworthy here is the substantial correlation of .65 between the percentage of elite law school graduates practicing in a field and the intellectual challenge score assigned to the field by our panel of scholars.

An intriguing finding on this dimension is that one of the highest percentages of elite school graduates is found in the civil rights/civil liberties field. (Since this field has one of the smallest case bases, however, we should be cautious regarding this result.) Civil rights ranks only twentieth in prestige on the original list of thirty fields. Given the high percentage of elite law school graduates practicing civil liberties law, what might account for its relatively low prestige? There is not a great deal that is noteworthy about the other characteristics of the lawyers practicing in the field, except that the percentage of solo practitioners who do civil liberties work is zero in our sample, a fact that would also tend to be associated with high prestige. We have already noted, however, that civil liberties was ranked highest on three of the five imputed characteristics—the public service score, the ethical conduct dimension, and the freedom of action score—and near the top of the ratings on the other two. Of those scores, particularly extreme ratings occurred on the freedom of action and public service dimensions (where the scores were 70 and 77, respectively), and these two imputed characteristics are the ones that are negatively correlated with prestige. On the face of these data, then, one interpretation might be that the prestige of civil liberties work suffers because its practitioners enjoy too much autonomy in their work and have an unseemly reputation for altruistic motivation! But perhaps it would be well to be tentative about this conclusion, having a decent regard for the limitations of our data—in particular, the sample size. We will have more to say about these general issues at the conclusion of this chapter.

Moving from data that concern demographic and recruitment characteristics of practitioners in each of the fields, we turn to characteristics of the work context of the fields. These include the nature of the organizations within which the fields are practiced, the type of clients served, and the stability of the attorney-client relationship in each of the fields. We might begin with four of these characteristics that constitute two more pairs of mirror images. The percentage of solo practitioners in a field is inversely related to the percentage of the specialists who practice in firms with more than thirty lawyers, and the two are correlated with prestige at -.58 and .63, respectively. (These are, of course, only two among several possible practice settings—the others include positions in smaller firms, as corporate house counsel, or as government lawyers at the federal, state, or local level. All of these other possibilities, however, have smaller correlations with prestige.) A similar relationship exists between the percentage of law practice income that the practitioners in the field receive from major corporations (defined as corporations with more than $10 million in sales per year, in 1975 dollars) and the percentage of their clients who are persons of lower social status. These two variables are correlated with prestige at .54 and −.86, respectively. (These are again, of course, only two among several possible client types, but these categories are mentioned because of their extremity of type rather than the degree of their correlations with prestige. The percentage of income derived from major corporate clients has, in fact, the lowest correlation with prestige of the five client type categories.)[30]

The securities field has one of the largest percentages of lawyers who practice in large firms, and in our sample its percentage of solo practitioners is zero. Its percentage of large-firm lawyers is surpassed only by that of the antitrust defendants' lawyers, another of the highest-prestige fields. These two fields are among those with the highest percentages of practice income derived from major corporate clients and the lowest percentages of clients who are blue-collar workers. The low-prestige fields, by contrast, reverse this pattern. Divorce, the lowest-prestige field, has the highest percentage of solo practitioners, one of the two lowest percentages of large-firm lawyers and of income from major corporations, and a percentage of lower-status clients that is well above the mean. The pattern of the divorce lawyers is repeated, in a degree that is only slightly less extreme, by criminal defense counsel and by the other lowest-prestige fields—in particular, general family practice and personal injury plaintiffs' work. The direction of these findings would certainly be anticipated, but the clarity of the pattern is impressive when one recalls that the practitioners included in these fields may have devoted up to 75 percent of their time to other types of work.

Public utilities practitioners do not fit this pattern. They include relatively small percentages both of solo practitioners and of large-firm lawyers. Instead, corporate house counsel and government lawyers are substantially overrepresented among the public utilities practitioners. Public utilities work also has by far the highest percentage of clients whom the lawyer has represented for three years or more. That is, again, perhaps attributable to its high percentage of house counsel and of government lawyers. In general, the higher-prestige fields tend to have greater stability of clientele, though the correlation of this variable with prestige just fails to achieve statistical significance at the .05 level (.33). Criminal defense has the lowest percentage of clients represented for three years or more, in spite of the well-publicized delay in bringing criminal cases to trial. But it is interesting to note that lawyers engaged in general family practice report that they have, on the average, represented about three-fifths of their clients for three years or more. Apparently the clientele of the neighborhood lawyer is fairly stable.

All of the respondents were asked to characterize the nature of the tasks involved in their legal work in terms of dimensions defined by sets of polar opposites. One of these dimensions dealt with the degree to which work in the field required arcane skills or expertise. Eighty-six percent of the securities lawyers responded that it would not be possible to train paraprofessionals to handle many of the tasks involved in their practice. Though this percentage was far higher than that of any of the other fields, there was a general tendency for the more prestigious fields to be relatively high on this dimension—it correlates .49 with prestige. The two sides of antitrust work were, however, both somewhat out of line on this dimension. In spite of their high-prestige standing, only a minority of each of those sorts of practitioners believed that a professional's skills were so uniformly required in antitrust work.

At the other end of the prestige order, 31 percent of the general family practitioners believed that professional expertise was indispensable in their work. Divorce, criminal defense, and personal injury plaintiffs' lawyers were slightly more likely to feel that a professional's training was essential to performing the tasks required in their practices—about two-fifths of the practitioners in each of those fields responded that paraprofessionals could not be trained to handle much of the work. And civil liberties had, again, a position on this dimension that was inconsistent with its relatively low prestige rank—nearly 70 percent of the civil liberties lawyers believed that their work required professional expertise. This result may be related to the high percentage of civil liberties lawyers who are graduates of the elite law schools or to the high rate of change in the law of the field.

Another of these work task dimensions dealt with the extent to which the practice of each of the fields requires skill in negotiating and in advising clients, rather than detailed concern with technical rules. Though this may sometimes be associated with the relative proportions of corporate and individual clients, that is not always the case. To the extent that the big business lawyer spends time putting business deals together, as many lawyers certainly do, he or she functions as a negotiator and advisor. The overall tendency, however, is for the negotiating and advising tasks to be inversely related to prestige; the correlation is –.42. The largest percentages of practitioners who define their tasks as negotiating and advising are to be found in such specialties as general family practice and divorce. Securities work, by contrast, has one of the lowest percentages on this dimension, the other conspicuously low ones being antitrust plaintiff's work, banking, and criminal prosecution. Apparently, the negotiation of plea bargains does not consume much of the prosecutors' time or attention.

A third work task dimension concerns the extent to which practitioners in the field find that the nature of their work requires them to concentrate on one field of law. This dimension is, then, a measure of the degree of specialization (or, at least, of the lawyers' perceptions of it). Securities has one of the highest percentages of practitioners reporting that their work is concentrated in one field. The only fields higher on this dimension are patents—a "classic" specialty that traditionally commands the exclusive attention of its practitioners—and labor union work, perhaps the purest of the newer specialties. Divorce has one of the lowest percentages on this dimension. Other fields low on this dimension are probate, commercial work, and—especially low—general family practice. The dimension correlates .52 with prestige.

On all three of these dimensions, general family practice is found at one of the extremes. Perhaps this is attributable to the fact that a general family practice is perceived as the sole remaining refuge of the general practitioner, the small-town lawyer in the big city. In fact, however, the range of problems handled by these lawyers is rather severely limited. They are highly unlikely to handle any antitrust law or securities or patents or municipal bond work or labor law. Still, it is no doubt true that the general family practice is as close as we come in major cities to the practice of law as it existed before the rise of specialization and of the large firm.

Finally, we turn to the extrinsic rewards of law practice—the percentage of practitioners in each of the fields who have incomes from law practice of $50,000 per year or more (recall that these are 1975 dollars).[31] The financial rewards of law practice do not quite achieve a significant correlation with the prestige of the fields and, when the income variable is included with others in a regression equation, it makes no additional contribution to the prediction of prestige (see table 4.4). Securities work, however, has one of the highest percentages of practitioners with incomes of $50,000 or more, and high income rates are also found in the banking, patents, and general corporate fields. The lowest percentages are found in criminal prosecution (where there is a system constraint on income—the practitioners are full-time, salaried public employees),[32] in consumer law, and in real estate. Real estate, thus, has fewer high-income practitioners than would be suggested by the more moderate prestige level of the field. The correlation of law practice income with the prestige of the fields is certainly in the expected direction, then, but it is important to note that the extrinsic reward system seems to affect the prestige judgments less than do several of the more intrinsic characteristics of the practice—including, specifically, client type, the nature of the work, and the characteristics of the lawyers engaged in the field.

The lack of a strong relationship between income and prestige has surprised some of the lawyers whom we have informed of this finding. It may not appear so surprising, however, if we consider the possible impact of field prestige on the market for legal services. Prestige may tend to increase the supply of lawyers in the high-status fields and to decrease supply in the types of work that have lower prestige. If these hypothesized effects of prestige on supply did occur, their impact on income would, of course, tend to increase remuneration in the lower-status specialties, and, conversely, decrease income in the high-prestige fields—producing, perhaps, a result like the one we observe. A study of the medical profession also found no significant correlation between income and the professional prestige of the medical specialties,[33] suggesting that some such general process may operate.

Multivariate Models of Prestige

Of the many possible attributes of a social position that might be grounds for differing prestige evaluations, we have included in this analysis only one or two representatives of each of the major varieties of deference entitlements recognized in the literature. Given the limited theoretical closure in the field and the limitations on the data that we could realistically gather, we can certainly make no claim that our list of attributes is theoretically or empirically exhaustive. The attributes imputed to the fields by the scholars whom we used as expert raters (see table 4.3) were, however, designed to tap what we thought were the most important, analytically independent characteristics of the work that might influence prestige, apart from the social characteristics of the persons who perform such work. (But we recognize, of course, that our panel's evaluations may have been "contaminated" by knowledge of the sorts of people involved in particular fields.) Four of these five attributes proved, in fact, to be significantly correlated with prestige, giving some support to our initial ideas. We can only appeal to face validity, however, to justify our claim that these five attributes are analytically independent of one another. In examining the intercorrelation matrix of the imputed characteristics, we found that five of the ten correlations were statistically significant, but these correlations were usually of only modest strength. (Only two of the ten coefficients were larger than .55.) Similarly, we analyzed a number of measures drawn from four broad categories of deference entitlements. Most of these variables also proved to have statistically significant associations with the allocation of prestige standing among the fields, but they too are correlated among themselves to varying degrees.

The crucial question thus becomes: given the extensive information that we have about the characteristics of the fields, many of which are known to covary in highly predictable ways, can we devise a parsimonious explanation of the differential allocation of prestige among the fields? In attempting to answer this question, we constructed three alternative theoretical models of the prestige allocation process in which we specified a set of characteristics that might determine prestige standing. We were then interested in calculating the net effect on prestige of each characteristic, holding constant the effects of all the other independent variables in the model. Multiple regression analysis is designed to do just this sort of task.[34]

Table 4.4 presents three regression models. Model I considers all five of the characteristics imputed to the fields because we believed at the outset that they all would make analytically independent contributions to our understanding of prestige allocation. Model II considers six selected characteristics drawn from the much larger set of attributes of the practitioners and their practices. The proportions of "Jewish origin" and "elite law school attended" are intended to represent social origins; proportions "working in law firms with thirty or more lawyers" and "professional training required for practice" tap the work context and work characteristics; percent "lower-status clients" represents client characteristics; while proportion "earning $50,000 or more" represents the extrinsic rewards associated with the fields. Of course, all these indicators are resultants of complex social processes and cannot, consequently, be expected to measure precisely only one hypothetical construct in our theoretical argument. The proportion working in large law firms, for example, is associated with the proportion reporting major corporations as clients, while the proportion in solo practice, which we have treated as a work context attribute, is associated with the proportion of Jewish origin, a putatively social origin attribute. Thus, since we expected some confounding and redundant effects among the various indicators, caution

TABLE 4.4

Multiple Regression of Selected Variables Predicting Prestige of Fields

	Unstandardized Coefficients	Standard Error	Partial F	Standardized Coefficients
Model I: Characteristics Imputed by Legal Scholars				
1. Public service	-.81	.27	9.18**	-.62
2. Intellectual challenge	.84	.32	6.80**	.62
3. Ethical conduct	.55	.32	2.95*	.33
4. Freedom of action	.16	.22	0.51	.11
5. Rapidity of change	-.15	.31	0.25	-.11
Multiple $R^2 = .88$; $F = 24.73$, $p < .001$.				
Model II: Selected Characteristics of Practitioners				
1. % lower-status clients	-4.63	1.03	20.07**	-.73
2. % professional training	1.41	.99	2.01	.20
3. % Jewish	-1.29	1.05	1.53	-.16
4. % law income $50,000 or more (age adjusted)	1.48	1.43	1.08	.16
5. % firm larger than 30	-.45	.86	.27	-.10
6. % elite law school	.02	1.33	.00	.00
Multiple $R^2 = .80$; $F = 10.90$, $p < .001$.				
Model III: Composite Model				
1. Public service	-.56	.14	16.56**	-.43
2. Ethical conduct	.54	.13	15.85**	.33
3. Intellectual challenge	.44	.14	9.51**	.33
4. % lower-status clients	-1.48	.85	3.04*	-.23
5. % Jewish	-1.43	.61	5.54**	-.18
Multiple $R^2 = .92$; $F = 41.77$, $p < .001$.				

NOTES: *Statistically significant at the .05 level.
**Statistically significant at the .01 level.

in interpreting the results is advisable. Model III is a composite that considers simultaneously the five variables in Model I and the six in Model II to construct the best predictive model.

Table 4.4 lists the variables for each model in the order of their standardized coefficients (see last column). These standardized coefficients may be compared with one another in a given model in order to determine the relative impact each variable has on the dependent variable, the standardized prestige score. The partial Fs in the third column permit one to test whether the independent variable in question still contributes significantly to the explained sums of squares once the effects of the other variables in the model have been statistically removed. The unstandardized coefficients in the first column are the b coefficients, or partial slopes, for the multiple-regression equation that can be used to predict the prestige scores. The second column gives the standard errors of these coefficients, providing a different way to evaluate the significance of a given unstandardized coefficient in the multiple-regression equation as a whole.

All three regression models are able to explain very high proportions of the total variance in prestige scores (the multiple R^2s range from .80, or 80 percent, for Model II to .92, or 92 percent of the total variance, for Model III). But in the case of models I and II, only one to three variables are required to achieve these high R^2s. In Model I the first two variables, public service and intellectual challenge, achieve a multiple R^2 of .80, which rises to .87 with the addition of ethical conduct. The remaining two variables, freedom of action and rapidity of change, do not make significant contributions to the explanation of the prestige scores once the effects of the first three variables are taken into account. In Model II an even more dramatic result emerges. Only the first variable, the percentage of lower-status clients, is significantly involved in explaining prestige, achieving an R^2 of .74. The addition of each of the other variables does not appreciably improve the prediction. Especially noteworthy is the absence of impact of the income of the fields on their prestige standing—a negative finding of considerable theoretical import.

Model III confirms the results of the other two models by selecting only the top three variables from Model I and the top two from Model II (from the eleven it was originally given) to construct the optimal prediction of the prestige scores. It also informs us, however, that our fears about the problem of disentangling the confounding effects of the various indicators were justified. The percentage of lower-status clients, the single most powerful predictor in Model II, drops to relative insignificance when the imputed characteristics are taken into account. To a considerable degree, however, this is probably attributable to the fact that the imputed characteristics may be themselves—like the prestige judgments—relatively abstract assessments of the goodness or social desirability of the fields.[35] They may thus be expected to be closer to prestige.[36] Moreover, the variables that are subject to the least measurement error and contamination will tend to have the greatest explanatory power in a given regression analysis.[37] For this reason also, then, the relative predictive contribution of the client type variables and of the other practitioner responses may be, in a sense, understated. Moreover, the client variable is clearly associated with several of the imputed characteristics of the fields, and perceptions affecting the prestige of the fields that serve lower-status clients are probably measured more directly by these more abstract, imputed characteristics. The sorts of cases that lower-status clients bring to their lawyers, for example, often call for relatively routine legal procedures, however much these cases may be of great personal moment to the clients. But this fact about the nature of practice for lower-status clients may be measured more directly by the inclusion of the intellectual challenge variable in the composite model. Similarly, we have noted that certain types of cases—for example, personal injury, criminal defense, and divorce—are perceived as more likely to be handled by lawyers who employ practices that are contrary to the prevailing ethical norms of the profession. These cases, too, tend more often to involve lower-status clients, but our measure of ethical conduct more directly addresses the issue. Finally, lower-status clients, being persons of limited financial means, are likely to be involved in the less profitable sorts of litigation and legal work—at times even requiring *pro bono* service. As Model III shows, such public service is negatively associated with the prestige of the fields of law. Indeed, according to the standardized coefficients, it plays the strongest role in predicting the prestige scores.

The negative impact of the percentage of practitioners of Jewish origin, a nonsignificant variable in Model II but of some importance in Model III, appears to be tapping an aspect of the prestige of legal specialties that is no longer masked by the effects of the other variables in the model. The negative impact on prestige standing of high concentrations of Jews in a specialty is probably due to the past and possibly continuing discrimination against the entry of Jews into the higher-status specialties that serve major corporate clients.[38] But since our data measure the state of affairs at only one point in time, we cannot be certain of whether this reflects an historical process that has run its course.[39]

Conclusions

Though it is difficult to sort out the elements of prestige within the legal profession because of the high degree of intercorrelation among several of the hypothesized independent variables, some interpretations of the findings seem relatively clear. The general pattern of the prestige ranking, with fields serving big business clients at the top and those serving individual clients (especially clients from the lower socioeconomic groups) at the bottom, is unambiguous. Here again, however, we may run up against a confounding of effects. The degree of intellectual challenge of the fields is highly correlated not only with their prestige (.65) but also with their percentages of lower-status clients (-.59). Thus, what may appear to be an effect of client type on the prestige rankings might, instead, be in large part an effect of peer opinions of the intellectual demands of the different sorts of practice.

Rather than resorting to further techniques of multivariate analysis to attempt to unravel the confounding of intellectual challenge and client type, a condition that may well exist in the real world, let us simply look at a few specialties where the degree of intellectual challenge is held constant. Our list of thirty fields includes six where the adversary system creates clearly distinguishable specialties representing the two sides of the case—antitrust, labor, environmental, personal injury, criminal, and consumer law. The intellectual challenge ratings of the two sides of each of these six areas are, of course, substantially identical.[40] (Dealing with the legal substance of a case requires the lawyer, on whichever side of the case, to anticipate and respond to the law on the other side.)[41] In each of these six fields of law, the side that represents the more "establishment" client is consistently rated higher in prestige. That is, those who defend criminals are given less prestige than those who prosecute; labor union lawyers rank lower in prestige than do the labor lawyers who represent management; lawyers who represent plaintiffs with personal injury, environmental, or antitrust claims are assigned lower prestige scores than the lawyers who represent the insurance companies and other businesses that are the defendants in such actions; and the advocates for buyers of consumer goods have less prestige than do those who represent the sellers. The consistency of result in these comparisons seems to us to be rather persuasive support for the hypothesis that client type has an effect on prestige that is independent of the intellectual difficulty of the subject matter. And that effect is, quite clearly, to enhance the prestige of work done for corporate, establishment, or big business clients and to derogate that done for small businesses or for individuals, particularly those from the lower classes.

In the practice of law—as on the assembly line and in many other sorts of work—an almost inevitable consequence of the division of labor has been a routinization of tasks for most of the workers.[42] There are few kinds of law practice where a high proportion of the problems call for truly creative solutions, and these jobs are likely to be at the top of the prestige ladder, in the service of the most influential, most wealthy clients; unique problems and unique solutions are more likely to be generated when the stakes are high.

Service to individuals is often repetitious and dull. Although a divorce, a limb wasted by an automobile accident or by medical malpractice, a home mortgage foreclosure, a sanity hearing, a criminal charge, a lost job, or an adoption or child custody proceeding may all involve anxiety and suffering for the client, the specialized lawyer finds most such cases routine. Thus, the value placed on intellectual challenge in the allocation of prestige within the legal profession has an inherent elitist tendency—that is, because the depth of the clients' pockets determines, in important part, the complexity of the legal issues with which their lawyers will be permitted to deal, the value placed on intellectual challenge will tend to lead lawyers into the service of a socioeconomic elite. In this respect, the legal profession differs from medicine. An exotic medical problem may afflict rich or poor (though such a problem is no doubt more likely to be detected in the well-to-do), and prestige within the medical profession may not, therefore, correspond so closely to the wealth of patients. Even poor people can have prestigious diseases.

The association between the public service scores of the fields and their prestige is similarly entwined with the nature of the clients served by the fields. The clients who receive legal services at no fee or at greatly reduced fees (the recipients of *pro bono* work) are, of course, likely to be either persons of lower social status who cannot afford service at the going rate or controversial clients who are served as a matter of principle. Thus, the highest public service scores were assigned to civil rights/civil liberties, poverty law, work for plaintiffs in environmental cases, and work for debtors in consumer cases. By contrast, the fields that receive the lowest public service scores, banking law and antitrust defense,[43] serve powerful corporate clients. While we doubt that altruism is directly or consciously derogated, even in the practice of law, it may well be that the profit motive and the values associated with it are given some weight in the allocation of prestige within the profession. The American legal profession seems to be preoccupied with economic enterprise—Karl Llewellyn observed long ago that the "main work" of the metropolitan bar was "in essence the doing of business," and he drew some further conclusions:

Now, any man's interests, any man's outlook, are shaped in greatest part by what he does. His perspective is in terms of what he knows. His sympathies and ethical judgments are determined essentially by the things and the people he works on and for and with.... Hence the practice of corporation law not only works for business men toward business ends, but develops within itself a business point of view—toward the work to be done, toward the value of the work to the community, indeed, toward the way in which to do the work.[44]

We do not mean to suggest that the many lawyers who are primarily concerned with the facilitation of business do not perform useful social functions—they obviously do. The values they serve are the core economic values of our society,[45] and the more a field of law serves these values, the higher its prestige will be within the profession.

In addressing theories of prestige generation in the professions more generally, Andrew Abbott has commented on our findings and has put the subject in an interesting light.[46]

Intraprofessional status is in reality a function of professional purity. By professional purity I mean the ability to exclude nonprofessional issues or irrelevant professional issues from practice. Within a given profession, the highest status professionals are those who deal with issues predigested and predefined by a number of colleagues. These colleagues have removed human complexity and difficulty to leave a problem at least professionally defined, although possibly still very difficult to solve. Conversely, the lowest status professionals are those who deal with problems from which the human complexities are not or cannot be removed.

The theoretical origins of this argument lie in anthropology.... [P]urity and contagion taboos are an extension of cultural systems. The impure is that which violates the categories and classifications of a given cultural system. Through amorphousness or ambiguity it brings together things that the cultural system wishes to separate. Nearly all writers agree that the application of esoteric knowledge of particular cases is characteristic of professions.... [P]roblems that fundamentally challenge basic professional categories are impure and professionally defiling. It is at once clear why Laumann and Heinz (1977) find that legal practice involving corporations in nearly all cases stands above that involving private individuals. The corporation is the lawyers' creation. The muck of feelings and will is omitted from it *ab initio.* Where feelings are highest and clients most legally irrational—in divorce—intraprofessional status is lowest.

Over time, professional knowledge develops a system of such relative judgments of purity and impurity. All these judgments follow the same pattern.

The professionally defined or definable is more pure than the undefined or undefinable. . . . The barrister stands above the solicitor because he works in a purely legal context with purely legal concepts; the solicitor links the law to immediate human concerns. The free-lance or associated professional stands above the employed professional because his work is not conditioned by employer policy. The academic professional's high status reflects his exclusively intraprofessional work.[47]

We find this an intriguing and appealing argument, and we believe that it merits further examination. It is, in fact, quite consistent with some of our observations. Abbott suggests, however, that our data provide an adequate test of his thesis. We doubt this. In an extended footnote to his article, Abbott asserts that our study "provides striking confirmation of the purity thesis." He continues:

The best correlate of prestige in their legal data is the degree to which a specialty implies work for altruistic or reformist motives (*pro bono* work). Such service for non-legal ends is a strong negative correlate of specialty status, while a subfield's legal (intellectual) challenge and reputation for professional ethicality are strong positive correlates. It is clear that professional ethicality, at least, is an aspect of professional purity. The low ethicality ratings of personal injury, criminal defense, and divorce lawyers reflect the profession's fear that their judgment will be corrupted by client concerns. The low status of *pro bono* work is a similar disparagement of extralegal motives.[48]

After noting that our definition of the intellectual challenge variable specifically distinguished the legal or doctrinal substance of the work from the "strategic considerations" and dealt only with the challenge presented by the former, Abbott argues:

Since only legal complexity is measured, the variable of professional purity is implicitly included. Given that issues of the exclusion of the nonprofessional seem to sustain the other two correlates of prestige, parsimony suggests their importance in this correlation as well. Given that these correlates account for 87 percent of the variance in intraprofessional prestige rankings, Laumann and Heinz's study seems strong evidence indeed for the place of purity in determining that status.[49]

One difficulty with this line of argument is that it is an incautious use of our regression analyses. As we noted, the relative contributions of the several variables to the prediction of prestige cannot be taken at face value. Because of the nature of the variables and their measurement and because of statistical properties of regression analysis itself, it is almost inevitable that the more abstract, imputed characteristics of the fields, as rated by a small group of scholars, will do better in the regression equations than will the "real-life" characteristics of clients and practitioners, as obtained from our interviews with 777 randomly selected respondents. Indeed, the remarkable fact is that the client and practitioner characteristics do as well as they do. Moreover, Abbott points to the public service score as the "best correlate of prestige," presumably referring to the regression analyses, but by far the strongest simple, bivariate correlation with prestige is that of the percentage of the field's clients who are persons of lower social status—a correlation of -.86. If one were primarily interested in parsimony, therefore, one could do quite well in predicting the prestige of a field just by knowing the proportion of its clients who are blue-collar workers. And Abbott's thesis does not account for the consistently higher prestige of the establishment sides of the split fields—that is, personal injury plaintiffs vs. personal injury défense; criminal prosecution vs. criminal defense; consumer/creditor vs. consumer/debtor, etc.—unless he wishes to argue that the corporate side of a given field or case is consistently more professionally pure than the personal client side of the same field or case. If one takes this latter position, the professional purity thesis becomes very similar to the client type thesis of the generation of professional prestige. It really amounts to a contention that the mixture of client type with public service, ethicality, and intellectual challenge, in our terms, cannot be decomposed.

Whatever the explanation of this distribution of prestige within the profession, however, it is important to inquire into whether it can be translated into more generalized influence, either within or outside the profession. Public office would, of course, provide one sort of opportunity for such influence. Another type of influence is almost a necessary consequence of the role of advisor to big business. Lawyers who influence the expenditure of many millions of dollars, who determine whether corporate acquisitions or mergers will or will not take place, undeniably have an important sort of power. But there is also the sort of influence that may come from control of the institutions of the profession, especially the bar associations. That is, who is given the authority to speak in the name of the profession as a whole? We have examined the extent to which lawyers in the several fields have held positions of leadership in the Chicago Bar Association (CBA), the principal professional association in

Chicago, and we find that the percentage of practitioners in a field who have held such positions correlates .56 with the prestige of the field. More than 20 percent of the securities, patent, and public utility lawyers in our sample had been CBA leaders, for example, while 5 percent or fewer of the criminal defense and of the personal injury lawyers had held such positions. The direction of the causation (if any) seems quite clear. It is not very plausible that the proportion of CBA officers in a field would enhance its prestige appreciably. Rather, it seems more likely that lawyers are chosen for CBA office on the basis of their prestige, some of which is attributable to the prestige of the sorts of work they do. Thus, there is evidence that the prestige of the field of law may be convertible into influence, at least within the profession.

Another important consequence of the prestige structure may well be its effects on the recruitment of lawyers into the various fields. Most of us value deference, and there will thus be an incentive to enter the types of legal work that will earn one that deference. Many of the lawyers who practice in the fields that serve persons of moderate means[50] are probably not as highly qualified as are those who serve the large corporations, and many probably entered the lower-prestige fields more from necessity than from choice. As we have noted, practitioners who attended the most prestigious law schools are more numerous in corporate practice than in the fields serving individuals and small businesses. The other side of this coin is that the percentage who attended law schools of only local repute ranges from a high of more than 70 percent in criminal defense and personal injury plaintiffs' work to a low of less than 20 percent in securities, antitrust defense, public utilities work, and business litigation. The local law schools have fewer resources to devote to legal education than do the elite schools,[51] and the lawyers who serve individuals are therefore likely to be less well trained than are those who serve corporations. Since the income that a lawyer receives from his practice is not significantly associated with the prestige of his field, the monetary rewards available may induce some lawyers—even some well-qualified ones—to enter a lower-prestige practice. A desire for service might also lead, of course, to that same result. But to the extent that lawyers making career choices are concerned with their prestige within the legal profession—concerned, that is, with receiving deference or respect from their fellow professionals—they will tend to choose service to big business rather than to poor people.

In sum, the distribution of honor or deference among the fields of law is entirely consistent with our observations about the organization of legal work and the structure of social differentiation of the fields. All three appear to be organized by the types of clients served, and the great divide occurs between the kinds of law practice that serve primarily corporate clients and those that serve primarily individual persons or small businesses. These are the two main sectors of the legal profession.

Chapter 5

THE CONSTITUENCIES

OF "NOTABLE"

CHICAGO LAWYERS

Lawyers—like other citizens, but perhaps more than many—may participate in a variety of public activities, creating overlapping networks of association. Many lawyers are involved in politics, and that will certainly bring some of them together. Similarly, some members of the bar meet and work with other lawyers in community activities such as school boards, hospital boards, or sundry charitable organizations. Some are active in fraternal lodges or veterans' activities, where they come into contact with yet other lawyers. Lawyers who have ties to close-knit ethnoreligious communities form relationships with fellow attorneys who share their membership in those communities. And some lawyers become acquainted through the industry groups of their client businesses. These various circles of acquaintance all provide opportunities for lawyers to achieve prominence of one degree or another since the participants in each of these realms of activity will constitute a potential constituency that may provide its leaders with varying amounts of recognition and other resources.

The lawyers who are prominent within the profession and outside it thus draw upon several distinct sources of prominence, which may or may not create distinct sets of "leaders of the bar." It is possible that the several sorts of constituencies might give rise to separate "spheres of influence" within the bar or, in the alternative, that the mechanisms and agencies of the profession might serve to integrate some or all of the various bases of leadership, making it possible to mobilize varying constituencies toward common goals. (Such political integration probably becomes less likely, however, as lawyers become increasingly specialized by type of client.) The identification of the leaders of the major constituencies—and of the extent of the overlaps among the constituencies and their leaderships—is, then, a preliminary step in charting the distribution of influence within the profession.

Accordingly, one of the objectives of our research was to identify and analyze the characteristics of the circles of acquaintanceship of various sorts of "elite" Chicago lawyers. We approached this objective by compiling a list of lawyers who were notable for one or more types of influence.[1] Informants who are knowledgeable about the Chicago bar were consulted during the preparation of the list, and efforts were made to represent several kinds of elites. Some were included because of positions they held. For example, the deans of three law schools and the five most recent presidents of the Chicago Bar Association were placed on the list, as were all four of the persons who had, up to that time (1975), served as president of the Chicago Council of Lawyers, a group of younger, reform-oriented lawyers.[2] Chicagoans who had held office in the Illinois State Bar Association were also included. Most of the lawyers chosen were, however, selected reputationally—that is, they were chosen because they were widely reputed to possess the sorts of influence that we wished to represent. Some were selected because they were known to hold power within one of the important political factions in the city, some because they were thought to be "pillars of the establishment" of the profession, and others because they were widely said to be among the best-known and most successful practitioners in particular fields or areas of the law, thus perhaps giving them influence based on their command of the respect of their professional colleagues.

An effort was made to represent the major ethnoreligious groupings, and the final list was also structured to include solo practitioners and partners in large, medium-sized, and small firms. No special effort was made to include government-employed lawyers or corporate house counsel, and none in fact appear on the list.[3] We deliberately excluded from the list all lawyers who were then in public office, such as judges, prosecutors, and legislators, because we wished to avoid confounding personal influence with governmental authority.[4] Because our population was deliberately selected to consist of elite, influential lawyers, it substantially overrepresents older persons,[5] graduates of the more prestigious law schools, and senior partners from large firms. Young lawyers, graduates of less prestigious schools, and solo and small-firm practitioners are, however, also represented. Few blacks or women had reached positions of great prominence within the bar by 1975, and our list includes only three blacks and two women, but in neither case do those numbers underrepresent their proportions of the total bar (see chap 1).

During the interviews with each of our 777 respondents, we handed the respondent a printed card containing the list of "notable" lawyers.[6] (The lawyers on this list are sometimes collectively referred to below as "the notables." This term has the advantage of giving a sociological grouping some of the cachet of a Motown recording group.) The respondent was asked to go through the list twice. On the first run-through, the respondent was asked to check the names of the notables with whom he or she was "personally acquainted." Among the names checked, the respondent was then asked to select those notables who "would find the time to advise" the respondent because of their "personal relationship." These procedures were intended to get at successively stronger levels of acquaintance. Both the looser, lower standard of acquaintance and the more stringent standard can be used to generate a network structure, and we have analyzed both levels. The two structures are highly similar. The main difference is that the lower standard produces a somewhat weaker, fuzzier solution, presumably because of chance acquaintanceships or very casual, weak relationships elicited by the less stringent question. We have, therefore, used the results based on the higher standard in the analyses presented here. Since the two questions were both intended to measure acquaintance, of differing levels or strength, we speak below of the stronger level in terms of whether or not the respondents "knew" the notables; this should be read, of course, to mean that they were acquainted with them to the specified degree.

The Likelihood of Knowing Notables

One of the most important things to note about our findings is that fully 38 percent of our random sample of respondents knew *none* of the forty-three notables. Another 37 percent of the respondents knew from one to three; the remaining 25 percent knew four or more. Only ten individuals claimed to know as many as half of the notables. These findings suggest that only a small minority of the bar is in close or regular contact with any substantial segment of the elites of the profession, even when one considers a broad range of types of elites. Such contacts as occur are highly differentiated by the social and practice characteristics of both the respondents and the notables, as we shall see below. For now, however, let us not concern ourselves with the patterns of differential association with varying elites but merely note some of the correlations between the respondents' characteristics and the probability that they will know any of the notables.

The type of law school attended by a respondent significantly affects the likelihood of acquaintance with notables.[7] Respondents who attended elite or prestige schools are overrepresented among those who know more notables, while those who attended regional or local schools are underrepresented among the better-acquainted respondents.[8] For example, graduates of elite schools constitute only 14 percent of the respondents who know none of the notables, but they make up 21 percent of the group who know from one to three and 31 percent of those who are acquainted with more than three notables. By contrast, lawyers who went to regional schools make up 25 percent of the group who know no notables, 14 percent of those who know one to three, and only 6 percent of those who know more than three notables. Similarly, respondents who have higher incomes are significantly overrepresented among those knowing more notables, while those with lower incomes are underrepresented.[9] The reasons for both of these tendencies are quite obvious.

Age is also correlated with the likelihood of knowing the notables.[10] The mean age of the respondents who do not know any notables is 41.5; the mean age of those who know more than three is 50.6.[11] The interpretation of this finding is, again, quite straightforward—it no doubt reflects both the age of the notables and the tendency to accumulate more acquaintances as one's life goes on. The existence of a correlation between age and the level of acquaintance with notables, however, suggests the desirability of reexamining the correlation between income and acquaintance to determine whether income has an effect that is independent of age or whether the effect is attributable merely to the tendency of income to increase with age. If we correlate income with the number of notables known while controlling for age, we find that the income effect is still significant.[12] Emphasizing the statistical significance of these correlations between income and acquaintance may, however, distort their substantive meaning. Whichever of the correlational methods we use, the relationships between respondents' incomes and the extent of their connections with the notables is not large—income explains only about 10 to 12 percent of the variance in acquaintanceship. Since superior access to notables (often thought of as "contacts") may be of value in increasing one's income over the longer term, this modest correlation between income and notable acquaintanceship is the more surprising. That is, the relationship between the variables may be reciprocal, higher incomes tending to increase access to notables and access to notables tending to increase income. Given the fact that these two tendencies may reinforce one another, the observed correlation is not as high as might have been expected.

Neither the religious affiliations of the respondents nor their political party preferences are significantly correlated with the extent of their acquaintance with notables.[13] Because the list of notables was deliberately structured to include a more or less balanced representation of the various religious and political groupings, there would be no reason to expect overall levels of acquaintanceship to be biased by these variables.

There is a significant correlation between the sort of organizational setting in which respondents practice and their levels of acquaintance,[14] but the only strong differences are that respondents from large firms (those with more than thirty lawyers) are overrepresented and house counsel are underrepresented among those knowing more than three notables. Both of these tendencies are probably attributable to the composition of the group of notables. Many of the most influential members of the legal profession are partners in the major firms, thus causing them to be substantially overrepresented on the list, and we have already pointed out that the list includes no house counsel.

The Characteristics of the Notables

Because the notables occupy a variety of social positions and possess a great many combinations of personal background characteristics, it is not possible to summarize the variables in brief compass and yet do justice to the data. The notables' network structure, as we analyze and present it, includes several broad features that are readily discernible, but other points of interest rest on observations that are more subtle, more fine-grained, and yet distinct.

Therefore, we will set forth the characteristics of each of the forty-three notables in some detail so that the reader may evaluate our interpretation of the features of the structure. In both the biographies of the notables and the presentation of the smallest space analysis that we have used to examine the patterns of relationships (see figure 5.1), each of the notables is given a pseudonym. This has been done to facilitate the depiction of the structure of the relationships among broad types of elites within the profession.[15] The initial letters of the pseudonyms indicate the major classifications of the notables.

Categories of Notables	No. in Each Category
B = Leaders of the organized bar	10
D = Law school deans	3
E = Establishment	5
L = Prominent liberals	7
La = Presidents of the Chicago Council of Lawyers	4
M = Miscellaneous	2
R = Regular Democrats	3
T = Trial lawyers	9

Biographical Sketches of Notables

ORGANIZED BAR (B)

Baer. A partner in a small, family firm with her husband and father-in-law, she is in the line of succession to the presidency of the Illinois State Bar Association. She will be the first woman to hold that post, and she is one of only two women on this list of notable lawyers. She has been active in organized bar work on civil rights. There are a great many lawyers in both her family and her husband's, and there are family ties to the Regular Democratic Organization. Age 40; Jewish; graduate of Northwestern Law School.

Baker. A name partner in a medium-sized firm with a general corporate practice, he specializes in securities work. He is a past president of the Chicago Bar Association. He has also been very active in the Boy Scouts, serving at the national level, and he is on the boards of some smaller corporations. Mid-60s; Jewish; Northwestern Law School.

Barents. A partner in an old-line firm, specializing in general corporate and probate work, he participated in drafting the Illinois Probate Court Act. He is a past president of the CBA. In his early 70s, he is one of the oldest persons on this list. Of Dutch ancestry; educated at Phillips Exeter Academy, Harvard College, and Harvard Law School.

Beiderbecke. A partner in one of the largest and most prestigious Chicago firms, he is the immediate past president of the CBA. Though his firm is general counsel for several major corporations, his own work is in the area of personal injury defense (representing insurance companies). Of German ancestry, he is 60 and a graduate of John Marshall Law School.

Behan. Probably the most celebrated personal injury plaintiffs' lawyer in Chicago. A past president of the CBA, he is an Irish Catholic; went to Loyola for both undergraduate work and law school; a Regular Democrat; age 51.

Behrman. A name partner in a medium-sized firm that does general corporate and probate work, he is a past president of the CBA. He and Behan got more press than other recent presidents of the CBA; Behrman's press coverage dealt with organized bar affairs, while Behan's dealt more with his personal injury work. Jewish; mid-60s; University of Chicago, both undergraduate and law school.

Bigard. A name partner in a small firm, doing personal injury defense and general trial work. Now in the line of succession to the presidency of the CBA, he has long been active in the Association and has held a number of lesser offices. Of northwestern European ancestry, he is in his early 60s and is a graduate of John Marshall Law School.

Blackburn. A senior partner in one of the largest and most prestigious firms, he was president of the CBA several years ago and is now the president-elect of the ABA. His practice is primarily in public utilities and other large corporate work. He has served on many important boards and commissions. He is a registered Republican; WASP; mid-60s; attended Dartmouth College and Columbia Law School.

Brendan. A name partner in a small firm doing general trial work, including some personal injury defense and some probate work, he is the current president of the CBA. Irish Catholic; attended Villanova for undergraduate work and Loyola Law School. He has been described in the Chicago newspapers as a "nominal North Shore Republican but loyal to the Daley Machine." He is in his mid-50s.

Bricker. A name partner in a medium-sized firm, he defends steel companies in environmental pollution actions, but he also does probate work and is a Fellow of the American College of Probate Counsel. He is a past president of the Illinois State Bar Association. He has served on the boards of the Chicago Association of Commerce and Industry and the American Judicature Society and is a member of the Episcopal Diocesan Council. Mid-60s; WASP; graduate of the University of Michigan Law School.

LAW SCHOOL DEANS (D)

Dodds. The dean of the University of Chicago Law School. His specialty is antitrust, and he maintains a consulting relationship with a downtown firm. Before joining the Chicago faculty thirteen years ago, he was on the faculty at Stanford. WASP; mid-50s; graduate of both Harvard College and Harvard Law School.

Dolphy. The dean of the Northwestern Law School. Like Dodds, his specialty is antitrust, and, also like Dodds, he maintained for several years an active relationship with a downtown corporate firm. Protestant of German descent; late 50s; Northwestern both undergraduate and law school; longtime member of the Northwestern law faculty.

Drootin. The dean of the DePaul Law School. He teaches and publishes in the area of property and future interests. He has been a member of the DePaul faculty for ten years, joining it only a year after graduation from Loyola Law School. At 36, he is one of the younger persons on this list.

ESTABLISHMENT (E)

Eldridge. The senior, name partner of one of the largest and most prestigious Chicago firms. He is well known as a civil litigator and he has held numerous important positions. He was a member of the National Commission on the Causes and Prevention of Violence in 1968–69, senior counsel to the Warren Commission, and minority counsel to the House Judiciary Committee during the Nixon impeachment hearings. He has served as president or chairman of the National Conference of Commissioners on Uniform State Laws, the U.S. Supreme Court's Advisory

Committee on the Federal Rules of Evidence, the Illinois State Bar Association, the American College of Trial Lawyers, and the American Judicature Society. A Republican, he also has strong ties to some Democratic officeholders in Chicago. His father was a Chicago police lieutenant. He is an Irish Catholic; graduate of the University of Illinois, both undergraduate and law school; age 68.

Eliot. The senior, name partner of a small, family firm specializing in probate and real property work, he is one of the most prominent probate lawyers in Chicago. In addition to his practice, he has for many years held an appointment to the faculty of the Northwestern Law School, where he regularly teaches property and estates (wills and trusts). He has published treatises in those fields. He is a past president of the American College of Probate Counsel. Republican; WASP; graduate of Dartmouth College and Northwestern Law School; mid-60s.

Ellington. A senior partner in one of the most prestigious firms. He is the principal lawyer handling the affairs of Chicago's largest bank, which is also said to be the largest client of the firm, and is the chairman of the board of trustees of Notre Dame University. Catholic; independent Democrat; Notre Dame undergraduate and Harvard Law School; mid-60s.

Ellsworth. A senior partner in a major, old, established firm (it has been termed the "toniest" in the city, though the point might be disputed), where he represents large corporations and public utilities. He is active and influential in Illinois Republican politics and has served as president of United Charities. Early 60s; of English descent; University of Chicago undergraduate and Harvard Law School.

Elman. The senior partner of one of the largest, most prestigious firms, his specialty is antitrust defense, representing very large corporate clients. He serves on a number of boards and is active in community and cultural affairs, including present service as vice-chairman of the board of the Chicago Symphony. Republican; Jewish; Harvard, both undergraduate and law school; late 60s.

LIBERALS (L)

Presidents of the Chicago Council of Lawyers (La)

Ladinsky. Practices corporate law in a large firm. She is one of two women in this group of notable lawyers and also, at age 33, one of the youngest. She is a member of the U.S. Tax Court bar and has taught real estate finance at DePaul. Jewish; graduate of Northwestern Law School.

Lang. A name partner in a small firm, he specializes in the representation of plaintiffs in employment discrimination cases. His late father was a federal judge. Lang was one of the principal founders and the first president of the CCL. Age 34; Jewish; graduate of the University of Chicago.

Lasser. Does general corporate work, including some real estate and some securities, in a large, traditionally Jewish firm. Counsel to the committee on style and drafting of the 1970 Illinois Constitutional Convention. Age 33; Jewish; graduate of Northwestern Law School; liberal Democrat.

Lawrence. A professor at Northwestern Law School, he was the second president of the CCL. He does some *pro bono* litigation, especially in the fields of broadcasting regulation and welfare reform. Age 34; Jewish; Harvard graduate; liberal Democrat.

Other Liberals (L)

Lewis. A name partner in a small firm with a general practice. He does some work in both employment and housing discrimination and represents minority businessmen and entertainers. He is prominent in black liberal political circles, was formerly counsel to Jesse Jackson's Operation PUSH, and was, briefly, a candidate for the Democratic nomination for mayor of Chicago. A graduate of Northwestern Law School, where he has also done some part-time teaching, he did undergraduate work at Tennessee A & I State. African American; in his mid-40s.

Liebling. Head of a public interest law organization. He has long been prominent in reform litigation, especially in the area of housing discrimination, and he was formerly a partner in a major corporate law firm. Jewish; graduate of Chicago; late 40s.

Lynch. Does corporate litigation for one of the most prestigious firms in Chicago, but has also been active in liberal Democratic politics. He was one of the lawyers for the Singer-Jackson delegation to the 1972 Democratic Convention (the pro-McGovern Illinois delegation that was seated in place of the delegation headed by Mayor Daley) and was a member of the 1970 Illinois Constitutional Convention, where he chaired the committee on style and drafting (see Lasser). He was a law school classmate of Lasser's at Northwestern; mid-30s; Irish Catholic origin.

Leventhal. A name partner in a medium-sized firm that represents smaller corporations and does a large amount of "commercial" practice. He has long been prominent in the ACLU and other liberal causes. He is also active in support of the arts and in the American Jewish Congress. Jewish; early 50s; Chicago graduate.

Leonard. A name partner in a small firm. Widely known for his labor arbitration work, he also handles general corporate matters. At age 70, he is one of the oldest of the notables. He has been very active for many years in liberal and reform-oriented associations. He also has strong ties to the academic community, having been a lecturer or visiting professor at the law schools at Yale, Northwestern, and Arizona State. Jewish; University of Chicago graduate.

Lonsdale. A partner in an old-line firm, where he does corporate litigation. Characterized by associates as a "liberal gadfly," he has undertaken *pro bono* work in environmental pollution, voting rights, and housing cases. He has been active in the organized bar, formerly serving as secretary of the board of the CBA, and was also a member of the first board of directors of the CCL. He sits on boards of several civic and cultural organizations, including the board of the Chicago Symphony. A graduate of Harvard Law, he has done some teaching at Chicago. Mid-50s; English ancestry; politically independent.

Locke. Does corporate litigation and securities work as a partner of a large firm, and is influential in independent Democratic politics. Headed the state's ethics board under Governor Daniel Walker. A graduate of Harvard College and Northwestern Law School; early 50s; WASP.

MISCELLANEOUS (M)

McShann. A name partner in one of the largest firms specializing in labor law, he is perhaps Chicago's most prominent labor lawyer on the management side. As might be expected due to his role with corporate management, he is a Republican, and he serves on the board of the United Republican Fund. Early 60s; University of Chicago, both undergraduate and law school.

Mingus. A name partner in a small to medium-sized firm, he specializes in state and local tax matters, especially property taxes. Prior generations of his family provided Chicago with lawyers who were among the first Jews to attain prominence in the bar, and his late father's name still has pride of place in the firm name of one of the city's largest traditionally Jewish firms. He married into another prominent, wealthy Jewish family. He is a patron of the arts and serves on the boards of literary and cultural associations and institutions, including the board of trustees of Lake Forest College. He attended Lake Forest College and the University of Virginia Law School; late 50s.

REGULAR DEMOCRATS (R)

Robinson. A solo practitioner, he is a trial lawyer who is often called upon to represent, as a special counsel, the city of Chicago, other Cook County governmental bodies, and the Democratic Party Organization. He is a trustee of the University of Illinois (an elective office) and was recently chosen by the board to serve as its chairman. His career was advanced by Mayor Daley, who took a liking to him. His father was a judge who was close to Congressman William Dawson, long the most powerful African American in Chicago's Democratic Organization. African American; late 40s; University of Illinois undergraduate and University of Michigan Law School.

Rosenbloom. A name partner in a small firm, he does general trial work. He is well connected in Regular Democratic circles, earning substantial fees as a special counsel to the Chicago Sanitary District. Jewish; mid-40s; Northwestern undergraduate and Harvard Law School.

Ryan. A name partner in a small firm, his specialty is eminent domain work, where his political connections are thought to be useful in negotiating compensation for the land condemned. He is a former United States Attorney and serves as counsel to the Cook County elections board. He has talked of running for governor. Irish Catholic; Regular Democrat; Loyola undergraduate and University of Detroit Law School; early 50s.

TRIAL LAWYERS (T)

Taft. A partner in a medium- to large-sized firm, where he specializes in civil litigation, especially personal injury defense work. He has represented several insurance companies and Phillips Petroleum. Republican administrations have appointed him to various positions of public service. WASP; Republican; University of Nebraska undergraduate and Nebraska and University of Chicago law schools; mid-50s.

Takas. Among the most highly regarded criminal defense specialists practicing in Chicago. He is now in partnership with one other lawyer. Though he formerly did a great deal of work in the state criminal courts, he now devotes more of his efforts to the federal courts, representing more affluent clients accused of financial crimes. Twenty-five years ago, he was an assistant state's attorney. Greek Orthodox; University of Chicago, both undergraduate and law school; mid-50s.

Tendler. A partner in one of the largest and most prestigious corporate firms, he specializes in libel law and represents several of the news media. He also does general corporate work and litigation. He is well connected in both Republican and Regular Democratic circles and is called on to represent politicians who find themselves in legal difficulties. Of Jewish origin, he is now a Presbyterian, and he married into a socially prominent family. He is a graduate of Northwestern, both the college and the law school, and is a member of Northwestern's board of trustees. He is in his late 40s.

Tristano. The senior, name partner in a small, family firm specializing in divorce. Five of the nine lawyers in the firm are Tristanos. He is one of the best-known divorce lawyers in Chicago. Italian Catholic; DePaul University, both undergraduate and law school; late 60s.

Tolman. The senior, name partner in a small firm specializing in antitrust plaintiffs' work. He is probably the most prominent anti-trust plaintiffs' specialist in Chicago. Very active in support of the arts, particularly music, he is a member of the board of and counsel to the Lyric Opera of Chicago. He has commissioned new musical compositions and operatic productions. Jewish; undergraduate work at Syracuse, graduate of Northwestern Law school; mid-60s.

Tower. A name partner in a medium-sized firm with a general commercial practice, he is a prominent trial lawyer. Known for his work as a courtroom advocate, he has served as a "special prosecutor" of prosecutorial officials accused of crimes. He has long been active in the ABA, serving as chairman and a longtime member of the House of Delegates. He has also been president of the Illinois State Bar Association and of the American College of Trial Lawyers. He is a graduate of Georgetown

Law School and did his undergraduate work at St. Thomas College in Minnesota. Catholic. At age 73, he is the oldest person on this list of notable lawyers.

Trumbauer. A name partner in a medium-sized firm specializing in personal injury defense work. He represents insurance companies, particularly in the defense of product liability claims. He was long active in the Chicago Bar Association and served as a member of its Board of Managers. Of German descent; he is a graduate of Chicago Kent Law School; late 60s.

Turpin. A solo practitioner, he specializes in criminal defense work. He served as president of the Cook County Bar Association, the black lawyers' association. African American; both undergraduate work and legal education at University of Illinois; mid-40s.

Tyrone. The senior, name partner of a small firm, he is one of the best-known personal injury plaintiffs' lawyers in Chicago. He has held the presidencies of four associations of trial and personal injury lawyers. He also gained some celebrity through his representation of Dick Butkus, the Chicago Bears' football star, in contract negotiations. Irish Catholic; undergraduate and law school at Loyola; early 60s.

Smallest Space Analysis of Notables' Networks

To determine whether these notable lawyers have distinct, regularly structured networks of association with other Chicago lawyers, we have used smallest space analysis to summarize the patterns of our respondents' reports of their acquaintances with the notables.[16] Each of the forty-three notables is represented as a point in space (see fig. 5.1), and the relative proximities of the points reflect the degree of similarity of their patterns of association within the profession. That is, notables who were known by many of the same respondents will be located close together in the space; notables who shared few acquaintances will be far apart. The solution is computed to optimize the simultaneous representation of the relationships among all pairs of points. Notables will tend to be near the center of the space if they are known by large numbers of respondents who are drawn from varying circles of acquaintance. It is also possible, though less likely, for notables to be centrally located even though relatively few respondents know them—if the few who do know them are approximately equally likely to know the notables who are located at the respective extremes of the space, this will tend to place them equi-

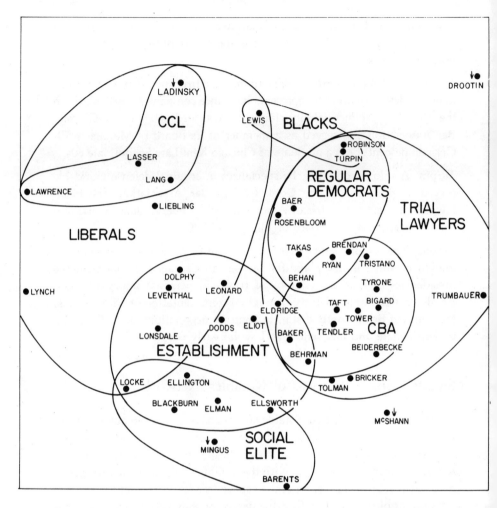

FIGURE 5.1
Patterns of Acquaintance with 43 Notable Chicago Lawyers (Three-dimensional Smallest Space Solution)

distant from those extremes, or at the center. Notables will be located in the margins or periphery of the space if the respondents who know them are highly homogenous in key social characteristics that differ from those of notables on the other side of the space. Since homogeneity is more likely among limited subsets of respondents, the notables in the periphery are also likely to be known by fewer respondents.

An accurate depiction of the relationship between notables X and Y that simultaneously represents the relationship of each of those points to that of notable Z—together with the exact relationships of those three points to and among each of the other forty—is highly unlikely in a space with only two or three dimensions. Unless the structure of the data is quite simple, a perfect depiction of the relationships among all of the pairs of points may well require a solution with only one less dimension than there are single points. It is difficult to think in terms of a forty-two-dimensional space, and it would not be particularly helpful even if one could. To develop a theory about the nature of a system, we need to seek a more parsimonious account of its properties. But because solutions with only two or three dimensions will be less than perfect, statistical tests have been developed to assess the extent to which the representation accurately portrays, or "fits," the actual data. One such measure is Kruskal's stress. Using that measure, we determined that a two-dimensional representation of the notables' networks does not depict the relationships among the points with sufficient precision to satisfy the usual criterion, but that the use of three dimensions produces a more satisfactory fit with the data.[17] We have already presented a three-dimensional diagram in this book (see chap. 4), and we are not eager to burden the reader with another. As it happens, that may be avoided in this case without sacrificing substance. The third dimension of the solution does not contribute much additional differentiation to the space. Ninety percent of the notables are located within only 42 percent of the range on that dimension, and they are rather evenly distributed around the most central actor's position on the dimension. Only four of the notables fall outside this restricted range; they appear to be providing most of the additional variance that is represented by the third dimension. All four of those points are located toward the negative end of the dimension, and they are separated from the other points by a relatively substantial gap. In the figure presenting the smallest space analysis, therefore, we are using the three-dimensional solution, but we represent the third dimension only by placing downward arrows next to these four points. Looking at figure 5.1, we see the arrows next to the points representing the positions of Ladinsky, Drootin, Mingus, and McShann—two being at the top and two near the bottom of the space, forming a rough square. These four persons were less widely known than most of the other notables, and that probably accounts for their low position on the third dimension.[18]

To aid the reader in using the figure, we have drawn rough ovals around some of the regions of the space that we believe can be identified with reasonable certainty. These boundaries are *not* determined empirically. Rather, they represent our interpretations of the nature of the primary affinity of the notables who occupy those regions. We have made those interpretations by observing whether notables who are proximate appear to share characteristics that might plausibly account for their proximity. That is, using the known characteristics of the notables, we have induced a proposition about the nature of the bond that ties these sets of notables. A particularly clear example is the four presidents of the Chicago Council of Lawyers, who are relatively close together at the upper left of the space (in the area labeled "CCL").[19] Because each notable occupies multiple role positions, a given notable may well have a characteristic that fits the region where he is located and yet have another characteristic that matches the label that we have given to some other region of the space. Lynch, for example, is a litigator. In that respect he is like Taft, Tendler, and Tolman, who are all located within the region labeled "Trial Lawyers." (But the sorts of litigation that all of those lawyers do is quite unlike that handled by Turpin, Takas, Tristano, and Tyrone; see their biographies.) The fact that Lynch is not located in close proximity to the trial lawyers, however, and that he is more proximate to other lawyers who are engaged in liberal political activities, suggests that his liberal affiliations are more salient than is his role as a litigator in structuring his relationships with other lawyers.

The fit of the notables with the labels given their regions is generally quite good, but it is not always exact. Tendler, for example, has never been closely identified with the CBA, but he does clearly belong within the broader "Trial Lawyers" region. Cases that do not fit are rare, and there is *no* such problem within the precisely defined regions such as those labeled "Blacks" and "CCL." Even when their region's characteristic is not the one that caused particular notables to be chosen for inclusion on the list, their characteristics almost always fit the region within which they are located. For example, Baer was included primarily because she was in the line of succession to the presidency of the Illinois State Bar Association. But she is found in the "Regular Democrats" area of the space (not far from some other bar leaders), which is consistent with her ties to the Regular Democratic Organization through family members. When a notable's point falls near the boundary of one of the regions, it might often have been plausible to draw the line either to include or to exclude that notable from the category. In such cases, we have used our judgment, which is certainly open to question.[20] But these close cases should not cause us great concern. The purpose of labeling the regions is only to suggest broad properties of the space. Two notables, Drootin and McShann, did not seem to us to be clearly assignable to any of these regions. We have, therefore, left them in limbo; these two persons—like others who are found in the outer ring or periphery of the space—are significantly less widely known than most of the other notables.

With the explanations and caveats in mind, we may now turn to our interpretation of the substantive significance of the results of the analysis. Some of the properties of the smallest space solution are readily apparent. Noting the general categories of the notables and their location in the figure, we find that the liberals (L) (including the presidents of the Chicago Council of Lawyers, as a subset of liberals) are located exclusively on the left, particularly at the upperleft. The leaders of the organized bar (B), rather thoroughly mixed in with the trial lawyers (T), tend to be located on the right, particularly at right center; the trial lawyers tend to be higher in the space and a bit further right than the leaders of the organized bar. The establishment is found relatively low in the space, most of them just left of center. But that should not be taken as a political statement; these dimensions (the vertical and horizontal axes) have no substantive meaning in themselves. If one wished to draw a line through the space that would separate the political right from the political left, that line should depart from the vertical, slanting from the upper right to the lower left and dividing the establishment area about in half (see fig. 6). This would still place some of the Regular Democrats on the right side of the line (though not so far right as it appears on the horizontal axis of figure 5.1), and that is probably correct in political terms.

The locations of the groupings labeled "Blacks" and "Social Elite" are illustrative of a general property of the structure of the circles of acquaintance of the profession's elites: social opposites—whether the source of the opposition is politics, social class, or law practice characteristics—tend to be found on opposite sides of the space. Thus, the location of the black notables is diametrically opposed to that of the social elite (i.e., those notables who have the closest ties to high society, to the world of private clubs and newspaper society pages). Similarly, the presidents of the Chicago Council of Lawyers are located about as far as is possible from the leaders of the Chicago Bar Association, the established, conservative organization that it was created to oppose. (While Bricker was president of the Illinois State Bar Association, he strongly resisted the seating of a representative of the CCL in the ABA's House of Delegates. This occurred during Lawrence's term as president of the CCL. The two are located opposite one another, Lawrence at the upper left and Bricker at the lower right.) And the criminal, divorce, and personal injury plaintiffs' lawyers among the notables tend to be found opposite those who do antitrust defense and the other sorts of work that serve the large corporations; the personal plight lawyers are located toward the upper right and the large corporate practitioners toward the lower left. As we have already observed, these represent the extremes of the two broad sectors of the profession (see chap. 3). In a sense, our findings confirm that these types are in fact social opposites—that they are separated by substantial "social distance," as measured by their circles of acquaintance. The smallest space solution, reflecting this social distance, assigns them to opposite sides of the space.[21]

One of the most striking findings is the proximity of the blacks to one another in spite of their quite different characteristics. Robinson is a fixture of the Daley organization (he is *the* African American who was most relied on by Daley for legal work, and he was reported to be personally close to the mayor), while Turpin is a criminal defense lawyer who had been active in the black lawyers' association. These two are so close in the figure as to be virtually on top of one another. The third African American, Lewis, is about as different from Robinson as it is possible to be in Chicago political terms—Lewis is a liberal independent Democrat who is affiliated with Jesse Jackson's sociopolitical activities. (In Chicago, such Republicans as existed in 1975 were probably closer to the Regular Democrats, in most ways, than were the independent Democrats.) Yet Lewis is located quite near to Robinson and Turpin in the figure, just to their left—toward the liberals. Given the extreme political differences among them, particularly between Robinson on the one hand and Lewis on the other, the fact that the blacks end up so close together suggests that they move within quite narrowly restricted circles within the bar. But we should note that these three notables also share some practice characteristics. They all do some sort of litigation, and they are all either solo practitioners or in small, rather informal partnerships. These characteristics alone, however, would not seem to account for their close proximity. Most of the litigators from small firms are located somewhat lower on the right side of the space (the vicinity of Takas, Brendan, Behan, Ryan, Tristano, and Tyrone). The most plausible interpretation of these findings is surely that race has a strong effect on lawyers' circles of acquaintance within the profession.

Lewis is located about halfway between the other two African Americans and the most proximate of the young liberals who had served as president of the Chicago Council of Lawyers. The four CCL presidents—Ladinsky, Lasser, Lang, and Lawrence—are also clustered within a relatively restricted region of the space, indicating that many of their acquaintances overlap or that the people who know them have very similar patterns of contact with the other notables, located in other regions of the space. There is a substantial gap between the CCL presidents and most of the other notables; only Liebling, the public interest lawyer, is very near them. Lewis, Lynch, a young liberal political activist, and Dolphy, the dean of the Northwestern Law School, are next closest. The relative segregation of the CCL leadership is probably explained by their youth and by the tendency for reformers, like other out-groups, to have a limited, homogeneous circle of acquaintances.[22] Persons opposing established interests or challenging conventional roles may well find that association with the like-minded is reassuring. It reduces dissonance.

Note that, though the liberals' region of the space is large, it is rather lightly populated. The dispersion of the liberals indicates that they are of varying types and perhaps that they tend to operate as free agents— that socially, as in the figure, they are not tightly clustered. Moreover, there appear to be distinct wings of the liberals. At the far upper left of the space is a group of liberals who tend to be younger, affiliated with the CCL, and probably more left in political terms as well. The four CCL presidents and Liebling are all Jewish; Lewis is an African American; Lynch is Irish. Lower and closer to the center of the space is the "liberal establishment." Though two of these liberals are also Jewish, the only WASPs in the liberal group are found here.

If the establishment region of the space has a liberal wing, the separation of that wing from the balance of the establishment notables is less clearly demarcated by any natural boundaries. But the establishment does include a group that is more certainly a part of the social elite. (In fact, the only notables in our social elite region of the space who are not also included within the establishment region are Mingus and Barents.[23]) Similarly, yet another wing of the establishment can be identified. Toward the upper right of the establishment region is a group of notables who derive some of their authority from the organized bar. Eldridge, Baker, and Behrman have all served as presidents of bar associations— Eldridge, of both the Illinois State Bar Association and the American College of Trial Lawyers, and the latter two, of the CBA.

These overlaps among the regions also suggest that individuals who are located within the areas of overlap or at the points of intersection of the various regions are well situated to serve as mediators among those spheres of influence. And a person who bridges two constituencies may not only act as a messenger between them but may also be able to mobilize the resources of both. Eldridge, again, is a prime example.

He is a member in excellent standing of both the establishment and the litigators' elite (the trial lawyers' region), and is located in their area of overlap. He is also situated in close proximity to both the Regular Democrats and the CBA leadership. Eldridge is thus in a fine position to serve as a go-between for these groups, to confer legitimacy on the proposals of each in dealing with the other, and to gain recognition and power by mobilizing these multiple sources of influence. As indicated in our simple biographical sketch, Eldridge has made good use of these opportunities. One of the statistics used in interpreting smallest space analysis is a measure of centrality. If all of the points in the space were equal weights resting on a weightless plane, the centroid would be the balance point. By this measure, Eldridge is the most central of the notables.

Most of the notables who represent the largest corporations are not located at the very center of the space. The corporate establishment is only one of the profession's power centers. Others are the Regular Democratic Organization (which controls City Hall and has the allegiance of most of the judges of the local courts), the organized bar (particularly, the Chicago Bar Association), and the independent liberal political forces (which have access to influence through state and national politics, particularly through the governor and through Illinois' United States senators, who of course control appointments to federal judgeships). Each of these constituencies or spheres of influence occupies an identifiable region of the profession's network structure, and these regions overlap to form a generally circular structure. The elites who are found close to the centroid of the space either lead multiple constituencies or play mediating roles (sometimes, of course, they can do both); those who are located farther from the center tend to be more closely identified with one or another of the distinct constituencies. Elites located in the periphery may be "pure types," each commanding the attention of a limited constituency. In the alternative, they may be notables who derive their influence primarily from relationships *outside* the profession, or their notability may be largely personal or symbolic, leaving them unable to mobilize any substantial constituency within the profession.

These social networks within the legal profession are not, then, linear or bipolar. Though the structure is oppositional in nature—social opposites are found on opposite sides of the space—other constituencies or groups within the profession mediate between the opposites, and these mediating groups are not necessarily located more centrally in the space but may themselves be peripheral, being located at other points around the rim of the structure.

The proposition that the notables' network structure has distinct regions—separate "spheres of influence"—may be examined through the use of another type of analysis, to which we now turn.

The Notables' Space as Defined by Respondent Characteristics

Rather than focusing on the characteristics of the notables in identifying the regions of the space, we may use the characteristics of the respondents who claim acquaintance with each of the notables to define the nature of the notables' overlapping circles of acquaintance. That is, if we continue to treat each notable as a point in space, as presented in figure 5.1, and then assign to each point the characteristics of the respondents who know that notable, we may observe the patterns of relationship among the points on those characteristics. To the extent that the notables' associations within the profession are random, we will see no clear patterns; to the extent that the notables' acquaintances are differentiated by these variables, we should be able to observe distinct patterns, distinct regions of the space. If a characteristic of the respondents varies systematically as we move along any vector that can be drawn through the points—that is, if the values of the points on that variable change in a consistent direction—it will suggest that the variable organizes that portion of the network structure, that it explains that dimension of lawyers' relationships with the notables. But a straight-line dimensionality is only one possibility. If, for example, the fields of practice of the acquaintances should change in an orderly fashion as we move around the circle from one region of the space to another, it would suggest that the notables' networks of association are influenced by that variable.

To present these data, we have prepared a number of additional figures, all of which duplicate the social space presented in figure 5.1. In figures 5.2 through 5.5, each notable's point in that space is labeled with a number that indicates the extent to which respondents who were acquainted with the notable differ from the norm of all of our respondents on the variable in question.

For example, figure 5.2 analyzes the extent to which respondents who were acquainted with each of the notables varied from our respondents overall in holding positions of leadership in the established organized bar.[24] That is, the variable is whether or not the respondent had held a leadership position in the Chicago Bar Association or the Illinois State

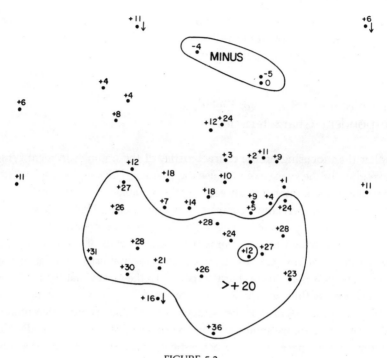

FIGURE 5.2
*Characteristics of Respondents Acquainted with Each of 43 Notables: Percentage
Difference from Total Percentage in Leadership Role*

Bar association. Only 10 percent of our respondents had played such a
role. The numbers by the notables' points in figure 5.2 state the extent
to which the respondents who know each notable depart from that
norm—that is, +5 indicates that 15 percent of the respondents who
knew that notable had, themselves, held positions of leadership in the
organized bar.

The most obvious lesson of figure 5.2 is that the lawyers who know
the most notables are disproportionately likely to have held leadership
roles. Leaders are more likely to know other leaders. Almost all of the
numbers in figure 5.2 are positive, indicating that the acquaintances of
almost all of the notables were more likely than were average respondents
to have held bar leadership positions. Recall that only 62 percent of our
respondents knew any of the notables and only 25 percent knew more
than three of them. One of the factors that appears to influence likelihood
of acquaintance with the notables is, then, the respondent's occupancy
of a leadership role. In a sense, this finding is probably a validation of

the selections that we made for our list of notables. We appear to have succeeded (in some measure, at least) in selecting leaders who are likely to have come into contact with other leaders in the course of organizing support for their causes or of basking in the same limelight.

But an equally striking—and far more interesting—feature of figure 5.2 is that the *only* points where leaders are not overrepresented are those of the black notables. (The three points, toward the upper right, are labeled "minus," though only two are actually negative. One is a zero, indicating no difference from the norm.) The obvious hypothesis as to why this should be the case is that blacks move within separate circles of acquaintance that do not include the sorts of lawyers who are likely to be active in the Chicago or Illinois bar associations. That the circles of acquaintance of black lawyers tend to be separate from the balance of the profession has already been suggested by the fact that the three quite different black notables are grouped so closely in the smallest space solution. The Chicago Bar Association was closed to blacks until 1945,[25] and black lawyers consequently formed their own organization, the Cook County Bar Association. Though a few blacks have more recently held office in the CBA, many no doubt continue to pursue alternative opportunities for professional recognition. Moreover, most black lawyers work in small firms or as solo practitioners, often doing "personal plight" work, and lawyers in these sorts of practice are, regardless of race, among the least likely to be active in the organized bar.

Following the general tendency for opposites to be located on opposite sides of the space, we find that the notables with the largest proportions of bar leaders among their acquaintances occupy a region that is directly across the space from that of the black notables. These are in the area labeled "> +20"; that is, over 30 percent of the acquaintances of each of the notables within the area have held bar positions, more than three times the overall proportion. (One notable found within the area, Tolman, does not fit that criterion. His acquaintances are only 12 percentage points higher on this variable. As with any point that does not fit the label given its area in figures 5.2 through 5.6, his point is circled.) This area overlaps the establishment and the CBA regions of figure 5.1. Since the types of leadership roles that were used in defining the variable were positions in the establishment bar associations (i.e., not in the Chicago Council of Lawyers, the Cook County Bar Association, or the American Trial Lawyers Association),[26] this pattern is easy to understand.

Figure 5.3 is a bit less clear-cut, but it is no more difficult to interpret.

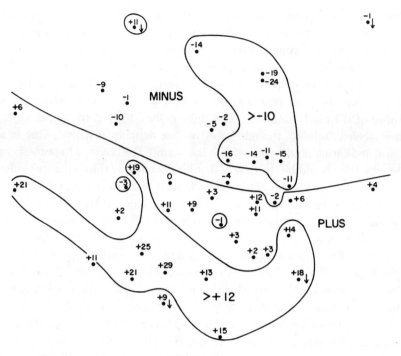

FIGURE 5.3

Characteristics of Respondents Acquainted with Each of 43 Notables: Percentage Difference from Total Percentage of Income from Major Corporate Clients

The variable analyzed is the percentage of law practice income that the lawyers receive from major corporate clients. The mean of all respondents is 34 percent, and the figure again indicates the extent to which each notable's acquaintances depart from that mean. As in figure 5.2, this variable organizes the space in a generally vertical direction, somewhat tilted from the upper right to the lower left. The blacks and the trial lawyers who are in fields like criminal defense, divorce, and personal injury plaintiffs' work are found in the area where the acquaintance's percentages of income from major corporate clients are more than 10 percentage points lower than the average of all respondents. (That is, the mean percentage for the acquaintances of each of the notables in that area is 24 percent or less.) The area with the highest percentages of income from major corporate clients (labeled "> +12") includes only one of the CBA leaders—Biederbecke, a personal injury defense lawyer who is a partner in one of Chicago's largest firms. The only notable in that area who is not a partner in a large firm is the dean of Northwestern law school.

The high degree of interaction between the establishment of the profession and the lawyers who represent the largest corporations is well documented by figure 5.3.

The variables dealt with in figures 5.2 and 5.3 are of quite different types, being organizational roles and client differences, respectively, and in figure 5.4 we analyze a variable that reflects yet another type of differentiation of lawyers, the differences in tasks that they perform. The task type variable that we have selected for analysis here is the frequency of litigation in state courts. We have found this to be a highly useful diagnostic variable, one that distinguishes among the fields of practice rather clearly (see tables 3.1 and 3.2). Here, again, the pattern is sharply defined. The notables who have acquaintances with above-average rates of appearance in the state courts can, with only one exception, be separated from those with below-average rates by a line drawn with a ruler. Of course, it matters little whether that line of separation is exactly straight or a bit irregular, but given that we are dealing with friendships among real people, who might be expected to behave idiosyncratically at times and who surely do not form even their professional relationships for instrumental reasons alone, the orderliness of these data is rather remarkable.

There is a general relationship between the pattern of the rates of state court appearances and that of the income derived from major corporate clients (see fig. 5.3), but the state litigation rate vector appears to be more sharply tilted than is the major corporate client vector. (The litigation vector would run at approximately a right angle to the line that separates the "plus" from the "minus" side of figure 5.4. That is, the vector would run from the lower left to the upper right, at about a 45-degree angle.) The area of the space with the higher rates of state court appearances is, again, the area where we find the notables who are criminal defense lawyers and personal injury lawyers, conforming once again to the principle of homogeneous choice of associates. The area with the lowest state litigation rates includes notables who practice antitrust, securities, public utilities, labor law, and probate—fields that either consist primarily of office practice or deal with federal rather than state courts.

Figure 5.5 is, if possible, even more sharply defined. It presents the findings for yet another basis of differentiation among lawyers, ethnoreligious differences. As figure 5.5 indicates, the notables who have the highest percentages of Roman Catholics among their acquaintances are concentrated at the right of the space. The degree of segregation of the

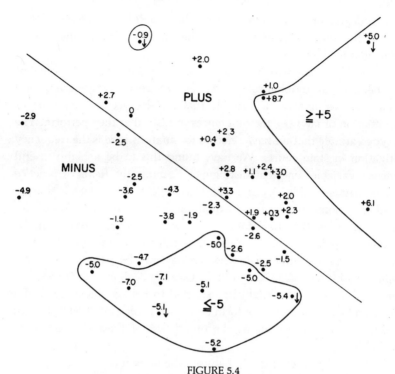

FIGURE 5.4

Characteristics of Respondents Acquainted with Each of 43 Notables: Difference from Total for Mean State Court Appearances per Month

above-average percentages from those that are below average is, again, quite remarkable. Moreover, the percentages of Catholic acquaintances decrease in a generally orderly fashion as we move from right to left in the space. The vector, here, is much more nearly horizontal than that in figure 5.4—the Catholic acquaintance vector appears to tilt only slightly from the lower left toward the upper right.

In progressing through figures 5.2 to 5.5, then, we have seen the directions of the vectors of each variable shift from nearly vertical in figures 5.2 and 5.3, to a 45-degree angle in figure 5.4, and to near horizontal in figure 5.5. The degree of the angles at the intersections of these vectors reflects the degree of the intercorrelations of the variables.

In figure 5.6, we present the analyses of six more variables in a simplified form. The space is the same, of course, but the scores that are given next to each point in figures 5.2 through 5.5 have been eliminated here. The reader has, by now, been exposed to four sets of such scores and is thus familiar with the meaning of the figures; the individual

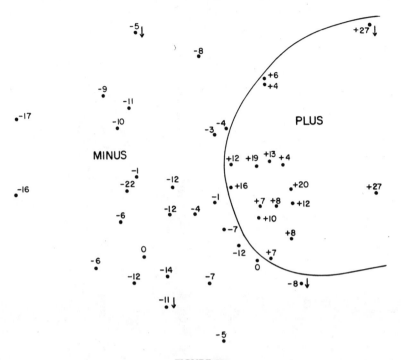

FIGURE 5.5

Characteristics of Respondents Acquainted with Each of 43 Notables: Percentage Difference from Total Percentage of Catholics

scores are not necessary to an appreciation of these general patterns of acquaintance.

Three of the variables presented here display, for the first time, vectors that are tilted in the other direction—that is, from the lower right to the upper left. These variables are the percentages of Republicans and of Jews among the notables' acquaintances and the extent to which the notables' acquaintances have high or low scores on a measure of "economic liberalism."[27] The Republican vector is the most nearly vertical of the three, while the Jewish vector runs at approximately a 45-degree angle (about perpendicular to the state court appearance vector). These three variables are obviously correlated. There is a strong negative association between the percentage of Republicans and the percentage of Jews or of economic liberals among a notable's acquaintances.[28]

Turning now to the other variables presented in figure 5.6, we see a clear relationship between the extent to which a notable's acquaintances are Regular Democrats and the extent to which they are likely to have attended one of the four "local" law schools. Both of these variables are,

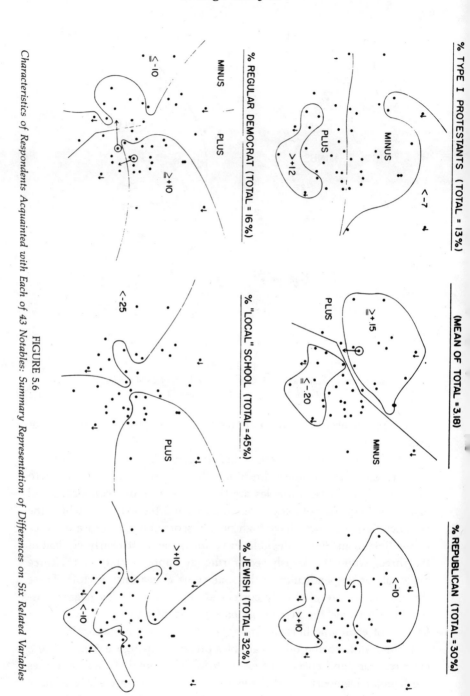

FIGURE 5.6

Characteristics of Respondents Acquainted with Each of 43 Notables: Summary Representation of Differences on Six Related Variables

in turn, also positively correlated with the percentages of Catholics among the notables' acquaintances[29] (see figure 5.5) and with the acquaintances' rates of state court appearances (see figure 5.4). The area at the right center of the space on both the local school variable and the Regular Democrat variable corresponds rather closely to the "plus" area, in the shape of a half circle, that we see on the Catholic variable (fig. 5.5).

The final variable presented in figure 5.6 is the percentage of type I Protestants among the notables' acquaintances.[30] The regions with the lowest percentages on this variable, understandably enough, are those with the highest percentage of Catholics (at the upper right) or of Jews (at the upper left). The area with the highest concentration of type I Protestants is at the bottom of the space, overlapping the establishment and social elite regions. This variable is obviously correlated with the tendency to represent major corporate clients (see figure 5.3), where the vector is also almost vertical (perhaps with a slight tilt toward the right, just as here) and where there is a clear separation between the top and the bottom of the space.

The multicollinearity of these variables once again makes it very difficult to determine whether one or another of them is "causal"—i.e., whether the patterns of acquaintance that we observe are to be attributed to one of these variables rather than another. It is likely that the variables reinforce one another. That is, multiple bases of similarity may be expected to enhance the likelihood of cohesion among the lawyers, and this no doubt helps to account for the quite orderly structure we have observed in the notables' patterns of acquaintance. The clarity of the organization of the space by the variables presented confirms the major findings of our other analyses. It indicates that, in yet another respect, the legal profession is a highly differentiated, quite stratified social system. The precision of the patterns of association, with so few of the notables failing to conform to the characteristics of their regions of the space, suggests that lawyers know their place—that they associate largely with those whose positions within the profession are similar to their own or with others whose roles are related to theirs in ways that are clearly defined, usually hierarchically ordered, and presumably functional.

The Spheres of Influence

One of the most important tenets of a pluralist view of politics is that not only will a large number and variety of different political interests have access to the locus of decisions but the demands made by each group will be constrained by the representation within that group of persons who have a wide variety of other interests, other social identities.[31] Each group will be likely to include a membership that cuts across some or all of the social distinctions created by differences in occupation, religion, ethnicity, class, values, or personal circumstances, and the overlap among the memberships of the various interest groups will thus serve to moderate the positions adopted by each group and to give the polity cohesion, to bind it together.

In his major synthetic work, *The Governmental Process*, David Truman stresses the importance of overlapping group membership as one of two crucial elements in his conception of the political process:

> The idea of overlapping memberships stems from the conception of a group as a standardized pattern of interactions rather than as a collection of human units. Although the former may appear to be a rather misty abstraction, it is actually far closer to complex reality than the latter notion. The view of a group as an aggregation of individuals abstracts from the observable fact that in any society, and especially a complex one, no single group affiliation accounts for all of the attitudes or interests of any individual except a fanatic or a compulsive neurotic. No tolerably normal person is totally absorbed in any group in which he participates. The diversity of an individual's activities and his attendant interests involve him in a variety of actual and potential groups. . . . Such heterogeneity may be of little significance until such time as these multiple memberships conflict. Then the cohesion and influence of the affected group depend upon the incorporation or accommodation of the conflicting loyalties of any significant segment of the group, an accommodation that may result in altering the original claims. Thus the leaders of a Parent-Teacher Association must take some account of the fact that their proposals must be acceptable to members who also belong to the local taxpayers' league, to the local chamber of commerce, and to the Catholic Church.[32]

To the extent that the varying constituencies within the Chicago bar are separated into distinct clusters, however, this tendency toward the moderation of demands may not obtain. There are, of course, some prominent lawyers who serve as intermediaries among several of the different interest groupings, but these tend to be exceptions. If there is little movement of either leaders or followers across the boundaries of the major constellations of interests within the bar, then the expression of narrow interests will be less constrained and the politics of the bar will be more likely to be characterized by divisive conflict, perhaps creating further barriers to the integration of the professional community. But it is difficult to be certain that our findings concerning these separate interest groupings are not, in part, an artifact of our research design. The nature of the patterns of acquaintance, after all, reflects categories that were used in the selection of our list of notables. Would liberals have emerged as a separate group if we had not consciously included a set of liberals among the notables? Even with our procedure, however, we might have found that the liberals were spread throughout the space. But they were not. A selection criterion might, then, prove to be irrelevant. But this one did not.

It would be very difficult to construct a list of influential lawyers that did not rest upon some preconceptions about the kinds of constituencies that might exist within the profession or the types of power that might be useful in mobilizing corresponding types of lawyers, and we do not believe that the mix of positional and reputational methods used to select our list was likely to distort any important reality of the relationships among lawyers. Assuming, therefore, that we are entitled to place some confidence in our findings, three principal spheres of influence appear to exist in the Chicago bar.[33]

The first of these is based in liberal politics. This sphere, which includes the leaders of the Chicago Council of Lawyers, is engaged in explicit political activity both inside the profession and in the broader polity. To the extent that partisan political activity is involved, these elites largely work through the independent wing of the Democratic Party in Chicago (i.e., *not* the Regular Democratic Organization) and, more occasionally, through moderate to liberal Republicans (e.g., Senator Charles Percy). Issues on which this sphere was active include "merit" selection of judges (i.e., selection by appointment rather than election and, more generally, selection in ways that would minimize the influence of the Regular Democrats), open housing, welfare reform, and abortion.

The second of the major spheres of influence is the corporate establishment. It includes the lawyers for the largest corporations, the deans of the prestigious law schools (both of whom, here, happen to be antitrust lawyers, which may enhance their inclusion in this group), and some, but a distinct minority, of the leaders of the organized bar. The principal basis of the influence of this sphere is its connections to the business and financial community. Though it is probably less directly involved in political activity, the party of choice for such activity is most often the Republican party. (If the Republican party had been healthier in

Chicago, this sphere might perhaps have been more active in partisan politics.) The public issues that concern it usually involve governmental regulation of business.

The third and last of these major spheres is a bit more amorphous but still clearly discernible. Its core is the trial lawyers who practice in fields such as personal injury and criminal law, and it includes many of the leaders of the Chicago and Illinois bar associations. Many Chicago lawyers believe that the personal injury bar made a concerted effort to capture the leadership of the local bar associations. If the personal injury lawyers have done so, their purpose may have been to enhance their prestige or to gain greater influence over such issues as "no-fault" compensation in automobile accident cases. The elites in this sphere concern themselves with a relatively broad range of public and professional matters, specifically including "no fault" and judicial selection. When they engage in partisan political activity, they usually work with the Regular Democrats.

In attempting to explain the patterns of acquaintance with the notables and, thus, the bases of these spheres of influence, we are faced with the fact that ethnoreligious differences among the acquaintances correspond to these spheres or regions of the space, thus rendering interpretation more difficult. The trial lawyers sphere is dominated by Catholics, Jews are overrepresented in the liberal region, and the corporate establishment sphere tends to overrepresent high-status Protestants. The problem, then, is to determine, if we can, whether the patterns of association among lawyers are attributable to the political, professional, and ideological affinities just described or, instead, to the selection of associates on the basis of ethnic homogeneity. It is unlikely, of course, that either factor operates without the influence of the other—it is almost certainly the case that ideological and ethnic affinities go hand in hand.

In previous chapters, we have emphasized the part that client interests play in determining the structure of the profession, though we have also noted substantial, systematic ethnoreligious differentiation among lawyers. The distinguishing characteristic of these notable lawyers is their public role. While lawyers' professional roles may be circumscribed by the interests of the clients that they serve, the *public* roles of lawyers may be determined more by their social background characteristics, including ethnicity and religion.[34]

By saying all of this, however, we do not mean to imply that client type variables have no relationship to the data on the notables' circles of acquaintance. The fit of client variables with the notables' smallest space solution is, in fact, at least as neat as that of the ethnoreligious variables (see, e.g., fig. 5.3). The daily legal work of the notables will, of course, tend to bring them into contact with other practitioners in their own fields. But the roles of these notables as leaders or even just as notables might be expected to give them a broader, more cosmopolitan range of acquaintances with whom they might confer on issues concerning the course of the organized bar or on extraprofessional matters, including partisan political activity, issues of public policy, and their personal investments and business ventures. Given that the notables' networks of association are subject to these important determinants that are largely unrelated to their clients' interests, it is striking to note the extent to which acquaintance with the notables corresponds to the fields or sectors of law practice.

Thus, political and client affinities will loosely correspond to religious ones.[35] But whether client interests, political allegiances, or social background characteristics (or, as is almost certainly the case, some combination of all of these) is thought to determine lawyers' patterns of acquaintance and networks of influence, the important point to note is that none of these organizing factors is rooted in the norms, doctrines, or organizational rules of the law or the legal profession. Instead, the spheres of influence within the legal profession draw upon sources of power that are located outside the profession. The liberal sphere has explicit ties to liberal candidates for public office and to ideologically based voluntary associations that are extraprofessional or far broader than the profession, organizations such as the American Civil Liberties Union. The trial lawyers/CBA sphere has clear political ties to the city and county governments, and thus may secure the benefits that it is within the power of City Hall to confer. This sphere is also associated with particular types of clients; its lawyers tend to represent individuals and smaller, family-owned businesses. The corporate establishment sphere is even more clearly identified with a particular type of client and less tied, perhaps, to public politics. The source of its power within the profession is its access to (and its presumed influence upon) the business and financial community.

Arthur Bentley, the father of the interest group approach to political science, contended that "the great task in the study of any form of social life is the analysis of groups. . . . When the groups are adequately stated, everything is stated. When I say everything, I mean everything."[36] Refreshing as this dose of certitude may be in a work of social science, one need not be so unequivocal as Bentley to recognize that identification of the affinities that organize lawyers into varying social groupings is a useful step in an analysis of the constituencies of the leaders of the profession. The interests that unite and divide groups of lawyers set limits on the freedom of action of the leaders both in their activities within the bar and in their roles in the broader community; the leaders overstep the bounds of their constituencies' interests only at the peril of weakening their own positions as leaders. Our findings concerning the patterns of relationships between Chicago lawyers and the elites of the profession thus suggest two principal conclusions. First, the rigidity of the structure of relationships indicates that, though the three major spheres of influence have some areas of overlap, for the most part their differing constituencies inhabit separate social worlds. The relative lack of shared members and of leaders whose influence extends across the boundaries of the major interest groupings suggests that tendencies toward conflict among the interests are less likely to be moderated than would be the case if there were a greater community of concern and more multiple memberships among the groups. Second, the sources of the interests that appear to organize the principal constituencies of the profession's elite lie outside the profession. The conflicts that occur between the major groups within the bar will thus reflect the agendas of the broader community rather than a set of issues that arise only in the professional context or that are peculiar to the norms or concerns of the profession. The bar, then, is likely to function less as a guild than as a sort of guild-hall—that is, as a forum within which the various external interests will press their cases and contend for advantage.

Chapter 6

THE HEMISPHERES OF

THE LEGAL PROFESSION:

SUMMARY AND

SPECULATION

As we noted at the outset of this book, it comes as no surprise that Chicago lawyers are not a solid phalanx, marching ahead in lockstep. The bar's variety and dissension have been made public with enthusiasm. But perhaps the types of lawyers are not quite so various as we might have supposed. As the analysis presented in this book has unfolded, we have advanced the thesis that much of the differentiation within the legal profession is secondary to one fundamental distinction—the distinction between lawyers who represent large organizations (corporations, labor unions, or government) and those who represent individuals. The two kinds of law practice are the two hemispheres of the profession. Most lawyers reside exclusively in one hemisphere or the other and seldom, if ever, cross the equator.

Lawyers who serve major corporations and other large organizations differ systematically from those who work for individuals and small businesses, whether we look at the social origins of the lawyers, the prestige of the law schools they attended, their career histories and mobility, their social or political values, their networks of friends and professional associates, or several other social variables. Though there certainly are distinctions among lawyers that cut across the line between the two broad classes of clients, this fundamental difference in the nature of the client served appears to be the principal factor that structures the social differentiation of the profession.

One might argue, however, that it is not the form of organization of the client that matters but rather the wealth of the client.[1] That is, one might contend that the fundamental distinction is that between rich clients and poor clients (or, because few of the poor ever get to be lawyers' clients, perhaps we should say "less wealthy clients"). Surely the representation of an individual Rockefeller must be fully as remunerative and prestigious as is legal work for a state government, a labor union, or even most corporations.[2] Rich people do, after all, tend to pay their bills, and mingling with the Social Register elite, at their hunt balls and polo clubs, will carry with it as much cachet as does association with the sorts of persons who are now likely to become the chief executive officers of American corporations.[3]

But our attempts at generalization here are just that; we do not mean to assert that there are no exceptions to the rule. And it would, of course, be a mistake to overdraw the precision of the cleavage between the corporate and personal client hemispheres of the Chicago bar. The client type distinction is too crude and too simple to account for the full complexity of the social structure of the profession. Any scholar who had the temerity to suggest that such a large bundle of social phenomena was anything less than polycrystalline and polymorphic would very likely be sent to stand in the corner with the journalists. One who wishes to look for variability, imprecision, or ambiguity in the structure of the legal profession would surely find it. It is there. There are, in some respects, larger differences within the hemispheres than between them. As we argue below, the different roles of litigators and office lawyers may create a systematic difference in the distribution of power between lawyer and client that cuts across the distinction between types of clients. Nonetheless, the distinction between corporate and individual clients is a very important one, and that distinction is probably key to an understanding of the social structure of the legal profession and of that structure's consequences for the distribution of power and influence.

Because an ever-increasing amount of social power has come to be concentrated in corporations, lawyers who are in a position to influence the affairs of corporations are now likely to have the most impact on the transactions that are of greatest consequence for our society. James Coleman has summarized the historical growth of the power of corporations:

[I]ndividuals in society, natural persons, show a general and continual loss of power to corporate actors. . . .

[L]ooking back at the thirteenth through the seventeenth centuries, [we can see that this was a period] when the feudal structure was breaking up, when natural persons were coming to have rights, that is, powers, before the law, and when the early corporations were conceived in the form of boroughs and churches. At that time, the corporation and the trust were outgrowths of the newly born "natural rights" of persons, extending their powers vis-à-vis the power of the state or the king. In effect, the law's recognition of boroughs as legal persons, the extension of this recognition to non-landed corporations, and the endowing of trusts with the powers of persons, legitimated the idea that an individual could extend his powers through combination. The increase in power by coalition-formation was brought about through this recognition. The nineteenth and twentieth centuries have witnessed a vast extension of these possibilities. Today we find ourselves confronted by a world of corporate actors to whom much of our sovereignty has gone.[4]

Thus, lawyers who represent corporations have access to the decisions that are most likely to have important effects on the allocation of scarce goods and resources, on the manner of development and use of both public and private property, and on the course of governments. This greater power of the corporate lawyer to determine social outcomes may be one of the reasons why corporate practice differs so fundamentally from that serving individuals.[5]

Our thesis that the profession is divided into two quite distinct, largely separate hemispheres therefore rests on the proposition that the principal independent variable is not a continuum, like wealth, but a dichotomy, the difference between corporate and personal clients.

In addition to the difference in social power associated with these two types of clients, the nature of the interaction between lawyer and client may also differ systematically with client type. Most individuals, even the wealthiest persons, will not devote any substantial portion of their time and energy to direct supervision of their lawyer's work. Persons who are not wealthy will usually be too busy earning a living to use their time for this purpose, and wealthy individuals will usually have better things to do. Organizations, however, will give an employee the responsibility for looking after the organization's legal affairs. Thus, lawyers are likely to have greater freedom of action, greater control over how they practice law, if their clients are individuals rather than corporations or other large organizations.

The professional's freedom from client control is often cited as one of the most fundamental of the characteristics that distinguish the professions from other occupations.[6] But our argument suggests, quite ironically, that the lawyers who serve the more powerful, corporate clients are likely to be less "professional" in this respect than are those who serve the less powerful clients, individuals. This inference needs to be examined further, and we will therefore return to this important issue, treating it in more detail.

Size, Separation, and Specialization of the Two Hemispheres

Though the two principal parts of the Chicago bar are not exactly equal in size, the total amounts of effort devoted to each and the total numbers of lawyers practicing in them are roughly comparable.[7] The corporate sector is somewhat larger, but not so much so as to overwhelm the personal client practice or to render it insignificant. More than three-quarters of the practicing lawyers devoted at least some of their time to fields in the corporate client sector, while more than three-fifths of them devoted time to personal client fields. There is, then, substantial overlap in these categories—that is, a number of lawyers practiced in both hemispheres—but a solid majority of the practicing lawyers worked exclusively in one hemisphere or the other. Only about two-fifths of them reported devoting any time to work in both hemispheres. And if we look not merely at whether they spent any time at all in fields in both sectors, but take the devotion of at least 25 percent of their time to a field as a measure of greater commitment to that area of practice, we find that only 101 of our respondents (i.e., only about one-seventh of the 699 practicing lawyers) devoted that much time to fields in both of the hemispheres. The two hemispheres thus tend to be largely separate, to be populated by different lawyers. Relatively few lawyers do substantial amounts of work in both.

Because of client demand for full service, a lawyer often works in a range of fields, encompassing various doctrinal areas, but this demand will be limited by the range of needs of the lawyer's particular clients, and the doctrines dealt with will therefore be confined within client type boundaries. Corporations seldom worry that their refrigerators will be repossessed.[8] The neighborhood lawyer may be called upon to do individual income tax returns, real estate transactions of modest size, wills, divorces, accident cases, debt collections, and perhaps some criminal defense work. The lawyer who practices in the corporate hemisphere is likely to work in a narrower range of fields, but the large firms in which most such lawyers practice will also feel some pressure to serve a broad range of the demands of the firm's clients. Thus, the large law firm that looks after a corporation's tax problems will also be likely to handle its securities issues, antitrust problems, and real estate development or zoning matters. The firm will often be reluctant to refer a portion of the client's business to a specialist in another firm, fearing that the client may develop too permanent or extensive a relationship with the specialist's firm and, perhaps, may then take more of its business to that firm or to another where it will receive full service.[9] There are, of course, a few true specialties among the fields of law, but we found that the only fields to which a majority of the field's practitioners devote as much as half of their time are criminal prosecution, patents, and labor law work for unions. While labor law practiced on the union side is included in this exclusive list of true specialties, it is instructive to note that lawyers who practice labor law on the management side are substantially more likely to spread their time across a range of fields. We suggest that the explanation for this difference may be that the legal problems confronted by management (that is, corporations) are more varied than are those faced by labor unions, and the organization of the lawyers' work responds to the demands of their clients.

The very meaning of the term "specialization" among lawyers is also worth examination. What is the nature or kind of specialization that lawyers have in mind when they say that they are "specialists"? Seventy percent of our sample of Chicago lawyers told us that they regarded themselves as specialists, but their self-labeling may be biased by the prestige that attaches to the term. It connotes expertise and special skill. One may, therefore, seek the label. But it is also possible that lawyers may regard themselves as specialists if they concentrate on service to a particular type of client. This is the sort of specialization that we observe in the Chicago bar, and it may be that the lawyers' perceptions of themselves as specialists are based on client type. Our respondents were significantly more likely to regard themselves as specialists if they practiced exclusively in either the corporate or the personal client sector, even though they might work in a variety of fields within their respective sectors.

Unlike the task specialization that Durkheim associates with mutual interdependence, the division of labor along client lines may mean that lawyers become devoted to such a narrow range of interests that they have little stake in or dependence on lawyers who serve other sorts of clients.[10] No less than task specialization (and perhaps more), client specialization thus may have consequences for the integration and coherence of the profession. If specialization has not only disaggregated lawyers' interests but created conflicts among them, we would expect these conflicts to emerge in disputes over "territory," over the monopolization or control of types of work or clients.

Fifty years ago, for example, the organized bar might readily reach a consensus that lawyers were the proper persons to search real estate titles and to handle the closings of home sales. Performance of these functions by anyone else would have been said to constitute "the unauthorized practice of law." Today, the bar is sharply divided on this issue. There is now a substantial interest group within the profession consisting of lawyers who regularly represent real estate brokers and title companies. It is, of course, these clients who would engage in that "unauthorized practice." Rather than retain lawyers to perform these routine tasks, the title companies would prefer to use their own, less well paid employees to do these jobs, keeping for themselves any profit that is to be made on the services. The paradigm of the general practitioner—the nineteenth-century lawyer or perhaps the present-day small-town lawyer—would represent home buyers or sellers one day and the local real estate agent the next. But specialization within the profession has now created, in addition to the group of lawyers who represent the brokers, a second distinct faction: neighborhood lawyers who almost never represent large real estate brokers or title companies but have many middle-class clients who buy and sell their homes and small businesses. For this second interest group, real estate closings are bread and butter. The two groups have reason to conflict. And they do.

The conflicts need not be motivated exclusively (or even primarily) by self-interest or client interest. Like other persons, lawyers have private causes. They may act as "moral entrepreneurs,"[11] and this may bring them into conflict with other lawyers who have opposing moral principles. But their principles may also be influenced by their areas of practice. The corporate lawyers who dominate the Association of the Bar of the City of New York advocate "no-fault" systems of automobile accident compensation. They never touch a personal injury case. And they are vigorously opposed by the personal injury plaintiffs' lawyers, whose voice is the American Trial Lawyers Association. The personal injury lawyers complain that the corporate lawyers "don't understand our problems."[12] It is certainly true that one of the consequences of specialization is that the different roles may come to exist in separate social worlds and that, as they lose contact with one another, the lawyers may also lose their sensitivity to one another's problems, thus diminishing consensus on the profession's goals.

Max Weber wrote extensively on the important role of specialists in rationalizing, systematizing, and codifying cultural belief systems and practical knowledge,[13] and he noted that it will usually be specialists rather than generalists who will have the impulse to reform. Generalists have relatively little investment or stake in each of the fields in which they practice, and they will therefore be relatively indifferent to improving the quality of practice in any field. This means that generalists will be unlikely to devote uncompensated time to the bar activities directed toward improvement or reform of any particular area of practice, and the fields that have few specialists will therefore tend to lack advocates for rationalization of the field—that is, for bringing order to its conceptual framework. But lawyers may well seek changes in the law— if they perceive that their regular clients have an important stake in such changes. It may not be necessary for the client to tell them or hire them to do this if the lawyer has a large enough investment in the client. Changes in the law that make things easier for the client will also often make things easier for the lawyer. To the extent that lawyers are specialized by client type, therefore, we may expect them to be organizationally or politically active, if at all, in areas that are defined by client interests.

The degree and kind of specialization within the profession is also likely to influence the nature and extent of the profession's internal social differentiation. If the division of lawyers' labor occurs along lines defined by social types of clients, the impulse toward social homogeneity between lawyer and client may tend to produce differences among lawyers that correspond, to a greater or lesser degree, to those among the client types.

SOCIAL DIFFERENTIATION OF LAWYERS AND CLIENTS

There are, of course, subdivisions within the two hemispheres of the profession. The most important of these is the distinction between litigation and office practice. In figure 6.1, the "corporate hemisphere" is at the right and the "personal hemisphere" is at the left, the circle being further subdivided into quadrants that engage in, respectively, corporate litigation, office practice for corporate clients, office practice for personal clients, and litigation for persons.

In our data, however, we do not find that the structure is so neatly circular. The two sorts of litigation fields—those representing corporate clients and those representing persons—are separated by a considerable social distance. A closer rendering of the arrangement of the fields in social space, therefore, more nearly resembles a U than an O. At the bottom of the U—that is, in the office practice fields—the difference between the hemispheres in wealth of clients, the nature of their legal work, and the character of the relationships among lawyers and clients is probably less pronounced than it is in the litigation fields at the top of the U. The great bulk of the office practice done for persons is no doubt work done for relatively wealthy individuals on such matters as estate planning, personal income tax avoidance, and real estate sales. There is also a considerable volume of commercial law work (debtor-creditor, contracts, Uniform Commercial Code matters) done for businesses owned or controlled by individuals. This work is probably much more like the office practice of law for corporate clients than is corporate litigation like personal litigation. Corporate litigators often represent the largest corporations, but personal client litigation is more likely to involve the low- to moderate-income end of the personal client spectrum.[14] Thus, defendants in criminal cases, evictions and repossessions, and plaintiffs in personal injury and civil rights claims are likely to have below-average incomes. Parties to divorce cases that consume much litigation time almost surely have above-average incomes, but they need not be wealthy. It is therefore likely that social distinctions will be greater between lawyers engaged in litigation for the two, broad sorts of clients than between practitioners in the two types of office practice.

The existence of this U-shaped social structure was first suggested by a multidimensional scalogram analysis that permitted us to examine the relationships among the fields on several variables considered simultaneously (see figure 3.1). In the resulting figure, which depicts the fields as points in a two-dimensional space, we found the points arranged in

FIGURE 6.1
General Structure of Law Practice

a rough U, with a cluster of corporate litigation fields at the upper right, a cluster of "personal plight" litigation fields at the upper left, and the office practice fields at the bottom, less widely separated but with corporate practice generally toward the right and personal matters toward the left.

We also found that the allocation of prestige to these fields of law, determined by an entirely separate set of questions asked of our respondents, was very highly correlated with the same U structure. The rank order of the fields along the U substantially reproduced the rank order of the prestige scores assigned to the fields by our respondents (see chaps. 3 and 4). Thus, the kinds of variables that were used in the multidimensional scalogram analysis—the types of clients represented, the mechanisms by which lawyers obtain business, the sorts of tasks performed, the organizational setting of the practice, the type of law school attended, and the religion of the practitioners—appear to create an overall structure that is strongly associated with the extent to which Chicago lawyers perceive that each of the fields has a claim to deference within the profession. Further analysis persuaded us that the nature of prestige within the profession largely reflected the types of clients served by the fields. It may be that the greater wealth of the corporate clients means that their lawyers are regularly able to devote greater resources to the issues and thus that the opportunities for creativity are consistently higher in the corporate fields even when the general doctrinal area of the law is held constant. But it is clear that fields that serve corporate, wealthier, more "establishment" clients are accorded more deference within the profession than are those that serve individual, poorer clients. This suggests the thesis that prestige within law is acquired by association, that it is "reflected glory" derived from the power possessed by the lawyers' clients.

We also found a strong relationship between the types of work that lawyers do and their social background characteristics, including ethnoreligious origins (see chap. 3). Lawyers from less prestigious social origins were overrepresented among those practicing in the less prestigious fields. A Catholic respondent was three times more likely than either a Protestant or a Jew to be working as a prosecutor. A respondent who was affiliated with a high-status Protestant denomination (that is, a type I Protestant—Episcopalian, Presbyterian, Congregationalist, etc.) was five times more likely than either a Catholic or a Jewish respondent to be found doing securities or antitrust defense work. Jews were more than twice as likely as were Catholics to do divorce work, and they were incalculably more likely to do so than were type I Protestants—in our sample, we found no one of high-status Protestant origin who did a substantial amount of divorce work. Other fields with particularly high concentrations of type I Protestants were banking, patents, municipal, and personal tax; Jews were disproportionately represented in labor law, both on the union and on the management side, in business tax, commercial work, criminal defense, and personal injury plaintiffs' work; and Catholics were greatly overrepresented in personal injury work, on both the plaintiffs' and the defendants' sides, and in both business litigation and general litigation. Generally, WASPs were more likely to be found in the corporate hemisphere, Jews in the personal client hemisphere, and Catholics in the litigation fields of both hemispheres.

As a "learned profession," avowedly devoted to high ideals, the bar professes the principle that attainment within the profession should be determined by merit. Talcott Parsons argued that the professions are a "sector of the cultural system where the primacy of the values of cognitive rationality is presumed,"[15] and Terence Johnson has observed that it is a part of the ideology of professionalism that "prestige within the occupation is dependent upon colleague evaluation and, as a result, technical competence is a significant criterion of individual worth."[16] Thus, proficiency in lawyerly skills should determine professional success if this ideal-typical model of the profession prevails. The Chicago bar does not appear to conform closely to the model. To illuminate some of the reasons why, it may be instructive to compare the law with medicine and to note how the two differ in respects that might influence their degree of conformity to the meritocratic model.

The Legal and Medical Professions Compared

Like the medical specialties, most fields of law are characterized either by a substantive concentration (nephrology and cardiology, antitrust and tax) or by a common technology or skill (radiology or surgery, drafting or litigation). The legal system's adversary mode frequently bifurcates areas of the law, however, causing lawyers to specialize according to the type of client or side of the case—this is a part of the more general tendency for legal specialties to be organized around the needs of clients who are distinguishable by social type, a pattern that is not so characteristic of medicine. A patient may be classified as a "kidney problem" without any reference to his wealth or social position, but only a wealthy client of a lawyer is likely to have antitrust or securities law problems. It is true that certain diseases disproportionately afflict the rich, and many others are more likely to be diagnosed in rich than in poor patients, but social implications seem likely to flow more naturally from the organization of legal specialties than from medical specialization. Certain types of legal problems can, by definition, afflict only corporations. Thus, lawyers who specialize in those fields of law will have a clientele with a disporportionate amount of economic power and, perhaps, social and political power as well. Beyond this necessary correspondence between some doctrinal areas of the law and particular social types of clients, however, the structure of the demand for legal services induces most lawyers to handle a variety of problems, a variety that cuts across doctrinal areas and reflects the perceived legal needs of the lawyer's set of clients, which usually includes only a narrow range of social types (see chap. 2). Substantive specialization in law has therefore lagged well behind that in medicine. Demand for medical services is not usually tied to the patients' social type; some doctors specialize in serving the poor, the rich, old people, young people, or one sex, and some diseases of genetic origin afflict persons of distinct racial or ethnic heritage, but most illnesses are shared broadly throughout the population, providing a considerable range of social types of patients even if the doctor specializes in a particular malady.

Apart from the economic pressure to make efficient use of scarce technology or technology that requires a distinct skill, the lines of specialization within medicine have largely been dictated by scientific theory. Medicine, engineering, and other professions in the sciences are structured around their conceptual bases, as developed by autonomous scholars in universities and scientific research institutions, and innovations in the knowledge bases of these professions usually account for changes in the organization of practice over time. This is not the case in law. We do not say that the law lacks theory but rather that its theory does not appear to organize the profession. The issue (for present purposes, at least) is not whether the law boasts some systematic body of knowledge or concepts corresponding to the scientific base of medicine but whether such systematic knowledge as exists structures the delivery of legal services. We are aware that concepts of "disease" may be defined, in part, by social variables.[17] Our contention, nonetheless, is that the structure of the delivery of medical services is organized in large measure by a body of scientific theory and empirical knowledge, while such division of labor as occurs in law tends to follow the boundaries between identifiable social groups who share distinct sets of legal needs.

This identification of lawyer with client may reflect the process and criteria by which clients select lawyers. The intimate nature of many medical problems notwithstanding, personal intimacy perhaps more often characterizes the relationship between lawyer and client than that between doctor and patient. Our relations with doctors tend to become routinized. In our early years we submit to preschool physical exams; later, as the indignities of age afflict us, we are told to have routine annual physicals. Though these occasions involve some procedures that are, in a sense, intimate, the interactions usually follow a standard format and become familiar. Doctors tend to adopt a matter-of-fact, somewhat laconic manner, perhaps designed to reassure the patient that his case is not exceptional and perhaps to speed case processing.[18] Even when we are ill, the doctor's questions are often standard: "Any nausea?" "Any abdominal cramps or pains?" Most of us see our lawyers, however, only when "ill"; we do not get routine annual legal examinations. When lawyers perform strictly legal functions, as opposed to general business or tax planning, the client has usually determined in advance that there is a problem, often some particular sort of "trouble."

It is important that the lawyer, in discussing a client's problems, speak the client's language, both literally and symbolically. The legal profession's greater reliance on extensive conversation between lawyer and client, rather than on a checklist of symptoms, may require that the lawyer and client share a range of discourse. But beyond this, the patient with nephritis is probably less concerned that the doctor share an outlook on life than that the doctor be well informed about kidneys. The client, of course, also wants his or her lawyer to be technically competent, but the matters that law addresses often require a trust that goes beyond confidence in professional skill. The client must trust the lawyer's discretion and may even feel a need to have the lawyer sympathize with the client's position. Clients may, therefore, prefer lawyers who share their social characteristics. It is probably more often important to clients than to patients that their professionals are of their own ethnic groups, went to the same sorts of schools, or belong to the same clubs. This, then, is another reason why social types of clients tend to produce corresponding groupings of lawyers.

DEFINING THE WORK IN LAW AND IN MEDICINE

Sociological thought concerning the professions has largely been shaped by the model of the medical profession[19] and has consequently identified freedom of occupational activity as one of the principal characteristics of a profession.[20] This autonomy is said to result, at least in part, from the professionals' possession of arcane knowledge that their patients or clients lack.[21] Since, by hypothesis, the client does not know the essentials of the professional's work and cannot evaluate it, the professional acts with a freer hand than do members of occupations whose customers have a broad understanding of the occupation's work. A professional's client will, of course, usually know whether the lawsuit has been won or whether the illness has been cured, but he may not know whether another result should have been expected. The law may differ from medicine, however, in the extent to which the problems it addresses are defined by clients rather than by professionals. Physicians use professionally defined standards to discriminate between cases that need attention and those that do not. The lawyer's client, by contrast, plays a larger role in defining legal problems, in deciding whether and when help is needed. Indeed, there may be a distinction between the role of "client," a person who employs an expert to perform more or less well defined services, and the role of "patient," a person whom the physician treats. It is only a bit too glib to put the point this way: the doctor decides when the patient needs an appendectomy, but the client decides when the client needs a divorce.

Within the legal profession, the extent to which the client defines the problems may well vary with the type of law and the nature of the client. Securities lawyers or corporate tax experts serve sophisticated business enterprises that can recognize and define their legal problems in considerable degree, while the generally less sophisticated clients of neighborhood lawyers are much less aware of their legal needs. Thus, the corporation planning a securities issue or a merger will present a relatively specific set of issues to the lawyer, while the blue-collar worker may not recognize the existence of a contract problem. This suggests somewhat ironically that lawyers doing high-prestige work are less likely to define their clients' problems than are lawyers doing lower-status work. On the other hand, in the legal work that enjoys high professional prestige, those who bring cases to lawyers will often be other lawyers. Large corporations that have significant securities and antitrust problems employ corporate house counsel who identify and analyze the businesses' legal problems and select specialized outside counsel to whom the work may be referred. Thus, though the client identifies the problems in such high-status work, a professional is still in control—it is a lawyer, not someone outside the profession, who defines the need for legal work. But these lawyers are full-time employees of the client corporations, answerable to corporate management and, no doubt, generally responsive to the management's wishes.

This observation suggests another important difference between the legal and medical professions. In medicine, the general tendency is that the less specialized practitioners, with lower prestige, refer difficult or exotic cases to more highly specialized, higher-prestige physicians. The typical referral is from the "family doctor" to a "specialist." In law, the cases flow in the opposite direction—higher-prestige lawyers more commonly refer work to lower-prestige practitioners. As we noted above, a large firm will usually refer out the divorce case of a corporate executive. The size of large law firms and the volume of business handled by them permits specialization within the firm, and the prominent specialists in corporate law fields such as tax, antitrust, securities, and real estate development will usually be found within such firms. Competition among these firms ordinarily induces each of them to provide a broad range of the services demanded by their clientele and, concomitantly, discourages them from referring cases to specialists in other large firms. When doctors practice in groups (or share a suite of offices), the groups are usually rather small and the practice is often limited to one specialty. A typical arrangement would consist of from three to five urologists, sharing a suite, consulting with one another, substituting for a colleague who is ill or on vacation, and referring cases to one another (usually from seniors to juniors) to even out the workload, but without a formal group practice or the sort of teamwork that characterizes the large law firms.[22]

The most prestigious doctors, as well as the family practitioner, are therefore likely to refer patients to specialists in other fields who are housed in other offices. That this sort of referral occurs far less often among lawyers deprives the legal profession of an important incentive for the maintenance of contacts among professionals and thus deprives it of one of the significant mechanisms for the enhancement of the profession's social solidarity.

But the differences in organizational character between doctors' patients and lawyers' clients are probably even more consequential than are the differences in organization of the firms that deliver services in the two professions. In the corporate client hemisphere, the clients are likely to be large organizations with substantial market power, and a law firm may depend heavily on the business of one large client. The consumers of medical services are, by contrast, individuals who are relatively seldom organized into groups or into the corporate form.[23] Thus, clients of the legal profession's corporate hemisphere will usually enjoy greater power vis-à-vis their lawyers than will patients vis-à-vis their doctors, while the autonomy of lawyers who practice in the personal client hemisphere may more closely approximate the doctor's degree of independence from client control. This is a view from another perspective, then, of the same irony that we have noted before—that lawyers doing less prestigious sorts of work for personal clients have greater "professional autonomy" than do lawyers performing more prestigious work for corporate clients.

There is at least one other reason, however, why clients may enjoy more control over their lawyers, in either hemisphere, than do patients over doctors. A primary method of control in any producer-consumer relationship is, of course, control of the purse strings, and clients seem likely to exercise more of that sort of control than do patients. It is common for clients to instruct their lawyers,

"Look into this estate for me, but don't run the bill up over $500 without first informing me about how much I may expect to inherit,"

Or,

"Let me know when your total billings to my company for the current fiscal year have reached $10,000, and we will then review our situation and decide how we wish to proceed."

By contrast, it is probably the rare patient who tells a doctor, "I am willing to spend $5,000 to have you take care of my heart and attempt to prevent another coronary." Most legal matters are primarily concerned with money, and it is possible to make a more or less rational calculation of the amount that it is prudent to spend in order to protect the amount at risk, given the probabilities. In medical cases, the costs of the exposure to risk are more difficult to calculate. This greater uncertainty will enhance the professional's power.

We should note at this point an important distinction between two quite different sorts of control that clients might exercise over lawyers. The first and more obvious of these is direct impact on decisions made about the nature of the lawyers' work, including positions taken and the extent to which particular problems are explored in depth. We have already argued that this sort of client influence is likely to occur more often in the corporate hemisphere where the clients are both more sophisticated and more powerful. The second, and perhaps even more important, sort of client influence on the profession is impact on the profession's total structure, on the patterns of differentiation of its component parts and thus on the form of organization of the delivery of legal services. We have much better evidence of the latter influence than of the former. Our survey of the Chicago bar was not designed to collect direct data on the substance of the relationships between individual lawyers and individual clients—that is, on the decision process through which various strategic judgments are made concerning the manner in which the clients' cases will be handled.[24] But we do have data on the relationship between client type and the profession's social structure. Though we will continue in the frankly speculative manner of this concluding essay, we might then return now to a systemwide analysis—more at the macro than at the micro level—focusing not on the dyadic relationship between lawyer and client but on more general characteristics of the social structure of the legal profession, still using medicine as a point of comparison.

THE CONCEPTUAL FRAMEWORKS OF LAW AND MEDICINE

Dietrich Rueschemeyer has observed that there is far greater societal dissensus about the "central value" of the law—justice—than about that of medicine—health:

Apart from borderline cases there exists a near-universal *consensus about the central value* toward which the medical profession is oriented. Physician and patient, the doctor's colleague group and the patient's family, his friends, and his role partners in other contexts, as well as the larger community and its various agencies, agree essentially on the substantive definition of health and on its importance compared with other values.

The situation is far more complex for the legal profession. Justice, like health, ranks high in the societal value hierarchy. In the substantive definition of justice, however, there are considerable ambiguities and wide discrepancies, . . . the notion of unjust law is by no means uncommon.[25]

The division of labor in the law will, then, tend to have consequences for the structures and legitimacy of the legal profession that are quite different from the consequences of specialization in medicine. The interests of a dermatologist and a cardiologist seldom conflict. But the distinct social types of clients served by most lawyers—even those who work in a number of fields—will often have conflicting economic and political interests. To the extent that the interests of lawyers' clients conflict,[26] the interests of the lawyers will also conflict and the social integration of the profession will suffer.

The conceptual framework of the law does little to bridge these gulfs. Just as a lawyer's clients tend to be limited to particular social types, the applicability of many legal doctrines is restricted to narrowly delimited social types[27]—broadcasters, landlords, or securities brokers, for example. Because the law has no overarching conceptual framework that is broad enough or strong enough to encompass all of these discrete doctrinal areas, scholarly contributions to legal theory and practice tend not to be cumulative. Even the broadest of the law's concepts—abstractions like the right to privacy—take on different colorations in different factual contexts, meanings that often differ systematically with the type of client.[28] Although the boundaries between many areas of the law are undoubtedly indistinct, this is less often due to the presence of a common core of theory than to the absence of any theory that might clearly define boundaries. In spite of plentiful ambiguity, the law is decidedly *not* a seamless web.[29] It has not only seams but darts, tucks, pleats, gaps, and open zippers. Is this as true of medicine? Some medical specialties are, of course, quite distinct from some others, and doctors certainly regard much of the literature that is produced in remote specialties as irrelevant to their own work, but all of medicine deals with a human body that is conceived of as a set of interdependent systems, subject to a relatively rigidly classified set of diseases, and studied by one set of general principles, "the scientific method." The procedures dictated by scientific method, whatever the ambiguities, are more clearly defined than those dictated by "due process." Because the elements of legal theory and knowledge are less clearly interrelated, the effects of the innovations of legal scholars are often felt only within separate, delimited doctrinal spheres, and law professors therefore play a lesser role than do academic scientists in determining the structures of their respective professions. We have already noted the existence of dissensus about the nature of justice. This dissensus may lead legal scholarship to be directed toward differing—perhaps conflicting—goals, thus contributing further to the lack of conceptual integration.

We will return briefly to a comparison of the legal and medical professions, assessing the extent to which some of their key institutions serve to promote social integration of the two professions. For now, however, let us close this catalog of the professions' differences and turn to a further analysis of the degree of autonomy or independence of the legal profession.

Interests from Within and Without

A critical issue in the study of any profession is this: to what extent does the profession manifest client interests (or, perhaps, the interests of others outside the profession) and to what extent does it reflect its own concerns, interests, or values? Common lore says that lawyers are "hired guns," that within the vague limits of "professional responsibility" they do their clients' bidding. But the lore also holds that some forces or agencies within the legal profession serve to unify it, to give it a sense of identity or coherence. Thus, the bar associations, the law schools, or the court-appointed boards that control lawyer discipline and admission to the bar may be thought to create or enforce norms and values that originate within the profession. How accurate is the lore?

As our statement of the question implies, the issue is one of degree. Every profession reflects to some extent the economic, social, and ideological interests of its clients. All the professions also reflect norms and values of the professionals qua professionals—tenets that spring from the profession's own interests, ideology, and socialization processes. To varying degrees and in varying ways in the different professions, the professionals sometimes speak for themselves and at other times advocate the interests of outsiders. Beyond their "hired gun" role (but by no means unrelated to it), lawyers and other professionals may adopt their clients' views and, thus, advocate client interests because they have accepted them as their own. Cancer specialists may campaign for the control of environmental carcinogens even though a successful campaign might reduce the number of their patients. Tax lawyers may seek to simplify the tax code even though simplicity would reduce the demand for their professional advice. If we are correct, however, lawyers are not likely to advocate the abolition of a tax shelter if that would conflict with their clients' interests.[30]

Professions may also reflect client interests in a more subtle, but perhaps more fundamental, manner. The interests may affect the social structure of the profession itself—they will influence the organization of the bar into groups or fields, the distribution of lawyers from different social origins among those groups, and the patterns of relationships among the lawyers. External influences that may shape the legal profession's social structure include the interests of clients and the baggage that the professionals bring with them into the profession. The attitudes and behavior of professionals as professionals are, no doubt, affected by their other roles—as spouses, parents, churchgoers, Daughters of the American Revolution, or Sons of Italy. The early socialization of professionals may also be relevant to their professions, as may their commitments to religious, political, or social values.

But what is the relevance of our findings to these issues, and what are their implications for the profession? One conclusion suggested by our findings is that the bar associations, law schools, and court agencies accomplish little social integration of the profession. While our research documents the divisions within the legal profession, however, it does not provide direct evidence about the internal processes of these institutions. A fair inference from our data is that client interests play, at the least, an important role in the failure of these institutions to achieve integration of the profession, but we have examined the functioning of the bar associations, the law schools, and the agencies that regulate the profession only in an exploratory, impressionistic fashion.[31] With this caveat in mind, let us proceed to speculate a bit about some of the reasons why these institutions might have failed as integrative mechanisms, using the medical profession again as a basis for comparison.

The principal integrative institutions of the medical profession are the medical societies, the major hospitals, and the medical schools.[32] These may be thought of as roughly analogous to the bar associations, the courts, and the law schools, respectively, but there are important differences. The medical societies appear to be much more effective as regulatory mechanisms than are the bar associations. Bar associations have, in fact, been losing their regulatory powers over the profession in recent years. In 1973, the Chicago Bar Association (CBA) voluntarily ceded its power to discipline lawyers to an agency of the Illinois Supreme Court, known as the Attorney Registration and Disciplinary Commission. The leadership of the CBA had concluded that the association had been generally ineffective in carrying out the disciplinary function, and the CBA had also found the process expensive to administer. The cost of retaining the disciplinary power outweighed the perceived benefits to the organized bar.[33] In 1980, the Association of the Bar of the City of New York also yielded its disciplinary authority to the courts, not so voluntarily.[34] In our survey of Chicago lawyers, we asked our respondents whether they thought that the investigation of unethical conduct by attorneys should be carried out by the professional associations or by a governmental body under the supervision of the courts. Only 29 percent of our respondents favored control by the professional associations. Thus, the profession's power of self-regulation—a power that is usually included among the characteristics that are thought to distinguish the professions from other occupations—was supported by only a minority of Chicago lawyers.[35]

In his classic work, *The Governmental Process*, David Truman remarked:

> In striking contrast to medicine, the legal profession in the United States has been notably lacking in cohesion.

> [T]he centrifugal effects of specialized practice and wide income differentials have placed limits on the effectiveness with which bar associations stabilize the relationships of their potential membership and upon the completeness of association among lawyers.[36]

We find ourselves in accord with Truman's observations. The organized bar appears to us to function less as an interest group than as a forum within which interest groups compete for power. Unless some coalition within the bar can mobilize powerful constituencies, often from outside the bar, and can thus impose its will on the profession as a whole, the profession is unlikely to take a definite stand on a consequential issue. The legal profession can and does take definite stands, however, on issues that lack moment for most of the profession and most of its clients, and the organized bar often delegates such decisions to the concerned subgroup.[37]

Unlike the bar associations, the medical societies and related organizations (such as certifying boards) retain tight control over the standards of medical competence, admission to practice, the certification of specialists, and ethical standards of conduct. David Truman also noted that "in a closely knit profession like medicine, where reputation is crucial to a successful practice and where access to hospitals and other medical institutions is essential, sanctions can be effective."[38] This points to the second of the medical institutions—hospitals—that we wish to examine and to compare to the integrative institutions of the legal profession. The law does not have any institution quite like the hospital. An affiliation with a hospital is an essential precondition of most sorts of medical practice.[39] A doctor will be unable to hospitalize patients or to treat them while they are in the hospital without a staff appointment or some sort of "hospital privileges." This gives the hospitals a significant form of control over individual physicians and standards of medical practice. Large law firms are important assemblages of practitioners and in that sense may be analogous to hospital staffs, but the law firms lack this sort of control. Lawyers can pursue a great many alternative arrangements that will permit them to practice, often quite successfully, even though they may be denied access to a large firm. Moreover, as we have seen, the large law firms are quite specialized institutions, serving only a narrow range of clientele, and they thus do not perform the integrative role that makes hospitals so important to the social solidarity of the medical profession. Large hospitals typically treat a wide range of ailments and serve patients from a variety of social classes, thus bringing together physicians from virtually the full spectrum of specialties who then make collective decisions about the managment of the hospitals and the allocation of resources, as well as about the treatment of patients. Because of their regulatory functions—their de facto control over entry into the practice of medicine and their role in setting and enforcing standards—the hospitals are probably more closely analogous to the courts than to the large law firms.

The large, corporate law firms do little to bridge the two hemispheres of the legal profession. They have little occasion to come in contact with either the clients or the lawyers of the personal client hemisphere. The growth of the large firms over the past few decades, the increase in salaried lawyers who are full-time employees of corporations and governments, and the simultaneous decline in the numbers of solo practitioners do represent a consolidation of a sort in the structure of law practice. But, because of the gulfs that separate lawyers who serve different types of clients, these trends have not enhanced the social integration of the profession. Indeed, the distinctions and divisions may be growing even sharper.

What, then, of the courts? Whether they are internal or external to the profession, why do they not succeed in giving the profession coherence, in creating social solidarity or integration among lawyers, in assuring that the lawyer will come closer to being a "standard model"? Unlike the English bar, which has always been self-governing,[40] the American legal profession is subject to the supervisory authority of the courts,[41] but the courts have seldom used their licensing and disciplinary powers to exact conformity to any one, clear vision of the "proper lawyer." Administration of the courts' rules governing bar admission and attorney discipline is sometimes delegated to bar associations or to other groups of practitioners, and the courts for the most part have been content to impose rather minimal, rather laxly administered requirements for admission to practice—requirements that applicants must be of suitable character, must have completed a specified number of years of professional education (with very few required courses),[42] and must have passed a comprehensive bar examination that varies from jurisdiction to jurisdiction and from time to time in coverage and in degree of difficulty. Recently, however, we have seen initiatives by some judges to exert a greater degree of control over the content of legal education. Reflecting the view that many advocates are incompetent (a view expressed by Chief Justice Burger, among others),[43] committees of both federal and state judges have recommended and adopted requirements for admission to practice that demand the completion of a more extensive list of substantive law school courses, thus establishing required law school curricula.[44] These requirements usually include a prescribed amount of "clinical" legal education (supervised work in a legal clinic), and some would make experience in a certain number of trials (sometimes distinguishing further between jury trials and bench trials) a precondition of full admission to the bar.[45]

For the most part, however, the courts have not attempted to set rigid or rigorous standards for the profession or to determine the characteristics that lawyers must possess. Note that the training and experience requirements just discussed deal only with litigation skills—the judges' expressions of concern about lawyer competence have largely been limited to competence as an advocate. Similarly, in the area of lawyer discipline, judges will punish lawyers who disrupt sessions of court or who are insulting or insubordinate in direct dealings with the bench, but the courts seldom concern themselves with the far greater volume of legal business that takes place outside the courtroom. Because most lawyers appear in court seldom or not at all, most of the profession is thus little subject to supervision by the judiciary. And because the organized bar is largely ineffectual, decisive action being blocked by the diversity of the bar and the resulting "veto groups," the authority delegated by the courts to the bar to control both discipline and admission to practice is little used to give the profession coherence or a distinctive character.

The remaining institution that might serve to enhance the social integration of the profession is the law school. The schools might inculcate norms that would endure through all or much of a professional career, influencing the way in which lawyers do their work and see their roles, or might train lawyers in habits of mind that would shape their definitions of the nature of legal work, their relations with clients, or even their perceptions of social reality.[46] Legal education is widely reputed to be an intensive, demanding, emotionally charged, anxiety-producing experience. It is replete with rites of passage and status degradation ceremonies. The traditional, though now seldom practiced, classroom style—the "Socratic method" as employed by mythological monsters like Professor Kingsfield[47]—is portrayed as intimidating and authoritarian, calculated to exact conformity to the professor's (and the profession's?) values, *or else.*[48] Moreover, and probably more important, American law schools are said to adhere closely to a standard model created by Dean Langdell at Harvard in the 1870s. Thus, almost all of the schools use appellate court opinions in actual cases rather than treatises or textbooks as the basic teaching materials; certain best-selling collections of these appellate opinions (assembled in edited versions in casebooks, bearing the names of professors at the better schools) are widely used across the full spectrum of law schools, from the most to the least prestigious; and the curricula of almost all of the schools include highly similar lists of standard courses in basic areas of the common law, taxation, and economic regulatory law.[49]

But there is little evidence that American legal education produces a standard product. As we have seen, Chicago lawyers differ substantially in their views on social and economic issues, and they do work that varies greatly in character, in the service of clients of a variety of social types. Assuming that certain habits of mind may be particularly useful in or well adapted to the performance of certain types of work, we might nonetheless expect to find little in common among the modes of problem solving used in the characteristic tasks of the litigator who tries personal injury cases, the business advisor who gives tax counsel along with investment advice, the scientist who drafts patent applications, the artist who drafts indenture instruments,[50] and the public relations lawyer who handles a corporation's dealings with the government. Law schools may prepare lawyers for only a narrow range of lawyers' roles, but the variety of jobs that lawyers are called upon to do in urban America guarantees that, as a practical matter, the notion of "thinking like a lawyer" will be largely meaningless.

In the first decades of the twentieth century, the Carnegie Foundation sponsored studies of both medical and legal education in the United States with a view toward improving quality. The report on the medical schools, known as the Flexner Report, succeeded in stimulating the profession and the political process to abolish the marginal schools and to subsidize the remaining ones.[51] By contrast, the analogous report on the law schools by Alfred Z. Reed failed to achieve any such objective. Reed may have erred in being too permissive, too democratic. The report called for a two-tiered system of legal education, one track (and perhaps one set of schools) designed to prepare students for membership in what he called the "Inner Bar," practicing largely corporate law, and another, less demanding track preparing other students to join the "General Body of Practitioners,"[52] practicing "conveyancing, probate, . . . criminal law, and trial work."[53] Though Reed's prescription sounds elitist enough today, it was regarded by the bar establishment at the time as a threat to the exclusivity of the profession. The defect in Reed's position was that it would not close the proprietary law schools and the night schools, and thus would not cut off the access to the profession of the new immigrants who had arrived in the United States in such large numbers in the late nineteenth and early twentieth centuries.[54] The statement of Professor Arthur L. Corbin of Yale that is quoted in the epigraph at the front of this book was one of the pieces of rhetoric brought forth by the controversy— he argued that the democratic tendency "to open wide the gates of a profession to 'the average man'" ensured the "utter mediocrity of judges and lawyers" and rendered a part of the profession "incompetent and dangerous to the public welfare."[55] Though the Association of American Law Schools sought to achieve educational hegemony, forcing the marginal schools out of business, it did not succeed. A number of proprietary schools, night law schools, and other opportunities for part-time law study persist to this day.[56] Thus, legal education never became as highly standardized as did medical education in the United States; a greater variety of institutions continued to train candidates for the bar, the number of seats available in law schools was far less limited than in the medical schools, and the law schools thus have produced a considerable volume and variety of graduates. As law schools have conformed less to a standard model than have medical schools, so too, very likely, have their graduates.[57]

Sources of the Profession's Social Organization

If the formal institutions of the legal profession—the bar associations, the courts, the law schools, and the large law firms—do not determine its social organization, what then is the source of its structure? It is surely not random; the data are far too clearly organized for that to be the case. We have argued that the primary determinant of the social structure of the profession is the interests and demands of the lawyers' clients, but we have also pointed to the role played by social origins— particularly ethnoreligious identification—in structuring the allocation of lawyers to varying professional roles.

The patterns of interaction among lawyers are influenced in significant degree both by the lawyers' fields of practice, a variable that is closely associated with the types of clients served, and by the ethnoreligious affiliations of the lawyers. Moreover, the ethnoreligious and client type variables overlap—lawyers' ethnicities vary systematically by the type of client served (i.e., lawyers of particular ethnicities tend to serve particular kinds of clients). This overlap of the two variables does not exist only in the allocation of lawyers to types of work; we also saw it in our analysis of the patterns of acquaintance with a list of selected "notable" Chicago lawyers, a set of the profession's elites. The patterns were divided into readily identifiable regions or networks, one area being composed disproportionately of WASPs who serve the largest corporate clients and another having a great preponderance of Catholics who do trial work for individuals and smaller businesses. We found that acquaintance with notable Jewish lawyers did not correspond quite so neatly to client type, however. The Jewish notables tended to be spread somewhat more evenly across the types of practice—some located in the corporate area with the WASPs and some with the Catholics in the region characterized by trial work for individual clients and general commercial work for smaller businesses. The variable that appeared to organize the patterns of acquaintance of Jewish lawyers was, rather, the lawyers' positions in the political spectrum. Jews were much more likely to be acquainted with leaders of liberal political view—with liberal Democrats rather than with Republicans or conservatives. Indeed, one quite separate, readily identifiable network of acquaintances where Jews clearly predominated was the network of lawyers active in liberal causes such as the ACLU and other reform-oriented organizations.

The most remarkable thing about all of this is that *intra*professional concerns, motivations, and interests appear to count for so little in the social structure of the profession. All of the organizing principles that have the greatest influence—client demand, ethnoreligious origin, and politics—arise outside the profession. Talcott Parsons contended that one of the identifying characteristics of the professions is that they are not "self-regarding" but externally oriented.[58] The sort of external orientation Parsons had in mind is rather different, however, from the one that we observe. He argued that the professions display a "collectivity orientation," that they are devoted to the commonweal. We find that Chicago lawyers are devoted to the interests of their clients, to ethnoreligious loyalties, and to political causes. There may be a substantial tendency for the advocate to equate client interests with "the general interest," but the adversary nature of the legal process prevents any professionwide consensus about the validity of such equations. Lawyers who represent Citizens for a Better Environment may differ from those who represent Commonwealth Edison in their view of the public interest concerning the development of atomic power, those who work for the Internal Revenue Service may not share corporate tax counsel's view that the general welfare will be served by a tax avoidance scheme, and those who represent insurance companies may not see the justice of the position, taken by personal injury plaintiffs' lawyers, that accident victims should be fully compensated for pain and suffering. But in spite of their differing views, it is important to note—as Parsons might have—that lawyers on both sides of all those disputes and many others seek to harmonize the commonweal with their clients' interests.[59] And the other sources of differentiation and conflict within the bar, ethnic and political loyalties, can no doubt be harmonized with a particular view of the general interest at least as readily as may client interests. But because the ethnic and political identities are associated with service to particular types of clients, such loyalties may serve to reinforce the homogeneity of outlook of the lawyers serving those clients, to enhance their adherence to a shared conception of the commonweal. Thus, the reinforcement of client interests by ethnic and political networks may strengthen the devotion of lawyers to their clients' causes.

Many who have written about the legal profession, however, have argued that the lawyer is the dominant party in the lawyer-client relationship.[60] Lawyers are said to use various sorts of powers—intellectual powers, mastery of legal learning, silver tongues, the monopoly of the license to practice, the formality and mystification of legal procedures (silk ribbons and sealing wax, black robes and, in England, wigs), impenetrable jargon (Latin, "law French," and polysyllabic neologisms), and general bluster and chicanery—to manipulate and control their clients. But these writers have usually had in mind the part of the profession that we have referred to as the "personal plight" practice, the representation of individuals with legal difficulties that are (at least in large part) personal rather than economic in nature—fields such as divorce, personal injury, and criminal law. In his widely cited article "The Practice of Law as a Confidence Game," Abraham Blumberg argued that lawyers manipulate their clients, but he was considering there the practice of criminal law, where the clients are particularly vulnerable, usually impecunious, sometimes dependent on the state for the provision of counsel, and often not in a position to take their business elsewhere.[61] Douglas Rosenthal's pioneering and suggestive empirical study, *Lawyer and Client: Who's in Charge?* was done within the context of personal injury cases.[62] Though Rosenthal found that plaintiffs who took an active role in the supervision of their cases were likely to obtain better results than those who did not, the plaintiffs in such cases are nonetheless seldom the wealthiest and most powerful clients. Those who lack the resources to pay their lawyers in advance and, therefore, must find lawyers who are willing to take their cases on a contingent fee basis[63] will usually be in a subservient or dependent relationship to their lawyers. Pursuing Blumberg's theme, James Eisenstein and Herbert Jacob have observed that defense counsel who are regulars in felony courts may be less concerned with pleasing their clients than with accommodating the other regulars in those courts, the judges, clerks, and state's attorneys with whom they deal on a continuing basis.[64] Though the clients who appear in felony court may be awesome in some ways, they usually do not have the sort of power that counts with their lawyers.

A lawyer who represents a lower-class person charged with a crime (and most criminal defendants are, in fact, impecunious) will usually be able to prevail if a direct conflict arises between the lawyer's interest and the client's interest. A common situation regards the payment of the lawyer's fee. Many, perhaps most, private criminal defense lawyers insist upon payment in advance because they have found that most defendants who are convicted (even if to a lesser charge, by plea bargain) will not pay later, particularly if they go to prison, and because the lawyers know that most defendants are, in fact, convicted. Even if the defendant is acquitted, it is notoriously difficult to collect fees from clients who are as mobile, unreliable, and, some might even say, untrustworthy as are criminal defendants as a class. Paid *in advance* means that the fee must be paid before the lawyer will try the case. The practical effect of this is that the defendant who lacks sufficient money for release on bail (perhaps because funds that might have been used for bail are needed to pay the lawyer) must remain in jail until family or friends have managed to pay the full amount of the lawyer's fee, often on the installment plan. This may take many months. Pending full payment, the lawyer will seek continuances of the defendant's trial on one pretext or another. Despite the obvious ethical problems raised by such a practice, it is said to be widespread.

But when a similar conflict arises between the interests of a corporate lawyer and a client's interests, what does that lawyer do? Let us consider another example. Lawyers who specialized in the representation of airlines in route and rate regulation cases were confronted with a proposal that federal law be changed to remove or greatly lessen regulation of airline competition. What position would such lawyers take on the proposal? Would they lobby against it? Because most airlines favored deregulation, open opposition might well have offended the clients. Would the lawyers, therefore, perhaps seek to work quietly behind the scenes to oppose deregulation? Apart from any political activity, what would the lawyers *think* about it? Would they identify with the interests of their clients, or would they worry about the effect of deregulation on their incomes?

After deregulation had occurred, we asked these questions of a lawyer who had devoted most of his career, nearly thirty years of practice, to airline regulation work. The lawyer had been extremely successful and had regularly represented one of the major carriers, but after deregulation his practice had fallen off drastically. In mid-career and middle age, he was thus confronted with the need to develop a new, entirely different specialty. Had he seen this coming, we asked? Well, he said, he had of course known that deregulation was being proposed and debated. Had he taken any part in that debate? No. We knew that he had held responsible positions in the federal government and was well acquainted in the executive branch—had he, therefore, attempted to use his contacts to express doubts about deregulation? No. Did he anticipate or worry about the decline in demand for his services that deregulation might bring? No; he had assumed that it "would turn out all right." He had believed the old lawyers' adage that whatever the government does creates work for lawyers—airline regulation had created work, and deregulation, if it occurred, would also create work. It did not. We are confident that the lawyer's responses were truthful, and we believe that he is not atypical.

Corporate lawyers are accustomed to talk as if they have more business than they can handle, as if there is an inexhaustible reservoir of clients demanding their services. It is certainly true that the large law firms serving corporate clients have expanded greatly in recent years. It may also be the case that the expansion of the firms has made them less dependent upon any one client or, perhaps, even upon any one type of work (though this is not necessarily true).[65] But the firms do need to maintain their volume of business in order to support the investment that they have made in plant and staff—in word-processing equipment, computers, copiers, and walnut paneling; in secretaries, technicians, paralegals, and lawyers—and the firm as a whole is no doubt less dependent upon the continued flow of any particular kind of legal business than is the partner, team, or department within the firm that handles that kind of business. Lawyers who work in large firms are compensated in accordance with their productivity (at least, the more senior ones are). If they are not very busy or are not bringing many clients into the firm, their compensation and their power and prestige within the firm will eventually suffer.[66] The individual lawyers who handle the work of major corporate clients are therefore usually wary of offending such clients.

Corporate lawyers seldom perceive any conflict between their interests and those of their clients.[67] In most cases, there probably is none—events that make the client stronger will usually make their lawyers stronger in the long run as well. Corporate lawyers may thus come to regard their own interests as inseparable from those of clients. After lawyers have advocated a client's position for several years—after they have, time and again, been called upon to think of and express all of the strongest arguments for the client—it may well be impossible for them to step out of that role and to consider and assert their own interests apart from those of their clients. Corporate lawyers may thus behave like the managers of boxers; A. J. Liebling, the Max Weber of the prize ring, observed that managers habitually use the first person singular in describing what their boxers will do to opponents—as in "I am going to jab him silly."[68]

But the criminal defense lawyers, in our first example, appear to have no difficulty in discerning where their interests lie, even when their interests clearly conflict with those of clients. What is the source of the difference in the nature of the relationships between lawyers and clients in these two situations? The answer seems to lie in the differing distributions of power. Criminal defense lawyers deal with clients who, typically, lack wealth, political power, prestige, rectitude, and other deference entitlements,[69] while the lawyers are members of a high-status profession, middle class, and relatively well connected. The criminal defense lawyer represents a large volume of clients with quite rapid turnover, and is therefore not much dependent upon any one client. The corporate lawyer deals, by contrast, with the most powerful class of client, the major corporation that has considerable economic and political resources and a voice that may make or break reputations. These lawyers are, themselves, usually of the highest standing, the cleverest, the best educated, the most prestigious, the wealthiest, and the best connected, but their power is modest compared to that of their clients, and their continued success is highly dependent upon the maintenance of their client base.

TERENCE JOHNSON'S TYPOLOGY

In his seminal essay *Professions and Power*, the British sociologist Terence Johnson distinguishes between "collegiate" and "patronage" occupations. In Johnson's typology, a collegiate occupation is one in which "the producer defines the needs of the consumer and the manner in which these needs are catered for," while a patronage occupation is one in which "the consumer defines his own needs and the manner in which they are to be met."[70] The ordinary notion would be that, in these terms, the classic professions should be "collegiate" because the arcane knowledge of the professionals will give them autonomy in their work, permitting them to define "the needs of the client and the manner in which these needs are catered for." But some of the professions clearly fit this better than others. That was Johnson's point.

The profession that probably is most often collegiate is medicine. Even doctors do not always prevail over their patients, and would not if they could, but they come closer to the pure collegiate type than does any other profession. Engineering, by contrast, is pretty clearly of the patronage type. Most engineers are full-time employees of a corporation; there are relatively few independent consulting engineers. As employees, answerable to one employer, most engineers probably have less control over defining the scope and strategy of their work. Architects and accountants fall somewhere between these two. Their roles are even more variable. Accounting has, perhaps, changed from being more of the patronage type to being more collegiate. Historically, the evolution of the bookkeeper employed by a business firm into the chartered public accountant was designed to reassure investors in stock companies, thus enhancing the growth of capitalism. That rationale required that the accountants possess at least the appearance of independence from the management of the companies, but a very large proportion of the accounting profession always consisted of full-time employees of businesses, and even the independent accountants typically served a few large clients, upon whom they were highly dependent.[71] The consolidation of the accounting profession in the United States into a few large firms may, however, have moved it into a more collegiate posture.[72]

But what of the law? Where does the profession of the bar fall along this spectrum? When we apply Johnson's distinction to our analysis of the Chicago bar, we find that the profession again splits along its major divide. Of the two great parts, the personal client hemisphere more nearly approximates the collegiate type—the ideal of a profession—while the corporate client hemisphere comes closer to fitting the definition of patronage. That is, in the personal client hemisphere, the lawyers largely define the needs of the client and the manner in which they will be met, but the corporate client has a much larger role in defining its own legal needs and the strategy that will be used in pursuing them. Thus, the personal client hemisphere is, in an important sense, "more professional." This contradicts the common assumption that the attributes of professionalism inevitably enhance social status. It is demonstrable that corporate lawyers enjoy greater prestige than do those who serve persons (see chap. 4), but professional autonomy from client control is greater in the personal sector. Thus, the "less professional" hemisphere is the more prestigious one, an observation that lends further support to the hypothesis that the principal source of the prestige of lawyers is their clients—that the status they enjoy or suffer is acquired by association, that what enhances the status of a lawyer is not autonomy as a professional but access to centers of influence and avoidance of service to the powerless and despised.

But while the characterization of the corporate client as the patron of its lawyer may be a suggestive way of thinking about that relationship, it does not quite ring true to describe the personal client hemisphere as collegiate. There is little collegiality among the practitioners in that sector, little collective decision making or social intercourse among the lawyers who handle divorces, personal injury claims, criminal charges, wills, taxes, repossessions, and sales of property. The social and professional relations of those lawyers are, to be sure, disproportionately likely to take place with others who are in similar lines of work, but that fact does not suggest that these relations are frequent or intense. The lawyer in the personal client sector probably has fewer and less regular occasions to interact with other lawyers, particularly with opponents or those from other firms, than does the lawyer who serves corporations. Collegiality in this sense, however, is not at all implied by Johnson's definition of a collegiate occupation. The essential element is that the decisions about the work are controlled by the members of the profession—by the professional colleagues—rather than by the clients. The lawyers might well dominate their individual clients without any collegial interaction among the lawyers.

Nonetheless, we may want to consider another possibility. In addition to the collegiate and patronage types, Johnson proposes a third category of occupations. He calls this type "mediative," and he places in it occupations in which "a third party mediates in the relationship between producer and consumer, defining both the needs and the manner in which the needs are met."[73] Principal mediating institutions have, historically, included the state and the church. As we have already noted, the state regulates the legal profession in certain respects, chiefly in licensing (admission to practice) and in the discipline of lawyers for ethical lapses, though both of these sorts of regulation may be in large part delegated by the state to elements of the profession itself. To the extent that regulation of the bar is effective at all, the main impact of it falls upon the personal client sector. Official screening of potential lawyers to eliminate the incompetent or unusually venal is, in effect, directed at protecting the interests not of corporate clients but of persons as clients, in relatively small cases. Few candidates for the bar who have only marginal qualifications for admission to practice or who have much to fear from the bar examiners manage to find employment in the large corporate law firms. The corporations and the corporate law firms are capable of protecting their own interests, and they have elaborate systems of gate-keeping that do so. Similarly, the disciplinary system of the profession is also mainly brought to bear on the personal client sector, as Jerome Carlin, Jerold Auerbach,[74] and others have observed. The Code of Professional Responsibility (formerly the Canons of Ethics) deals for the most part with ethical issues at the level of ambulance chasing, not with issues that may arise in the practice of corporate law.[75] Critics of the code have observed that it covers handing out business cards in the hospital's emergency room but does not address the solicitation of business on the golf course at the country club.[76]

If the degree of regulation of the personal client sector makes it substantially mediative in character, that raises another interesting possibility. Carlin and Auerbach have argued that the regulatory power of the state is delegated to high-status, corporate lawyers, who then use the power to control lawyers who serve persons. If this is true, we have a patronage-type occupation—the corporate bar—serving as a mediating institution that intervenes in the relationship between lawyer and client in the personal client sector. Thus, a part of the bar that is lacking in autonomy, being itself subject to the influence of patrons outside the profession, regulates a subordinate part of the profession. The entire profession is therefore subject, directly or indirectly, to control by extraprofessional sources of power.

But there is a good case for the proposition that the formal regulatory mechanisms of the profession—the control of admission to practice and of disciplinary proceedings—are so little used and so generally ineffectual that their impact on the character of the profession may safely be discounted.[77] Even if this is so, however, the personal client sector might still be mediative rather than collegiate in nature.

Some third parties other than the profession's regulatory authorities may well intervene in the relationships between personal sector lawyers and their clients. In many cases, those lawyers may be answerable not to their clients but to bailiffs, court clerks, insurance claims adjustors, real estate brokers, title insurers, and so on. The lawyers will often be dependent upon these third parties for the continued flow of business; they are principal sources of client referral. The third parties may also control the lawyer's practice environment in ways that can make the work easy, difficult, or impossible. It may be within the power of these persons to expedite the settlement of cases, to move the lawyer's file to the top or the bottom of the pile, and thus to determine the volume of business that the lawyer can handle. Because the profitability of the work of these lawyers depends upon their ability to process large numbers of cases, the lawyer may be more concerned with cultivating and accommodating an insurance claims adjustor than with obtaining the maximum possible settlement for a client. The lawyer is likely to deal with that claims adjustor again soon, but may never see the client again. Though word-of-mouth among clients may be an important source of business for some lawyers, even those lawyers may well feel that they need the continuing goodwill of the adjustor if they are to make clients happy in the future. The fact that personal sector lawyers regularly exercise control of their clients does not, therefore, imply that they enjoy complete professional autonomy. They will often be dependent upon and constrained by other actors with whom they deal in the course of their practice.

Thus, the personal client hemisphere might plausibly be classified, in the alternative, as a mediative occupation. The corporate hemisphere could not be. The control of the corporate patrons is sufficient that the state, the professionals who act for the state, and other third parties are unlikely to interfere significantly.

Though there is little point in manipulating definitional categories, this characterization of the set of interrelationships among lawyers and clients seems to us to be useful and not unrealistic. The most problematic and the most controversial portion of this analysis, however, will no doubt be our suggestion that corporate clients often dominate their lawyers. We may, therefore, want to give that point a bit more attention.

Corporate Lawyers and Their Clients: Further Thoughts on the Allocation of Autonomy

To what extent are the needs of corporations for legal services and the strategies to be used in pursuit of those needs determined by the corporations rather than by their lawyers? One of the problems in addressing that question is the difficulty of deciding how to treat corporate house counsel. Are officials of the corporation who are themselves lawyers to be counted as part of the corporation or as part of the bar? They might, of course, plausibly be regarded as either or both. Whichever they are, they are a factor of great and increasing weight. According to a study by a management consulting firm, the legions of corporate house counsel quadrupled between 1950 and 1978, in the latter year numbering about

50,000 of a total United States lawyer population then estimated at 450,000.[78]

Terence Johnson would expect this development:

> Patronage, where it is the rule, creates the "housed" practitioner. The aristocratic patron "keeps" his artist, architect, doctor and priest; he maintains them on his estates or in some location socially or politically controlled by him. The practitioner is a courtier and must share the social manner and social graces of the courtier. Similarly, corporate patronage gives rise to the "house" man, either directly as an employee or within the organizational context of a professional bureaucracy.[79]

Corporate executives explain the growth of their legal departments somewhat more prosaically. They point to the very substantial increases in fees paid to law firms and note that it appeared rational to attempt to cut (or, in any case, to slow the increase in) those costs by doing more of their legal work within the corporation, thus retaining for the corporation the profit that would otherwise have been made on the work by the outside firms.[80]

A certain amount of the legal work that arises in the course of any corporation's busiess is quite routine—documents to be prepared following standard forms, recurring personnel matters, or routine reports that must be filed with the government periodically. Rather than pay the high hourly rates charged by large law firms, corporations increasingly use their own staffs to handle these matters. Beyond this routine work, however, corporate house counsel often perform tasks for their corporations that are more subtle and more consequential for the structure of the corporate sector of the legal profession. One of those is the identification of legal issues that might not have been noticed if a lawyer were not present in the organization, scrutinizing the daily operations. Thus, house counsel may see potential tax or antitrust consequences in a proposed business transaction, consequences that would not have been identified by a corporate officer who lacked legal training. This is said to enable the corporation to anticipate legal problems before they become acute. But there will also be cases where the problem would never have become acute—that is, if it were left untreated, it would go away. And there will be times when the potential problem identified by house counsel turns out, upon further examination, not to be a real problem at all. It is probable, therefore, that a net effect of the growth of corporate house counsel is to define more of the corporation's problems as legal problems, thus increasing the amount and expanding the range of work done in the corporate sector of the bar.[81]

Another important function of corporate house counsel is to select, or at least to participate in the selection of, outside counsel to handle the complex legal work that calls for a specialist. Traditionally, corporations maintained long-standing relationships with large law firms. One law firm often did all or most of the corporation's legal work, and a close working relationship was established over the years between the corporation's executives and the lawyers in the firm. In some cases, the lawyers served not only as lawyers but as general business advisers. This is probably less often true today. With the greater mobility of corporate executives, increasing specialization of lawyers, and growth of house counsel, corporations are less likely to maintain such close ties with their law firms.

It is important to note that house counsel have reason to discourage established connections between their corporations and outside law firms. Inside and outside lawyers compete for the blessings that their patrons can bestow. A corporate executive who does not have a close, personal relationship with an outside lawyer is more likely to turn to the insider for advice, thus increasing the dependence of corporate management on house counsel and, consequently, enhancing the power of the inside lawyer. If access to centers of influence is the principal source of the prestige of the corporate sector, then the lawyer who has the ear of the corporate officer has a superior claim to that prestige. And access to the powerful is, of course, itself a kind of power.[82] The role of corporate house counsel in distributing to outside firms the legal work that will not be done by the corporation's own legal staff places them in a good position to see to it that no one firm is able to establish close and continuing ties with the corporation's management.[83] It is probable, then, that the increase in numbers of house counsel preceded rather than followed the weakening of the established relationships between corporations and outside law firms. Whichever is cause and which effect, however, the corporation that once regarded a single, large firm as outside general counsel, to which it returned again and again with a wide variety of its legal problems, now often articulates a policy of selecting the "best qualified lawyer" (whether qualified by special expertise or by being well situated or well connected) to represent the corporation with respect to each discrete legal problem.

This greater tendency to distribute corporate legal work among a number of firms makes the firms less secure. While large law firms could formerly count on receiving a continuing, steady volume of business from each of their major corporate clients, the flow of work may now be less certain. As a result, the power relationships between lawyer and client—the claims that each can make upon the other—are altered somewhat. The older pattern of close, continuing ties between the corporate clients and their law firms more nearly resembled a traditional system of patronage. The firms were, to some degree, sheltered by their clients; it was natural for them to become dependent on continuing patronage. While the present situation bears less resemblance to the patron-servant model, the lawyers do not enjoy the sort of liberation that might be characterized as capturing the manor house. The corporate lawyer is no longer, so much, the loyal retainer, but the new entrepreneur role is probably more precarious.

If large law firms are, in fact, unsure of their clients' commitment to them, we would expect to observe some behavior manifesting that insecurity, to see some demonstration of their need to go out of their way to curry favor with their clients. Are there any such signs?

One manifestation might be found in the fact that so many firms have, quite literally, gone out of their way for their clients by opening branch offices. The increase in the numbers of branch offices of large law firms is one of the most notable developments in the corporate sector of the bar. We examined the branching histories of the dozen largest Chicago law firms—that is, the twelve firms that had the largest numbers of lawyers in 1979. The total number of branch offices of these twelve firms in 1960 was two. By 1970, they had four. In 1980, the dozen firms had a total of twenty branch offices. In 1960, only two of the twelve firms had branches; by 1980, only three did not.[84] If these branch offices were always profitable and caused no great problems for the firms, then this expansion would prove little about the sensitivity of the firms to their clients' wishes. But they are not always profitable and they do give rise to other problems in the management of the firm. The mere fact that one or more major clients of a Chicago law firm would find it convenient if the firm had an office in Los Angeles or in London does not assure that there will be sufficient demand for the firm's services there to make the branch office profitable. Some firms have opened branch offices as an accommodation to a few major clients without much knowledge of the demand that might be expected, though no doubt hoping that it would prove to be adequate, and they have in some cases been disappointed to find those branches unprofitable.[85] Moreover, the branch offices often pose serious problems of management control. If the Washington branch of a Chicago firm is successful and attracts new clients, it may begin to develop a life of its own, independent of the parent. That is, it may become more difficult to set policy in Chicago that will govern the Washington office's decisions about the types of clients and work that will be accepted, the fees to be charged, the hiring of personnel, the handling of ethical issues, and so on. In at least one or two well-publicized cases, a successful branch has seceded from the parent firm, taking clients with it.[86] The problems of managing and controlling a branch office mean, then, that it is rational to open one only if the firm is quite sure that the branch will be profitable or if the need to satisfy particular clients is compelling. Because branches have been opened when profitability was not assured, client considerations appear to loom large. Indeed, when partners in large firms are asked why they decided to open branches, their usual answer attributes the decision to pressure from clients.[87]

Another manifestation of the insecurity that large law firms may feel about their relationships with their major clients is the firms' avoidance of certain types of work and certain smaller clients. That is, an important factor influencing the firms' decisions concerning the types of work and clients that they will take on is their expectation about how such work or clients would be regarded by their important, major clients. Many large firms perceive that criminal law work, for example, would be regarded by their corporate clients as unseemly, and that corporate management would not wish to be associated with the sort of person who is charged with a crime. (This was especially the case before criminal antitrust and securities prosecutions became more common.) Divorce work was traditionally regarded in the same way,[88] as was work done *pro bono publico*. A principal reason large firms have given for their reluctance to represent the poor, downtrodden, friendless, and despised, or to take on various public interest causes, is that this sort of thing would give offense to their regular clientele. The defining characteristics of the friendless and despised are, after all, that they lack important friends and that many persons find them distasteful, and the difficulty with reformist causes is that they may well be controversial. This is, of course, closely akin to the rationale used by large firms for many years (less so now) to explain their failure to hire women lawyers or those from certain ethnic groups. "The clients wouldn't stand for it!" "The clients would not want to deal with them." The preferences ascribed to clients probably corresponded quite closely to those of the lawyers themselves, but there is also little doubt that the lawyers correctly perceived their clients' preferences and that those preferences were, in fact, given weight by the law firms.

This avoidance of work that might be offensive to major clients is not merely an excuse for declining to take cases that would not pay. If the new client or the work is likely to alienate a corporation that is important to the firm as a source of income, influence, or prestige, the firm will often refuse the work even if the potential client could well afford to pay the firm's bills. Certain criminal defendants are obvious examples, but there are also more subtle ones. Thus, for many years most of the law firms that regularly defended antitrust claims refused to accept antitrust plaintiffs' work.[89] When very large corporations began to use antitrust claims as weapons against one another, especially in takeover situations, this old taboo eroded, but the traditional defense firms worried that their regular corporate clients, corporations that found themselves defending antitrust claims, would see the firm's representation of an antitrust plaintiff as trading with the enemy. The defendant corporations objected to the use of the law firm's knowledge and resources in aid of a litigant that threatened the general legal stance and the public policy positions of the defendant corporations. This was almost a matter of ideology. For the law firm to align itself with a party that attacks the defendant corporations' brethren—corporations situated similarly to themselves—may therefore be perceived as a symbolic defection, as an act of apostasy.

A Chicago lawyer recounted to us an example of this thinking that is, perhaps, somewhat ludicrous in its extremity but that illustrates the point very clearly. Following the reformist ferment of the late 1960s and early 1970s, when law students and young lawyers increasingly expressed a desire to devote a portion of their effort to public service, a large, prestigious Chicago firm adopted a policy permitting its lawyers to spend some of their time on *pro bono* work, including the defense of criminal cases. All went well until a young lawyer reported to the firm that he had been assigned to defend a man accused of bank robbery. It happened that one of the principal clients of the firm was a major bank. The bank that was the firm's client had no connection with the bank that had been robbed (the two were widely separated both in space and in kind), but the firm nonetheless ordered the young lawyer to withdraw from the representation of the defendant. It was inconceivable that the case would make new law on bank robbery that would then permit other felons to steal from the client bank with less fear of retribution. As in most cases of bank robbery, the only issues were questions of fact. The reason for the firm's order to withdraw, apparently, was that bank robbers are the enemies of banks, and for the firm to permit one of its lawyers to represent a bank robber might therefore be seen as disloyalty to a major client.

That law firms are so cautious about giving offense to their major clients suggests that they are in a rather vulnerable, subordinate position. If the firm's expertise were of special value to the corporate client and not easily replaced by that of other firms, the firm might feel more confident that the client would continue to need and use its services, regardless of its representation of the occasional bank robber or labor union. The firm might then feel free to discharge its professional responsibilities as it saw fit, resting its decisions solely on its own criteria, whether those were professional norms or the profit motive. But that is not usually the case. Our data indicate that fewer than 5 percent of the lawyers who devote a quarter or more of their time to the defense of criminal cases work in firms with ten or more lawyers, and only 15 percent of the lawyers who devote as much as a quarter of their time to work for labor unions work in firms of ten or more, none of them in firms with thirty or more lawyers. One of the effects of the firms' reluctance to take on clients who might be regarded with distaste by their regular clientele is to limit the large firms to a very narrow range of potential clients, thus further heightening both specialization by client type and the firms' anxiety about continuation of the demand for its services. An end product of all of these tendencies is, then, enhancement of the power of the patron and reduction of the power of the professional in the lawyer-client relationship in the corporate sector.

Functional and Conflict Perspectives Reexamined

This discussion of the nature of the relationships between lawyers and clients has emphasized the distribution of power among the parties and has not given much notice to the system maintenance functions of the bar's social stratification. At the beginning of this book, we noted that both the "power" or "conflict" school of thought on social inequality and the "functionalist" school have distinct and appreciable contributions to make to our understanding. We have focused in this concluding essay, however, more upon the perspective of the conflict school than upon the functionalist school. Let us try to restore some balance between the two approaches, drawing upon themes already stated.

The greater recent role of corporate house counsel as the purchasers of services of lawyers in large firms suggests further rationalization of the market for legal services in the corporate sector. Corporate house counsel probably behave as better-informed, more rational consumers of those services than did the corporate executives who previously purchased them. The greater tendency to pick and choose among lawyers and firms for the handling of particular pieces of work, rather than using the same outside counsel for all of the corporation's legal problems, suggests that more discriminating judgments are being made. To the extent that decisions about the allocation of work among practitioners of corporate law are made by "professional" criteria—by criteria based in knowledge of law and in expert judgment concerning the competence of the lawyer or firm to handle the matter—the distribution of legal work within the corporate sector and the resulting social structure of lawyers and clients will be less subject to idiosyncratic variation produced by personal caprice or by random events. Though stable and predictable outcomes may also be produced by a system that is dominated by close adherence to traditional norms and the maintenance of established relationships, or by an autocratic system of authority based in great concentrations of power, the outcomes produced by an economic calculus that is based in the nature of the work itself will be more "functional." Because the logic of the allocative decision proceeds from the work that is to be done and the skills or competence of those who are to do it, productive efficiency should be increased. Though functional interdependencies also exist under a traditional system, those of a more economically rational division of labor will enhance what Durkheim called "organic solidarity,"[90] and the maintence of the system should be enhanced.

The dominance of corporate lawyers by their clients may also facilitate the formation of new business relationships. For a business firm to enter into a transaction with another organization that is not well known to it or with whom it does not have a history of dealings may entail substantial risk. It will help to bring such transactions about, therefore, if the lawyers who are acting for the companies are in a position to be able to reassure them that the risk is within acceptable limits. If the lawyer is thought by the client to be acting independently, then the client may well feel that the lawyer's advice should be given less weight because the lawyer may have an interest in seeing the transaction go ahead. It will create work for the lawyer. On the other hand, if the client knows that the lawyer is highly dependent upon the client's favor and would be vulnerable if the client should be injured or displeased, then the client may have greater trust in the lawyer's assurances. The dependence of the lawyer on the corporate client may thus serve the function of enhancing the likelihood of transactions in a large, mobile, national, and multinational business environment, where the transactions cannot be based upon personal ties.

Though concepts drawn from both functionalist and power theorists contribute to an understanding of the social structure of the legal profession, then, the power perspective may be peculiarly appropriate to the case of the bar. Lawyers are accustomed to deal in the allocation of power. They are regularly confronted in their work with situations of conflict, and the relative power of the competing parties is relevant to their strategic decisions. Lawyers may, therefore, be predisposed to think about social relations in power terms and to react to social stimuli in ways that reflect their assessment of power differentials. If this is true, as seems to us likely, then social relations within the legal profession may be unusually sensitive to the differential distribution of power, and the structure may be especially likely to evolve in ways that manifest power relations.

A conflict model of sorts is, after all, built into the adversary process. The American notion of due process of law specifically includes, for example, such elements as the right of confrontation of one's accuser and the right to cross-examination. The research of Thibaut and Walker and their associates[91] suggests the existence of a general preference for adversarial modes of legal procedure rather than for an "inquisitorial" system—that is, for the decision of contested legal issues through the clash of competing parties rather than through an impartial inquiry by a detached fact finder. But the right to confront one's accuser, Thibaut and Walker's research, and much of the general public's thinking about the legal process all take place within the context of the personal client hemisphere of the legal profession, and particularly in what we have called the "personal plight" cluster of fields. Conflict is, indeed, the preferred mode for the handling of many criminal, divorce, and personal injury cases, though even in those fields the greater share of the cases are disposed of by negotiated settlements.

The adversarial, conflict model is probably an especially inappropriate way of characterizing the actual process of the practice of law in the corporate hemisphere, however. The practice of corporate law far more often deals with negotiation, with drafting, with office practice that is directed not toward prevailing in conflict but toward the avoidance of conflict. Corporate lawyers often serve a mediative or facilitative function—they bring corporate organizations together to form relationships among them. Though there is, of course, an area of conflict in the negotiation of a contract, it is important to note that that conflict takes place within the context of a larger, shared interest of the parties, the interest in consummating a productive business transaction. The advice lawyers give to corporations that are merging is intended not only to secure advantage for their own clients, though it surely is often intended to do just that, but also to minimize conflict between the parties in the longer run, to avoid disputes with the government over antitrust, tax, or securities matters, and to reduce the likelihood of litigation with investors or customers of the merging companies.

Much of the work of the personal client hemisphere has a similar goal, of course. Wills and trusts, real estate closings, and commercial transactions between individuals and small businesses are all areas where the principal concern is with the avoidance of conflict. But the personal plight area is much more characterized by litigation and other forms of disputes, and such cases—particularly criminal and personal injury matters—dominate much of both academic and popular thought about the work of the legal profession. Litigation is, of course, also an important part of the corporate sector of law practice and is probably becoming more so, but it does not yet preoccupy corporate practitioners and has not come to dominate the ethos of the sector.

If the corporate sector is, at least in large part, concerned with a facilitative rather than an adversarial role, with negotiation, persuasion, and putting deals together rather than with formal disputes, does that fact carry implications for the relations between lawyers and clients? Will the distribution of power or advantage between lawyer and client in a predominantly adversarial setting differ from that in a predominantly facilitative one? It may. Most clients will probably feel more competent to deal with the issues that arise in office practice than with the conduct of litigation. There is less lay understanding of procedures in the courtroom and in other formal hearings—of the rules of evidence, and of whether it is better to challenge or not to challenge a potential juror— than there is of the terms that should be insisted upon in a contract negotiation. The contract negotiation is more likely to involve matters of business judgment and hunches about which tactic is likely to be most successful, and clients may well feel comfortable challenging their lawyers' judgments on these matters. (Litigation may, in fact, involve similar hunches about tactics, but it will often be less clear that that is what they are.) Even on matters as technical as tax law, clients and corporate house counsel may feel better informed and thus more competent to question their lawyers' judgments than they would on a matter of litigation procedure—on whether it is or is not advisable to take the deposition of a particular potential witness, for example. If we are right about this, clients in the adversarial, litigation setting will perceive a greater disparity between their knowledge and that of their lawyers than will be the case in the facilitative, office practice setting, and the portion of the lawyer's power vis-à-vis clients that is derived from the lawyer's possession of special expertise will therefore be less in the office practice areas. This is, then, yet another reason why the relation between client and lawyer in the corporate sector might often resemble that between patron and servant, while the relation in personal plight work does not.

Conclusion

Any profession will surely include disparate parts, but we doubt that any other is so sharply bifurcated as the bar. Only, perhaps, in architecture is there a similar fundamental division between types of clients that has such inevitable consequences for the nature of the work and for the relative power positions of professional and client—and in architecture the number of individual clients is trivial. The difference between serving corporations and serving individuals is, for a lawyer's work and career, a difference that has important, highly predictable implications, several of which have been explored in this book. That there is a fundamental split of some sort within the American legal profession has been recognized at least since the Reed report of the early 1920s distinguished between the "inner bar" and the "general body of practitioners." The difference between litigators and office lawyers has, of course, also been widely noticed for a long time; it has been formalized in England in the distinction between barristers and solicitors. But that is a task or skill difference, analogous to that between physicians and surgeons. The distinction within the American bar that is based in service to corporations, on the one hand, and to individuals and their small businesses, on the other, is quite another sort of phenomenon, with quite different consequences.

It would clearly be a mistake to assert that these two sectors of the legal profession are entirely separate, but the extent to which the complexity of the social structure of the Chicago bar may be sorted out by the fundamental difference between the two types of clients is nonetheless remarkable. The two hemispheres differ significantly both in practice and in social background variables. We have noted the very substantial difference in the prestige of the two sectors, lawyers serving corporate clients being much more likely to be accorded deference within the profession. We have also noted that lawyers who work in one hemisphere relatively seldom form friendships or close personal relationships with those who practice in the other. This, in turn, corresponds to the differential connections of the two hemispheres to the several spheres of influence in Chicago politics, community affairs, and the organized bar. The probability that a Chicago lawyer will know other lawyers who are influential in each of these realms differs systematically with the fields in which he or she practices and the nature of his or her clients. The client-based structure of the profession is, then, directly related to the structure of various sorts of power in the broader community.

In sum, the Chicago bar consists, to an extent that is quite striking, of two separate professions, quite different in type and content and both of substantial size. The more prestigious is, ironically, the less independent. It is a patronage-type occupation, in Terence Johnson's terms, where corporate clients to a large degree dictate the nature of the work done. The other profession, serving individuals and small businesses, is either a collegiate occupation by Johnson's definition, because the lawyers dominate their clients in the decisions that are made about the work, or mediative in type because governmental authorities and other parties mediate the relationship between lawyer and client, intervening in or regulating some aspects of that relationship.

The claims to professionalism of the lawyers in the two sectors are thus based in fundamentally different sorts of social power. Lawyers who practice in the personal client sector usually have the greater degree of authority vis-à-vis their clients because the wealth and social standing of the lawyers more often exceeds that of the clients and because the clients are ordinarily more dependent upon the lawyers than are the lawyers upon any one client. But what is it, precisely, that these personal sector lawyers have that their clients need so badly? The lawyers' knowledge and skills are not widely shared by the public at large, perhaps, but the skills required for many of the tasks performed by personal sector lawyers are not really all that abstruse, surely a good deal less so than those regularly needed by lawyers in the corporate sector, and the requisite knowledge could often be mastered by reasonably diligent non-professionals who had a sufficient incentive to do so. Obviously, what the client often needs, at least in part, is the license to practice law. The officially sanctioned monopoly that is granted to licensed lawyers limits the entry of unlicensed persons into this market—it excludes nonlawyers from the performance of some, but only some, of the tasks regularly done by the personal client sector of the bar. Plea bargaining on behalf of defendants in criminal cases is, for example, effectively restricted to lawyers, even though nonlawyers might conduct the bargaining equally well, but searches of real estate titles are often now done by employees of real estate brokers, title insurance companies, and the like, who may or may not be lawyers.

In other portions of their market, personal sector lawyers may compete with marriage counselors or women's centers that provide assistance in divorce cases, with freelance accountants or franchised tax return pre-parers, or with do-it-yourself probate kits. In these latter situations, the lawyers' monopoly of the relevant services is imperfect, at most. To the extent that clients choose to employ lawyers in such matters, therefore, they may have some affirmative reason to do so.

The reason for that preference is probably often the belief—one that sometimes, at least, has a sound basis in fact—that the lawyer will have superior access to networks of authoritative decision makers, networks that include the persons who have the power to solve the client's problem, to confer the benefit the client seeks or to relieve the client of the unwanted burden. This belief is commonly expressed as some variant of a statement that the lawyer knows the ropes at the criminal courts building or has friends at City Hall or has clout in the zoning board. Scholarly research on the criminal courts has confirmed the existence of "courtroom work groups" that consist of the judge, the lawyers who regularly appear in that court, whether for the prosecution or the defense, the bailiff, and the court clerk.[92] In such circumstances, it can, indeed, be advantageous to be a member of the work group and disadvantageous to be an outsider. The stock-in-trade of the lawyer in the personal client sector may therefore often be perceived, by both the client and the lawyer, to be his "connectedness." Access to the relevant networks may be im-proved by a license to practice law; it may enhance acceptance as a member of the club. Ethnicity or political affiliation, however, may also be important criteria for membership in such networks, and this fact helps to account for the salience of ethnic and political group member-ships in the social organization of the profession.

The types of social power that can be mobilized by lawyers in the corporate sector are quite different. Connectedness is probably less highly valued by them and by their clients, though their contacts will surely sometimes be useful. The corporations that are the clients of this sector of the bar more often maintain their own networks of relationships with the authoritative decision makers whose actions are most often relevant to the conduct of their operations. Corporate officers are themselves often persons of considerable influence, political and otherwise. Thus, what corporations need and expect from their lawyers is in large measure the lawyers' special skills and arcane knowledge. The skills and knowledge that are valued are not, of course, always *legal* skills or knowledge of legal doctrine narrowly defined. Rather, knowledge of business circumstances or of the cast of characters participating in a particular matter, skill as an advocate or a negotiator, or simply good judgment may recommend the lawyer to the corporate client. Such power as corporate lawyers have over their clients is power of the sort that derives from the client's belief in the lawyers' skills and from the correlative need of the clients to have some external expert to believe in. Corporate executives often operate in conditions of great uncertainty. The assistance of a sage or a conjurer is one of the classic means used by persons in precarious positions to reduce the uncertainty, to gain control.[93] In such situations, faith in the powers of the savant or shaman is crucial.

Similarly, the power of lawyers may be based largely in their repute. (This may be true of both corporate and personal sector lawyers, though the types of repute that will be important to them will be quite different.) To nurture the appropriate sort of repute and to conserve it once it has been attained, corporate lawyers engage in various kinds of status display. Their furniture is often upholstered in leather and their walls are lined with books, whether those books are often consulted or not; where the walls are not covered with books, they are often covered with hardwood paneling or with sophisticated paintings; the lawyers dress conservatively and they behave with circumspection[94] (much like bankers, though perhaps not carrying this to quite such an extreme); and a certain type of prestigious corporate lawyer tries hard to keep the firm name out of the newspapers, knowing that some clients retain the firm in the belief that it has the ability to keep their names out. The style of the corporate bar is, thus, designed to reassure its clientele, and the power of that sector of the bar is highly dependent on the clients' confidence in the sagacity, discretion, and stability of the corporate lawyer.

Assuming that corporate lawyers succeed in gaining the confidence of their clients, however, what sort of power have they then? As Edward Shils points out, persons are accorded deference corresponding to the degree to which they serve the central value system of the society.[95]

Because corporate lawyers advise persons who make the most consequential decisions regarding the allocation of economic resources and because modern, industrial societies attach great importance to economic values, we might expect corporate lawyers to be accorded deference to the extent that they are perceived to influence these allocative decisions.

The social power of the corporate sector of the bar is, then, based in its perceived influence on the distribution of the wealth of the society, influence that is derived from the belief of corporate officers in the wisdom and arcane skill of these lawyers, while the claim to professionalism of lawyers working in the personal sector is based less in special skills and more in their superior access to networks of relatively minor, relatively low visibility decision makers, such as insurance claims adjusters, police, state judges, court clerks, building inspectors, zoning commissions, and aldermen. The social origins of the practitioners in the two sectors are, as Shils predicts, consonant with the degree to which they are perceived to be entitled to deference on other grounds.[96] That is, Shils observes that the deference to which one is thought to be entitled on the basis of one's social origins is not likely to be greatly inconsistent with the deference that one's occupation is thought to warrant.

The two sectors of the legal profession thus include different lawyers, with different social origins, who were trained at different law schools, serve different sorts of clients, practice in different office environments, are differentially likely to engage in litigation, litigate (when and if they litigate) in different forums, have somewhat different values, associate with different circles of acquaintances, and rest their claims to professionalism on different sorts of social power. For the most part, these lawyers find themselves unable to cooperate in the organizations of the bar. Only in the most formal of senses, then, do the two types of lawyers constitute one profession.

Why should the degree of cohesion among lawyers be of concern? Some reasons will already be apparent. The social structure of any occupation that places so many of its members in positions where they can influence the allocation of scarce resources is of interest because the nature of the bonds and the divisions among the occupation's membership may have consequences for who gets what—in the case of lawyers, consequences for the distribution of legal services and for values that may be affected by the distribution of legal services. If the members of an occupation are so influentially placed, the ability to mobilize them toward a common purpose will carry the potential for great political and societal power. If, on the other hand, the social composition of the occupation suggests that it will be able to unite on common goals only rarely or only within a narrow range of issues, then the relative impotence of the occupation *qua* occupation is also of interest. But there may be another, less obvious consequence of the lack of social integration of the legal profession. To the extent that the public perceives the separation of lawyers into two hemispheres or two occupations, the symbolic unity of the law, and thus its legitimacy, will be weakened. The efficacy of law depends, in very large measure, on voluntary compliance with its requirements, and the disposition to comply depends, in turn, on the existence of a consensus that the legal system is legitimate. To secure this public support, a legal system will need to honor the society's central ideals, including those concerning equality of treatment that are manifested in such legal standards as "equal protection of the laws." The perception of equality is served by the symbolism of a unitary legal system—that there is only one law, one set of rules and procedures that determines justice for all. If lawyers of distinct social types work in distinct realms of law, serve separate sorts of clients, and deal with separate systems of courts and government agencies, symbolic unity can be maintained only with mirrors and smoke, and then unreliably. Ethnic diversity within the bar, reflecting the pluralism of the broader society, might enhance the legitimacy of the system if lawyers from the full range of social backgrounds were well represented and if they were all participating in the same system. But if the reality is that large cities like Chicago have two legal professions, one recruited from more privileged social origins and the other from less prestigious backgrounds, while yet other social groups are almost entirely excluded, and if the first kind of lawyer serves corporate clients that are quite wealthy and powerful, and the other serves individuals and small businesses that are far less powerful, then the heirarchy of lawyers suggests a corresponding stratification of law into two systems of justice, separate and unequal.

Notes

Preface to the Revised Edition

1. Coleman, "Loss of Power," *American Sociological Review* 38:(1973), 1–17.

2. "The lawyer stands before the community shorn of his prestige, clothed in the unattractive garb of a mere commercial agent—a flexible and convenient go-between, often cultivating every kind of equivocal quality as the means of success." John Dos Passos, *The American Lawyer: As He Was—As He Is—As He Can Be* (New York: Banks Law Publishing Co., 1907), p. 33, quoted in Marc Galanter and Thomas Palay, *Tournament of Lawyers* (Chicago: University of Chicago Press, 1991), p. 16.

3. Karl N. Llewellyn, "The Bar Specializes—With What Results?," *Annals of the American Academy of Social and Political Sciences* 167 (1993): 117.

4. Bette H. Sikes, Clara N. Carson, and Patricia Gorai, *The 1971 Lawyer Statistical Report* (Chicago: American Bar Foundation, 1972), pp. 10–12.

5. Jerome E. Carlin, *Lawyers on Their Own* (New Brunswick: Rutgers University Press), 1962.

6. Richard H. Sander and E. Douglass Williams, "Why Are There So Many Lawyers? Perspectives on a Turbulent Market," *Law & Social Inquiry* 14 (1989): 440, note 20, and 474–77.

7. *American Lawyer,* July/August 1992, p. 1.

8. Altman and Weil, Inc., *The Survey of Law Firm Economics,* 1987, cited in Sander and Williams, *supra* note 6, pp. 466.

9. National Association of Law Placement, *Employment Report and Salary Survey,* Washington, D.C., 1992.

10. James B. Stewart, "Death of a Partner," *New Yorker,* 21 June 1993, p. 54.

11. See Robert G. Eccles and Dwight B. Crane, *Doing Deals: Investment Banks at Work* (Boston: Harvard Business School Press, 1988).

12. See Michael J. Powell, "Professional Innovation: Corporate Lawyers and Private Lawmaking," *Law and Social Inquiry* 18 (1993): 423.

13. U.S. Department of Commerce, Bureau of the Census, "Illinois Census," *1970 Census of Population* (Washington, D.C.: Government Printing Office, 1973), pp. 907 and 1011.

14. State of Illinois, *Annual Report of the Attorney Registration and Disciplinary Commission*, Springfield, Illinois, 1992.

15. *Martindale-Hubbell Law Directory*, MS-DOS ed., New Providence, N.J., 1992.

16. Barbara A. Curran and Clara N. Carson, *The U.S. Legal Profession in 1988* (Chicago: American Bar Foundation, 1991), p. 77.

17. *Annual Report of the Attorney Registration and Disciplinary Commission*, *supra* note 14.

18. ABA Section on Legal Education and Admission to the Bar, *Review of Legal Education*, American Bar Association, 1991.

19. Richard Abel, *American Lawyers* (New York and London: Oxford University Press, 1989), p. 288.

20. Curran and Carson, *supra* note 16, p. 21; National Association of Law Placement, *Employment Report and Salary Survey*, Washington, D.C., 1992.

21. Curran and Carson, *supra* note 16, p. 21.

22. Nelson, "The Futures of American Lawyers: A Demographic Profile of a Changing Profession in a Changing Society," unpublished paper, 1993, p. 45.

23. National Association of Law Placement, *supra* note 20.

24. Michael McWilliams, President of the American Bar Association, letter to the U.S. House of Representatives, 29 June 1993.

25. Jerry L. Van Hoy, *Prepackaged Law: The Political Economy and Organization of Routine Work at Multi-Branch Legal Services Firms*, Ph.D. dissertation, Northwestern University, 1993.

26. Bates and O'Steen v. State Bar of Arizona, 433 U.S. 350 (1977).

27. Goldfarb v. Virginia State Bar, 421 U.S. 733 (1975).

28. Sander and Williams, *supra* note 6, p. 452.

29. *Id.*, p. 440–41.

30. Bureau of Economic Analysis, U.S. Department of Commerce, *Business Statistics*, 27th ed., 1992, p. A-94.

31. Robert Nelson, *supra* note 23, pp. 5–15.

32. *Id.*, p. 15.

33. Marc Galanter, "Reading the Landscape of Disputes: What We Know and Don't Know (and Think We Know) about Our Allegedly Contentious and Litigious Society," *UCLA Law Review* 31 (1983): 71.

34. Chicago: University of Chicago Press, 1987.

35. New York: Russell Sage Foundation, 1988.

36. Berkeley and Los Angeles: University of California Press, 1988.

37. New York, Oxford: Oxford University Press, 1989.

38. Richard Abel and Philip S. C. Lewis, eds., *Lawyers and Society* (Berkeley and Los Angeles: University of California Press, 1988 and 1989).

39. New York: Praeger Publishers, 1990.

40. Chicago: University of Chicago Press, 1991.

41. Ithaca and London: Cornell University Press, 1992.

Preface to the Original Edition

1. Erwin O. Smigel, *The Wall Street Lawyer: Professional Organization Man?*, 2d ed. (Bloomington: Indiana University Press, 1969).

2. Arthur L. Wood, *Criminal Lawyer* (New Haven: College and University Press, 1967).

3. H. Laurence Ross, *Settled Out of Court: The Social Process of Insurance Claims Adjustments* (Chicago: Aldine Publishing, 1970); Douglas E. Rosenthal, *Lawyer and Client: Who's in Charge?* (New York: Russell Sage Foundation, 1974).

4. Jerome E. Carlin, *Lawyers on Their Own: A Study of Individual Practitioners in Chicago* (New Brunswick: Rutgers University Press, 1962).

5. Jack Ladinsky, "Careers of Lawyers, Law Practice, and Legal Institutions," *American Sociological Review* 28 (1963): 47–54; Jack Ladinsky, "The Impact of Social Backgrounds of Lawyers on Law Practice and the Law," *Journal of Legal Education* 16 (1963): 127–44; Jack Ladinsky "The Social Profile of a Metropolitan Bar: A Statistical Survey in Detroit," *Michigan State Bar Journal* 43 (1964): 12–24.

6. Dietrich Reuschenmeyer, *Lawyers and Their Society: A Comparative Study of the Legal Profession in Germany and the United States* (Cambridge: Harvard University Press, 1973).

Chapter 1

1. Bette H. Sikes, Clara N. Carson, and Patricia Gorai, *The 1971 Lawyer Statistical Report* (Chicago: American Bar Foundation, 1972), page 5, table 1. In the same year, only about 9 percent of all lawyers resided outside the U.S. Census's "urbanized areas" (U.S., Department of Commerce, Bureau of the Census, *1970 Census of Population*, [Washington, D.C.: Government Printing Office, 1973] part 1, Sec. 2, table 222, "Detailed Occupations of Employed Persons by Residence and Sex," p. 725; for definition of "urbanized areas," see appendix A, p. 9, of report.) A lawyer might well, of course, *reside* in a small town or suburb, but *practice* in a city. In 1980, more than 22,000 of the 37,100 lawyers registered with the Supreme Court of Illinois resided in Cook County (Chicago) (Annual Report of Attorney Registration and Disciplinary Commission for 1980 [1981]). Moreover, small-town lawyers usually handle far less than the full range of legal work—they do not often get the most sophisticated corporate work, antitrust cases, securities work, or complex issues of corporate tax. Their practice might, therefore, be thought of not as truly general but as a type of limited specialization, a sort of "family practice."

2. Only 3 percent of our sample of Chicago lawyers report that more than half of their clients come from their own residential neighborhoods.

3. With elegant simplicity, Harold Lasswell defined "the influential" as "those who get the most of what there is to get" (*Politics: Who Gets What, When, How* [New York: McGraw-Hill, 1936], p. 3).

4. Kingsley Davis and Wilbert E. Moore, "Some Principles of Stratification," *American Sociological Review* 10 (1945): 242–49.

5. Talcott Parsons, "Equality and Inequality in Modern Society, or Social Stratification Revisited," in Edward O. Laumann, ed., *Social Stratification: Research and Theory for the 1970s* (Indianapolis: Bobbs-Merrill, 1970), pp. 13–72.

6. Ralf Dahrendorf, *Class and Class Conflict in Industrial Society* (Stanford, Cal.: Stanford University Press, 1959), "On the Origin of Inequality Among Men," in *Essays in the Theory of Society* (Stanford, Cal.: Stanford University Press, 1968), pp. 151–78.

7. See S. F. Nadel, *The Theory of Social Structure* (London: Cohen and West, 1957).

8. See Edward O. Laumann and Franz Urban Pappi, *Networks of Collective Action: A Perspective on Community Influence Systems* (New York: Academic Press,

1976) pp. 11–12. See also John Walton, "A Systematic Survey of Community Power Research," in M. Aiken and P. Mott, eds., *The Structure of Community Power* (New York: Random House, 1970), pp. 443–64.

9. See William J. Goode, "Community Within a Community: The Professions," *American Sociological Review* 22 (1957): 194–200.

10. The sample was drawn by strict random sampling procedures intended to eliminate systematic distortion or bias. The total number of names drawn randomly from the lawyer directories, *Sullivan's Law Directory for the State of Illinois, 1974–75* and *Martindale-Hubbell Law Directory, 1974*, was 1,142. Of those, 196 proved to be deceased, to have moved from Chicago, or otherwise to be ineligible for inclusion in the population. That left 946 lawyers as the total meeting the criteria that were used to define the sample universe.

11. An indication of the reasons why we were unable to schedule interviews with some of the lawyers in the sample may be gleaned from the following article that appeared in the *Chicago Sun-Times:*

> The 100 N. La Salle Building is full of lawyers. On the 21st floor there are a half-dozen lawyers' names on the door, painted gold on little wooden plaques. But none of them is ever in. The switchboard is among the busiest in town, but the answer is always the same: "Mr. Sherman isn't in," or "Mr. Wilson isn't in, would you like to leave a message?" Because it's not really a lawyer's office at all—it's Telephone Secretaries Unlimited, one of the 200 answering services in the Chicago area. It's run by Rosee Torres, who answers the phone for 4,000 Loop lawyers. "We also have 50 doctors," she said. "We're just starting on doctors." It's a busy office.
>
> She also rents out office space, beginning at $10 an hour, to lawyers who are from out of town or who have just got out of law school and don't have their own offices yet. "Our offices are set up like a law office and no one can tell the difference," she said, and she is right. "If they look at the switchboard, they might think there are hundreds of offices back there." Rosee has helped many young lawyers get started. "When they're just out of law school, they'll rent an office here for an hour and then try to interview as many clients as possible during the hour, not realizing that it takes hours to really sit down and interview a client nicely and get everything they need to know," she said. . . . [Paul McGrath, "Answering Services Go Beyond Call of Duty," *Chicago Sun-Times*, September 5, 1976, p. 5.].

12. While 64.7 percent of the respondents included in our sample were members of the Chicago Bar Association, for example, 60 percent of the nonrespondents were members, according to their listings in the *Martindale-Hubbell* directory. Forty-six percent of our respondents had attended one of four local schools, while 51 percent of the nonrespondents had attended those schools, again according to *Martindale-Hubbell.*

13. Information regarding the race of the respondent was missing in eight instances.

14. See Cynthia Epstein, Women in Law (New York: Basic Books, 1981); Robert B. Stevens, "Law Schools and Legal Education, 1879–1979," 14 *Valparaiso University Law Review* 179–259 (winter 1980), p. 254.

15. Stevens, *supra* note 14, pp. 252–53. See also James P. White, "Law School Enrollment Continues to Level," 66 *American Bar Association Journal* 724–25 (June 1980).

16. Three books provide information on contemporary Chicago politics. Two of

them, Mike Royko, *Boss: Richard J. Daley's Chicago* (New York: E. P. Dutton, 1971), and Len O'Connor, *Clout: Mayor Daley and His City* (Chicago: Henry Regnery, 1975), are quite explicitly anti-Daley, and the other, Milton L. Rakove, *Don't Make No Waves—Don't Back No Losers: An Insider's Analysis of the Daley Machine* (Bloomington: Indiana University Press, 1975), is more sympathetic to the Regulars.

17. As the data are presented here, then, respondents of "northwestern European" origin and "southern and eastern European" origin mean non-Jewish respondents of such descent. Our data also permitted us to distinguish, if the analysis appeared to require it, among Orthodox, Conservative, and Reform Jews. A majority of our Jewish respondents were Reform, another large group were Conservative, and only a small minority were Orthodox. In some analyses not reported in the book we distinguished between western European Jews, primarily German Jews, and eastern European Jews, primarily Russian and Polish Jews, but that distinction adds little that is of use for our purposes.

18. Bruce L. Warren, "Socioeconomic Achievement and Religion: The American Case," in Edward O. Laumann, ed., *Social Stratification: Research and Theory for the 1970s* (Indianapolis and New York, Bobbs-Merrill, 1970), pp. 130, 152; Liston Pope, "Religion and the Class Structure," *Annals of the American Academy of Political and Social Sciences* 256 (March 1948): 84, 89.

19. Ibid.

20. Peter M. Blau and Rebecca Z. Margulies, "A Research Replication: The Reputations of American Professional Schools," *Change in Higher Education* 6 (winter 1974–75): 44.

21. The various ratings of the law schools are collected in E. Epstein, J. Shostak, and L. Troy, eds., *Barron's Guide to Law Schools*, 4th ed. (Woodbury, N.Y.: Barron's, 1980), pp. 39–59.

22. Of the 126 respondents in the regional category, 48 attended the University of Illinois, 12 went to Notre Dame, 7 to George Washington, and 6 to Iowa. The remaining respondents in that category attended a total of 33 other law schools, each represented in our sample by 5 or fewer graduates.

The prestige category is even more heavily dominated by graduates of Northwestern; 107 of the 135 respondents in that category attended Northwestern, 12 went to Georgetown, 8 to Wisconsin, and 6 to Virginia.

In the elite school category, there are 67 graduates of Chicago, 49 from Harvard, 21 from Michigan, 12 from Yale, 5 from Columbia, and only 1 from Stanford.

Among the local schools, our sample includes 155 graduates of DePaul, 76 from John Marshall, 67 from Chicago Kent, and 55 from Loyola.

23. The "government" category here includes 21 judges and judicial clerks. In many of the analyses reported later in the book, we deal only with "practicing lawyers." For purposes of those analyses, we do not include judges or their clerks. Thus, combining the 57 lawyers found to be doing "nonlegal" jobs with the 21 judges and clerks, we get a total of 78 "not practicing law," leaving a remainder of 699 practicing lawyers. It is that base of 699 that we use in most of the analyses presented in chapters 2, 3, and 4.

24. Sikes, Carson, and Gorai, *supra* note 1, pp. 10 and 11.

25. Ibid.

26. This category includes 10 teachers of law.

27. See B. Peter Pashigian, "The Number and Earnings of Lawyers: Some Recent Findings," 1978 *American Bar Foundation Research Journal* 51–82 (winter).

28. In 1975, median family income in the U.S. was $13,719. Only 5 percent of

U.S. families in that year had incomes exceeding $34,138. In 1977, the median income of families in metropolitan areas of more than 1,000,000 population was $18,196. U.S. Department of Commerce, Bureau of the Census, *Social Indicators III* (December 1980), pp. 480, 486–87, tables 9/13 and 9/20. See also, U.S. Department of Labor, Bureau of Labor Statistics, *Area Wage Survey* "Chicago Metropolitan Area, May 1975" (Bulletin 1850–32, September 1975), pp. 3–30.

29. See American Bar Association Code of Professional Responsibility, DR 2–105(A)(1) (1977); see also Richard Zehnle, "Specialization in the Legal Profession," in *Legal Specialization*, American Bar Association, Specialization Monograph no. 2 (Chicago, 1976), pp. 20–33. (The Zehnle paper was also published separately by the American Bar Foundation, 1975.)

30. See Zehnle, *supra* note 29. See also Jerome A. Hochberg, "The Drive to Specialization," in Ralph Nader and Mark Green, eds., *Verdicts on Lawyers* (New York: Thomas Y. Crowell, 1976), pp. 118–26; Marvin W. Mindes, "Proliferation, Specialization, and Certification: The Splitting of the Bar" 11 *University of Toledo Law Review* 273–301 (winter 1980).

31. See John H. Dickason, "What Is Specialization?," 68 *Illinois Bar Journal* 714–15 (July 1980).

32. Karl N. Llewellyn, "The Bar Specializes—With What Results?" *Annals of the American Academy of Political and Social Science* 167 (1933): 177.

33. Sikes, Carson, and Gorai, *supra* note 1, p. 10; Jack Ladinsky, "The Impact of Social Backgrounds of Lawyers on Law Practice and the Law," 16 *Journal of Legal Education* 127, 139 (1963).

34. Sikes, Carson and Gorai, *supra* note 1, p. 10.

35. Sikes, Carson, and Gorai, *supra* note 1, p. 5, is the source of the 1951, 1960, and 1970 figures. The 1975 and 1980 figures are ABA estimates.

36. Sikes, Carson, and Gorai, *supra* note 1, p. 6, for the 1951 and 1970 estimates. The 1979 figure is from Murray Schwartz, "The Reorganization of the Legal Profession," 58 *Texas Law Review* 1269, 1270 (1980).

37. According to the U.S. Census, there were 13,400 lawyers and judges in the city of Chicago in 1970, out of only 16,087 in the entire State of Illinois; U.S. Department of Commerce, Bureau of the Census, *1970 Census of Population*, "Illinois Census" (Washington, D.C.: Government Printing Office, 1973), pp. 997 and 1011. The *1971 Lawyer Statistical Report*, however, published by the American Bar Foundation, counted 14,375 Chicago lawyers in 1970 and a total of 22,036 for the state. The ABF also reported that the *Martindale-Hubbell* directory listed 13,281 Chicago lawyers in that same year. See Sikes, Carson, and Gorai, *supra* note 1, pp. 22 and 55.

38. See Marc Galanter, "Larger than Life: Mega-law and Mega-lawyering in the Contemporary United States," (unpublished paper, 1980) n. 36.

39. C. Wright Mills, *White Collar: The American Middle Classes* (New York: Oxford University Press, 1951), p. 121.

40. See generally Heinz Eulau and John D. Sprague, *Lawyers in Politics: A Study in Professional Convergence* (Indianapolis: Bobbs-Merrill, 1964); Michael Cohen, "Lawyers and Political Careers," 3 *Law and Society Review* 563–74 (May 1969); Irwin H. Bromall, "Lawyers in Politics: An Exploratory Study of the Wisconsin Bar," 1968 *Wisconsin Law Review* 751. For more recent scholarship, see Paul L. Hain and James E. Pierson, "Lawyers and Politics Revisited—Structural Advantages of Lawyer-Politicans," *American Journal of Political Science* 19 (February 1975): 41–51.

41. See esp. Talcott Parsons, "Professions," *Encyclopedia of the Social Sciences*, vol. 12 (1968), pp. 536–47; Joseph Ben-David, "Professions in the Class System of

Present Day Societies: A Trend Report and Bibliography," *Current Sociology* 12 (1963–64): 247–330; William J. Goode, *supra* note 9, pp. 194–200.

42. Talcott Parsons, "Introduction to Part I," *Action Theory and the Human Condition* (New York: Free Press, 1978), p. 13.

43. Magali Sarfatti Larson, *The Rise of Professionalism: A Sociological Analysis* (Berkeley: University of California Press, 1977), p. xi.

44. See esp. Everett C. Hughes, *Men and Their Work* (Glencoe, Ill.: Free Press, 1958).

45. Eliot Freidson, *Profession of Medicine; A Study of the Sociology of Applied Knowledge* (New York: Dodd, Mead, 1970); idem., *Professional Dominance: The Social Structure of Medical Care* (New York: Atherton Press, 1970).

46. Jerome E. Carlin, *Lawyers on Their Own: A Study of Individual Practitioners in Chicago* (New Brunswick, N.J.: Rutgers University Press, 1962).

47. See, e.g., Larson, *supra* note 43; Richard Abel, "The Rise of Professionalism," 6 *British Journal of Law and Society* 83–98 (1979); "Socializing the Legal Profession: Can Redistributing Lawyers' Services Achieve Social Justice?" 1 *Law and Policy Quarterly* 5–51 (1979); Maureen Cain, "The General Practice Lawyer and the Client: Towards a Radical Conception," 7 *International Journal of the Sociology of Law* 331–54 (1979).

48. In addition to Larson, *supra* note 43, and the articles of Richard Abel, *supra* note 47, the theoretical works include most especially Dietrich Rueschemeyer, *Lawyers and Their Society: A Comparative Study of the Legal Profession in Germany and the United States* (Cambridge: Harvard University Press, 1973), a thoughtful and suggestive work on the two systems. Brian Abel-Smith and Robert B. Stevens, *Lawyers and the Courts: A Sociological Study of the English Legal System, 1750–1965* (Cambridge: Harvard University Press, 1967), and Michael Zander, *Lawyers and the Public Interest: A Study in Restrictive Practices* (London: Weidenfeld and Nicolson, 1968), are incisive analyses of the English legal profession, both of them quite critical in intent. More general descriptions and analyses may be found in Quintin Johnstone and Dan Hopson, Jr., *Lawyers and Their Work: An Analysis of the Legal Profession in the United States and England* (Indianapolis: Bobbs-Merrill, 1967); and in Albert P. Blaustein and Charles O. Porter, *The American Lawyer: A Summary of the Legal Profession* (Chicago: University of Chicago Press, 1954).

Important historical studies of American lawyers include J. Willard Hurst, *The Growth of American Law: The Law Makers* (Boston: Little, Brown, 1950); Lawrence Friedman, *A History of American Law* (New York: Simon and Schuster, 1973); and Jerold S. Auerbach, *Unequal Justice: Lawyers and Social Chagne in Modern America* (New York: Oxford University Press, 1976).

Additional primary data on Chicago lawyers are reported in Frances Zemans and Victor Rosenblum, *The Making of a Public Profession* (Chicago: American Bar Foundation, 1981). Though that study is primarily concerned with legal education, its findings about the characteristics of Chicago lawyers are quite consistent with ours. Their data were collected by mailed questionnaires in the fall of 1975, just after our survey, and their response rate was 66.4 percent. The Zemans and Rosenblum book was a part of the American Bar Foundation's larger program of research on legal education, which was conducted under the general direction of Spencer Kimball and Felice Levine.

49. Jack Ladinsky, "Careers of Lawyers, Law Practice and Legal Institutions," *American Sociological Review* 28 (1963): 47; idem., "The Impact of Social Backgrounds of Lawyers on Law Practice and the Law," 16 *Journal of Legal Education* 127 (1963);

idem. "The Social Profile of a Metropolitan Bar: A Statistical Survey in Detroit," 1964 *Michigan State Bar Journal* 12 (February).

50. Jerome E. Carlin, *Lawyers' Ethics: A Survey of the New York City Bar* (New York: Russell Sage, 1966).

51. Douglas Rosenthal, *Lawyer and Client: Who's in Charge?* (New York: Russell Sage, 1974).

52. Stewart Macaulay, "Lawyers and Consumer Protection Laws," 14 *Law and Society Review* 115 (1979).

53. Richard A. Watson and Rondal G. Downing, *The Politics of the Bench and the Bar: Judicial Selection Under the Missouri Nonpartisan Court Plan* (New York: John Wiley, 1969).

54. Zemans and Rosenblum, *supra* note 48.

55. The study, first published in 1964, has been published in a second edition, which includes a chapter updating the original data: Erwin O. Smigel, *The Wall Street Lawyer: Professional Organization Man?*, 2d ed. (Bloomington: Indiana University Press, 1969).

56. Hubert J. O'Gorman, *Lawyers and Matrimonial Cases: A Study of Informal Pressures in Private Professional Practice* (New York: Free Press of Glencoe, 1963).

57. Arthur L. Wood, *Criminal Lawyer* (New Haven: College and University Press, 1967).

58. Joel F. Handler, Ellen Jane Hollingsworth, and Howard S. Erlanger, *Lawyers and the Pursuit of Legal Rights* (New York: Academic Press, 1978).

59. A. J. Liebling, *Chicago: The Second City* (New York: Alfred Knopf, 1952), pp. 96–100.

60. See Stanley Lieberson, *Ethnic Patterns in American Cities* (New York: Free Press of Glencoe, 1963), pp. 44–91.

61. Ladinsky, *supra* note 49.

62. Carlin, *supra* note 50.

Chapter 2

1. E.g., Jack Ladinsky, "Careers of Lawyers, Law Practice, and Legal Institutions," *American Sociological Review* 28 (1963): 47; idem., "The Impact of Social Backgrounds of Lawyers on Law Practice and the Law," 16 *Journal of Legal Education* 127 (1963); idem., "The Social Profile of a Metropolitan Bar: A Statistical Survey in Detroit," 1964 *Michigan State Bar Journal* 12 (February); Jerome E. Carlin, *Lawyers' Ethics: A Survey of the New York City Bar* (New York: Russell Sage, 1966); Joel F. Handler, Ellen Jane Hollingsworth, and Howard S. Erlanger, *Lawyers and the Pursuit of Legal Rights* (New York: Academic Press, 1978).

2. E.g., on large law firms, Erwin O. Smigel, *The Wall Street Lawyer: Professional Organization Man?*, 2d ed. (Bloomington: Indiana University Press, 1969); on divorce courts, Hubert J. O'Gorman, *Lawyers and Matrimonial Cases: A Study of Informal Pressures in Private Professional Practice* (New York: Free Press of Glencoe, 1963); on solo practice, Jerome E. Carlin, *Lawyers on Their Own: A Study of Individual Practitioners in Chicago* (New Brunswick: Rutgers University Press, 1962).

3. Talcott Parsons, *The Social System* (Glencoe, Ill.: Free Press, 1951); Robert K. Merton, *Social Theory and Social Structure*, rev. and enlarged ed. (New York: Free Press, 1968).

4. See J. Willard Hurst, *The Growth of American Law: The Law Makers* (Boston:

Little, Brown, 1950); Magali Sarfatti Larson, *The Rise of Professionalism: A Sociological Analysis* (Berkeley: University of California Press, 1977).

5. Indeed, the type of client may even determine in good measure the recognized doctrinal categories. And doctrinal areas with no corresponding type of client—constitutional law, for example—may not produce any distinct specialty or field of practice. By noting that the fields of practice often correspond to courses taught in law school, we do not intend to imply that the treatment of a subject as a unit of law school instruction establishes that it is proper to regard that subject as a coherent body of doctrine, analytically severable from other bodies of legal theory. Law schools may well organize their curricula in response to demand, which may in turn be structured by client type.

6. Specification of levels of effort by field of practice could well be a useful element in the comparison of professional communities or in the analysis of changes in patterns of practice. One might compare, for example, the allocation of effort by field among the bars of Chicago, Boston, and Houston to gain some insight into the differing bases of their concerns. Identification of points of stability and change in those patterns of allocation at differing times would be a good indicator of developments in the markets for lawyers' services.

7. Michael T. Hannan and John Freeman, "The Population Ecology of Organizations," *American Journal of Sociology* 82 (1977): 929.

8. Jerome E. Carlin, *Lawyers on Their Own: A Study of Individual Practitioners in Chicago* (New Brunswick: Rutgers University Press, 1962).

9. We used relatively fine-grained categories with the intention of combining them if our sample proved to contain insufficient numbers of respondents in any field to permit separate analysis.

10. There are a number of ways one might have framed this question, each with some important advantages and disadvantages. After some pilot work, we chose to ask the question in terms of the past year because we found that a shorter time period (e.g., the past week or month) tended to elicit a misleading degree of concentration of effort. A single matter—e.g., trying a major case or negotiating a merger—might well consume the lawyer's time for a week or even a month. From the perspective of a year, however, the practitioner was often seen to have handled a variety of cases in several fields of law. Thus, we were willing to sacrifice the accuracy of recall of recent events for a somewhat less reliable but substantively more significant characterization of a practitioner's work life.

11. Several other such sources of ambiguity exist. The most important one, undoubtedly, is the "civil litigation" category, which may include litigation in any of the fields other than criminal. This problem is compounded by the fact that "litigation time" may well include not only the actual time in court but also the time spent preparing for trial or attempting to negotiate a settlement. It seemed advisable to include litigation as a separate field, however, because many large firms have separate litigation departments and many lawyers think of themselves as "litigators" of a variety of types of cases.

Since we asked a number of other questions concerning the respondent's activities, we are in a position to make somewhat finer distinctions within certain selected fields of law. We have distinguished between those attorneys who handle corporate tax matters and those who handle personal tax matters, between those who handle corporate real estate transactions and those who primarily handle residential real estate matters, and between litigators who represent corporations and those who litigate private claims against corporations, governmental units, or other individuals.

For those practitioners who reported doing any tax, real estate, or litigation work, we determined whether they received 80 percent or more of their professional income from corporate clients. Persons receiving the bulk of their income from such clients were designated as being active in corporate tax, corporate real estate, or corporate litigation. All others were assigned to the "general" tax, real estate, or litigation categories.

12. Every practitioner was first assigned 20 tokens, each worth 5 percentage points of his working time in a year, to "spend" on various fields of law. Tokens were allocated to a field according to the following schedule:

Percentage of Time Allocated to Field	Tokens (k)
0–4	$k = 0$
5–25	$k = 1$ to 4
25–50	$k = 5$ to 9
More than 50	$k = 10$ to 20

Two examples may illustrate the procedure. Suppose, first, that a respondent checked 3 fields as follows: field 1=5–25 percent, field 2=5–25 percent, field 3=25–50 percent. The following number of tokens would be assigned $k_1=4$, $k_2=4$, $k_3=9$. Seventeen of this respondent's tokens were thus assigned to specified legal work; the remaining 3 tokens were assigned to a "general" category. In the second example, a respondent checked 3 fields as follows: field 1=5–25 percent, field 2=5–25 percent, field 3=50 percent or more. Tokens would be assigned as follows: $k_1=4$, $k_2=4$, $k_3=12$. In this case, the maximum number of tokens is assigned to the first 2 fields, subject to the constraint that at least 10 tokens are assigned to field 3. This token assignment rule may understate somewhat the extent of "specialization" since more units are assigned to the smaller categories (fields with lower percentages). On the other hand, the rule is also biased against the allocation of tokens to the general category, and in this respect its tendency will be to overstate the degree of specialization.

13. This finding is generally consistent with the evidence presented in Pashigian's work on lawyers' incomes, which suggests that about half of the total earnings of the legal service industry comes from individuals and the other half from businesses or governments. See B. Peter Pashigian, "The Number and Earnings of Lawyers: Some Recent Findings," 1978 *American Bar Foundation Research Journal* 51, 77–81, tables 10 and 11.

It may be that, if the effort of persons other than lawyers were considered, the share of total effort devoted to the legal work of corporations would more greatly exceed that devoted to individuals and small businesses. The large law firms that serve corporate clients have very sizable staffs of supporting personnel, often far larger numbers than the number of lawyers in the firm. (A few years ago, the ratio of staff to lawyers in the big firms often approached two to one. With the growth in the use of word-processing equipment, staff efficiency has increased greatly; a more usual ratio now appears to be about one and one-half to one.) These support personnel include paralegals of various sorts, secretaries skilled in the use of legal forms and the preparation of documents, librarians, private investigators, computer technicians, file clerks, and expert consultants in several fields. The solo practitioners who serve many individual clients may, by contrast, get by with one part-time secretary. (Two or more lawyers, not necessarily joined in a formal partnership, often share a single suite and a single secretary. Some lawyers even hire offices and secretaries only by the hour; see chapter 1, note 11.) The total human resources purchased by corporate clients might, therefore, be thought to outweigh that allocated to individuals by a considerable margin. But Pashigian's evidence is that, at least as measured by compensation in the marketplace, any additional effort devoted to corporate clients is either only a minor increment or not very highly valued.

14. The measure of "exclusive attention" used here is that the respondents counted as full-time specialists in a field must have checked the "more than 50 percent" time category for that field and must have checked no additional field. Under this criterion, a respondent might have devoted up to 5 percent of his time to each of a number of other fields. This measure is probably the best approximation possible, given the categories available in our data.

15. It may surprise some lawyers to find that criminal prosecution is not always a full-time job. But only 9 of our 18 respondents who reported devoting some time to criminal prosecution did not also report at least 5 percent of their time being devoted to some other category of work. There are several explanations for the time allocation patterns of the other nine. Two of them were employed by federal agencies other than the U.S. attorney and did some enforcement work that they coded as criminal prosecution, as well as doing administrative law work and civil litigation. One was a supervisory official in the office of the state's attorney and was responsible for overseeing some criminal prosecution as well as civil litigation. One was an assistant state's attorney who did some consumer fraud work that he reported in the "consumer law" category, and another was an assistant state's attorney who had started the job within the past year so that a portion of the time period covered his previous work as a solo practitioner. Another respondent had moved in the other direction during the reporting period—from a position as a prosecutor to private practice in a firm. Three assistant state's attorneys were "moonlighting," doing small amounts of divorce, real estate, and "general family" practice on the side for private clients.

16. Cf. Rosemary Stevens, *American Medicine and the Public Interest* (New Haven: Yale University Press, 1971).

17. This technique is known as a hierarchical clustering analysis. The specific method used was the "minimum average diameter method." See Stephen C. Johnson, "Hierarchical Clustering Schemes," *Psychometrika* 32 (1967) 241; Kenneth D. Bailey, "Cluster Analysis," in *Sociological Methodology: 1975*, ed. David R. Heise, Jossey-Bass Behavior Science Series (San Francisco: Jossey-Bass, 1974), p. 59; Ronald S. Burt, "Power in a Social Topology," in *Power, Paradigms, and Community Research*, ed. Ronald J. Liebert and Allen W. Imershein (London: Sage Publications for the International Sociological Association, 1977).

18. When very high average conditional probabilities occur between fields, one would suspect that the field with fewer practitioners is a more specialized subfield of the larger field.

19. Tables 2.1 and 2.3 list the fields of law that are included in these broader "sectors." The figures presented in the text here, however, were derived by a separate analysis rather than from the analyses presented in those tables.

Chapter 3

1. There are two kinds of "social distance"; see Edward O. Laumann, *Prestige and Association in an Urban Community* (Indianapolis: Bobbs-Merrill, 1966); David

McFarland and Daniel Brown, "Social Distance as a Metric: A Systematic Introduction to Smallest Space Analysis," in Edward O. Laumann, ed., *Bonds of Pluralism: The Form and Substance of Urban Social Networks* (New York: John Wiley, 1973), pp. 213–53. One is the extent to which two or more phenomena (in our case, the fields of law) differ on any number of social variables. Thus, this sense of the term simply describes the degree to which the phenomena are socially distinct. For an indication of this type of social distance among the fields of law, see figure 3.1. The other kind of social distance refers to the extent of social interaction among specified persons or groups. The first kind of social distance may, of course, influence the second. Thus, the differences or similarities in the fields' substantive law, in their characteristic tasks, in the settings of their practice, in their practitioners' social origins, or in their clients may serve to increase or decrease the social interaction among the practitioners of those fields.

2. See Laumann, *supra* note 1, pp. 134–35.

3. For a discussion of the prestige of the fields of law, see chapter 4.

4. See chapter 1 at notes 29–31.

5. Since we also asked the respondents several other questions about their practices, we can distinguish somewhat more finely within certain fields of law. Within the tax field, for example, we can distinguish between corporate tax attorneys and personal tax attorneys. Similarly, we can distinguish between lawyers who handle corporate real estate transactions and those who primarily handle residential real estate matters, and between litigators who represent corporations and those who represent individuals. To accomplish this, we determined whether practitioners who reported doing tax, real estate, and litigation work received 50 percent or more of their professional income from business clients. If they did, we designated those lawyers as active in business tax, business real estate, or business litigation. We assigned all others to the personal tax, real estate, or litigation categories. Government lawyers in these fields were assigned to a residual category.

6. The extent of this double counting is discussed briefly below, and chapter 2 deals in detail with the extent of overlap among fields of law.

7. If the respondent changed jobs within the reporting year, however (or was engaged in moonlighting), a prosecutor might report work for some other sort of client.

8. See Hubert M. Blalock, *Social Statistics*, 2d ed. (New York: McGraw-Hill, 1972), pp. 454–64; Robert A. Gordon, "Issues in Multiple Regression," *American Journal of Sociology* 73 (1968): 592, 596.

9. By design, the 6 fields of law presented in table 3.1 include 1 from each of the 6 groups, listed in the same order.

10. Specifically, we used MSA-1. See James C. Lingoes, ed,. *Geometric Representations of Relational Data* (1977) (hereafter cited as *Geometric Representations*); Edward O. Laumann and James House, "Living Room Styles and Social Attributes: The Patterning of Material Artifacts in a Modern Urban Community," in E. Laumann et al., eds., *The Logic of Social Hierarchies* (Chicago: Markham, 1970), p. 195.

11. The Euclidean distances are assumed to be a monotonic function of an underlying multidimensional construct, "legal role," that creates social distance among the fields of law because of dissimilarities in some specialized set of their characteristics. We have already argued in chapter 2 that we can conceptualize the fields of law as a set of differentiated social roles and that an individual lawyer may occupy a number of these roles simultaneously.

Figure 3.1 portrays the two-dimensional solution, which had a very satisfactory coefficient of contiguity of .994 (a perfect fit would be 1.00) after only 12 iterations. The one-dimensional solution does not reach .99 (though it comes close) even after 50 iterations, and its fit is no longer improving appreciably at that point.

12. The intercorrelations among the 9 variables used in this solution are relatively modest. We did not use some interesting and important variables (e.g., the percentage of blue-collar clients) because they are too strongly associated with one or more of those included in the solution. Of the variables used here, the pair that is most highly correlated is percentage Jewish with percentage Type I Protestants. Pearson's coefficient for that pair is –.53, which means that one variable accounts for 28 percent of the variance in the other.

13. Recall that the field labeled "Public Utilities" on the figure includes "Administrative Law" and other sorts of government regulation work. It has, in fact, one of the highest percentages of government-employed lawyers (see appendix B).

14. One might wonder why litigation fields should be high on both ends of the U—meaning that corporate litigators have higher prestige than many of the other corporate fields, while litigators in the personal sector have lower prestige than other personal client fields. It may be that the greater visibility of litigators enhances their prestige if the substance of their cases is regarded as prestigious and enhances their derogation if the kinds of cases and clients with which they deal are derogated; see Robert Merton, chapter on "Continuities in Reference Group Behavior," in *Social Theory and Social Structure,* revised and enlarged ed. (New York: Free Press, 1968).

15. Including civil rights work among the personal plight fields greatly increases the heterogeneity of that group on most of the variables. The civil rights field is atypical in that a substantial portion of the cases are handled as a public service without fee (*pro bono publico*). Ideological motivations may thus attract to this work lawyers who are unlikely to be found in the other personal plight fields. For example, the distribution of civil rights lawyers among law school types looks much more like that of a field from the "large corporate" group than like any of the other fields in the personal plight group—the percentage of civil rights lawyers who attended elite schools is more than twice that of the next highest personal plight field.

We do not wish to make much of all this, expecially since our sample includes only 14 civil rights lawyers at the 25 percent level of activity, but the most interesting point to be noted is that civil rights work, rather than being motivated by noblesse oblige, appears to be in large part a public function, performed by government employees who are compensated by tax funds. Accordingly, we could with almost equal justification place the civil rights field in the corporate client sector with other government work. Though this reclassification would increase the sectors' homogeneity on several variables, the conceptual reasons already advanced have induced us to sacrifice this tidiness. The work of the profession is, in fact, a bit untidy in places, and it is important to note where points of ambiguity or overlap occur. The civil rights field presents one of the relatively rare opportunities for full-fledged corporate lawyers to practice law that deals with personal plight, with human suffering. Thus, the civil rights field, with a few others, is a point of intersection in the profession. Though quite a small field, it is one of those special places where residents of the profession's two hemispheres may meet one another.

16. During the sixteenth century, the Crown increasingly granted favored individuals monopoly privileges or exclusive licenses through proclamations known as "letters patent" (that is, open or public letters). The Statute of Monopolies (1623, 21 Jac. I, c. 3) curbed this practice. It voided the licenses or "patents" previously granted and provided that persons injured by a monopoly in the future could sue for treble

damages, but it excepted patents granted to "the first and true inventor or inventors of ... manufactures." Thus, Holdsworth observes that the Statute of Monopolies was "the foundation of the patent law of the present day" (William Holdsworth, *A History of English Law* [London: Methuen, 1924], vol. 4, p. 353).

17. See, e.g., United States v. United Shoe Mach. Co., 247 U.S. 32, 52–55 (1918) and the dissenting opinion, 247 U.S. 77–78.

18. See, e.g., United Shoe Mach. Co. v. United States, 258 U.S. 451, 460–64 (1922).

19. Similarly, if we compare "personal litigation" with litigation for business clients, thus holding the task type constant, we find business litigation at the far upper right but personal litigation diagonally across the space at the middle left. In this case, however, the substantive law differs systematically with the kind of client.

20. The personal injury defense lawyers in our sample reported that on the average 60 percent of their income from business clients came from "major" corporations (which we had defined in the survey as corporations with sales in excess of $10 million annually). This percentage may sound modest, but it is quite large when compared with most fields—"general corporate" lawyers, for example, reported an average of only 39 percent of their income from major corporations—and it is roughly equal to the average percentage of the corporate litigators, who reported 57 percent from major corporations.

21. Personal injury defense lawyers derived 25 percent of their law practice income from work for persons (rather than businesses); for personal injury plaintiffs' lawyers, the figure was 76 percent. The percentage of blue-collar workers among the clients of personal injury plaintiffs' lawyers was 43 percent—the highest in any field.

Chapter 4

1. Social standing outside the profession, of course, may not be identical to that within it. Some of the lawyers who enjoy the highest repute—or, at least, the greatest fame—among the public at large may not be so highly regarded within the bar, while others may be "lawyers' lawyers"; see Andrew Abbott, "Status and Status Strain in the Professions," *American Journal of Sociology* 86 (1981): 819. The prominence of a Lee Bailey or Melvin Belli or even of a Dean Acheson or Cyrus Vance is not what we mean by prestige, however. We are not concerned with cases of conspicuous individuals. Sociological usage restricts the term "prestige" to the evaluation of the standing of a general social position when compared with others (each of which has a number of incumbents). The esteem in which a given individual is held in the legal community is a combination of the prestige of the several social positions that he simultaneously occupies (including his work specialties, ethnic group membership, seniority, etc.) and the social evaluation of the personal competence and skill with which he occupies them. Thus, we are concerned here only with the general social evaluation of legal roles or the fields of law and not with the relative esteem or personal reputation of individual lawyers.

2. The amount and range of choice that lawyers enjoy in selecting their cases will always be more or less constrained, of course, demand being both limited and structured.

3. John H. Goldthorpe and Keith Hope, "Occupational Grading and Occupation Prestige," in Keith Hope, ed., *The Analysis of Social Mobility: Methods and Approaches* (Oxford: Clarendon Press, 1972), pp. 19, 21.

4. Ibid., p. 25.

5. Cf. Talcott Parsons, "Equality and Inequality in Modern Society, or Social Stratification Revisited," in Edward O. Laumann, ed., *Social Stratification: Research and Theory for the 1970s* (Indianapolis: Bobbs-Merrill, 1970), p. 13; Davis and Moore, *supra* note 9; Shils, *supra* note 5; Piotr Sztompka, *System and Function: Toward a Theory of Society* (New York: Academic Press, 1974).

6. Ralf Dahrendorf, "On the Origin of Inequality Among Men," in his *Essays in the Theory of Society* (Stanford, Calif.: Stanford University Press, 1968), p. 151; Alvin W. Gouldner, *The Coming Crisis of Western Sociology* (New York: Basic Books, 1970); Randall Collins, *Conflict Sociology: Toward an Explanatory Science* (New York: Academic Press, 1975).

7. Cf. Albert J. Reiss, Jr., *Occupations and Social Status* (New York: Free Press, 1961); Robert W. Hodge, Paul M. Siegel, and Peter H. Rossi, "Occupational Prestige in the United States: 1925–1963," in Reinhard Bendix and Seymour Martin Lipset, eds., *Class, Status, and Power*, 2d ed. (New York: Free Press, 1966), p. 322; Paul M. Siegel, "Prestige and the American Occupational Structure" (Ph.D. diss., University of Chicago, 1971); Goldthorpe and Hope, *supra* note 3; Paul M. Siegel, "Occupational Prestige in the Negro Subculture," in Edward O. Laumann, ed., *Social Stratification: Research and Theory for the 1970s* (Indianapolis: Bobbs-Merrill, 1970), p. 156; Anthony P. M. Coxton and Charles L. Jones, *The Images of Occupational Prestige: a Study in Social Cognition* (New York: St. Martin's Press, 1978). Of course, there is yet another important microstructural tradition growing most recently out of Erving Goffman's work, *The Presentation of Self in Everyday Life* (Garden City, N.Y.: Doubleday, 1959), and his *Interaction Ritual: Essays in Face-to-Face Behavior* (Garden City, N.Y.: Doubleday, 1967); Collins, *supra* note 6, sensitively portrays the dynamic interplay between status display and deference-demanding or -avoiding behavior in face-to-face interaction. This approach requires a set of data-gathering and analytic techniques radically different than those employed here. It is very much our impression, however, from our extended informal observations of lawyers with different practice characteristics, that the empirical results generated by the two approaches are broadly compatible and mutually reinforcing.

8. Cf. National Opinion Research Center, "Jobs and Occupations: A Popular Evaluation," in Reinhard Bendix and Seymour M. Lipset, eds., *Class, Status and Power: A Reader in Social Stratification* (Glencoe, Ill.: Free Press, 1953), p. 411; Hodge, Siegel, and Rossi, *supra* note 12.

9. In the survey instrument, the fields were listed in alphabetical order (see appendix A, question A1).

10. See Edward Shils, "Deference," in J. A. Jackson, ed., *Social Stratification* (Cambridge: Cambridge University Press, 1968); and Goldthorpe and Hope, *supra* note 3.

11. Peter Rossi has brought to our attention the fact that interpretations of correlation coefficients of this nature are somewhat ambiguous. If, on the one hand, all the respondents agreed on their prestige evaluations of the fields there could only be small correlations between judgments across fields. This is so because correlation is based on covariation and, in this case, covariation would be minimal. Such small correlations among the prestige evaluations of a cross section of occupations in the labor force are, in fact, typically observed. On the other hand, when respondents are in agreement concerning the attributes on which they evaluate fields (e.g., type of client) but disagree in the evaluations they make on the basis of these attributes, substantial correlations of the sort observed in our study are the result. Other analyses we have done support this speculation. For example, in examining the data using analysis of variance techniques, we found that characteristics of the respondents

themselves, including such things as their type of field, law school, and value orientations, were related to systematic differences in their prestige judgments. See Charles Cappell, "Differential Evaluations of the Status of Legal Specialties: A Detailed Analysis with Theoretical Implications" (unpublished paper, American Bar Foundation, 1977).

12. Cf. Louis Guttman, "A General Nonmetric Technique for Finding the Smallest Coordinate Space for a Configuration of Points," *Psychometrika* 33 (1968): 469; David D. McFarland and Daniel J. Brown, "Social Distance as a Metric: A Systematic Introduction to Smallest Space Analysis," in Edward O. Laumann, *Bonds of Pluralism: The Form and Substance of Urban Social Networks* (New York: John Wiley, 1973), p. 213; James C. Lingoes, *The Guttman-Lingoes Nonmetric Program Series* (Ann Arbor, Mich.: Mathesis Press, 1973).

13. In principle, one can always represent exactly the interpoint distances among *n* points in *n* minus 1 dimensions in a Euclidian space. Of course, since we cannot physically represent a space having more than three dimensions, we are usually interested in seeing if it is possible to sacrifice some accuracy of representation in order to have a minimum number of dimensions, ideally three or fewer, consistent with an acceptable level of distortion between the "real world" distances and those represented in the model of the real world. Two-dimensional maps are examples of representing a three-dimensional object, the earth, in a more convenient and easily comprehended form. Note, however, that distortions result from such an expedient.

Similarly, smallest space analysis tells us whether we have found an acceptable fit between the original matrix of proximity estimates, treated here as providing information only about the rank order of the distances among the points, and the calculated Euclidean distances between the points of a particular smallest space solution; cf. Peter V. Marsden and Edward O. Laumann, "The Social Structure of Religious Groups: A Replication and Methodological Critique," in Samuel Shye, ed., *Theory Construction and Data Analysis in the Behavioral Sciences* (San Francisco: Jossey-Bass, 1978), pp. 81–111. When the coefficient of alienation (the measure of fit) is zero, it indicates a perfect congruence between the real world proximities and the distances portrayed in the smallest space solution. As the coefficient increases in value, it indicates growing distortions or discrepancies between the real world data and the smallest space solution. Experience has shown that a coefficient of alienation of .15 indicates a satisfactory or acceptable smallest space solution.

14. See discussion of SSA–1 in Lingoes, *supra* note 12.

15. Cf. Shils, *supra* note 10.

16. The coordinates of the smallest space solution are themselves completely arbitrary and can be rotated to any other orientation without changing the order of the Euclidean interpoint distances—a feature that facilitates interpreting the generating principles organizing the space (cf. Edward O. Laumann and Franz U. Pappi, *Networks of Collective Action: A Perspective on Community Influence Systems* [New York: Academic Press, 1976], pp. 6–9). Being arbitrary, the coordinates are not always substantively interpretable (although, for the case in hand, the first axis of the solution reflects the general prestige rank order).

17. Cf. Edward O. Laumann and Franz Urban Pappi, "New Directions in the Study of Community Elites," *American Sociological Review* 38 (1973): 212, 221–23.

18. A physical analogy gives an intuitive sense of the meaning of the "centroid" of a smallest space solution: if all points in a two-dimensional smallest space solution were a set of equal weights resting on a weightless plane, the centroid would be that point on which the plane would balance. For a technical discussion, see E. Roskam

and J. C. Lingoes, "A Mathematical and Empirical Study of Two Multidimensional Scaling Algorithms," *Michigan Mathematical Psychology Program* 1 (1971): 1.

19. Cf. Laumann·and Pappi, *supra* note 17, pp. 221–23.

20. An alternative research strategy would have been to have the practitioners who rated prestige also rate these characteristics, thus permitting us to compare their prestige judgments to their ratings of the individual characteristics. To have done so would have greatly extended already crowded interviews, however, and it was thus not practical to pursue this strategy. We do not regard this as a great loss. We are not so much interested in analyzing the interrelationships among various evaluations by the individual rater—i.e, among the individual's ratings of field prestige and his or her ratings of the fields on other evaluative dimensions. Rather, we were concerned to examine whether some "real" properties of the types of work might be discovered that would help account for the differences among field prestige at the aggregate level. Thus, we used independent experts to judge the presence or absence of these properties.

21. Harold D. Lasswell and Abraham Kaplan, *Power and Society: A Framework for Political Inquiry* (New Haven: Yale University Press, 1950).

22. See, e.g., Ernest Greenwood, "Attributes of a Profession," *Social Work*, July 1957, p. 45; Richard H. Hall, *Occupations and the Social Structure* (Englewood Cliffs, N.J.: Prentice-Hall, 1969).

23. Note that the question on which the public service dimension is based did not ask for an assessment of the "social worth" or "contribution to the public good" of each field. Such a question would be even more difficult to answer than the one that we did, in fact, pose. Rather, our question asked the panel of scholars to judge the extent to which practitioners in each field were likely to undertake the work because of the money to be made in it rather than because of "altruistic" or "reformist" motives. We recognize (and think it safe to assume that our panel of scholars did, as well) that the choices open to any lawyer may well be limited both by opportunity and by personal circumstances. Some lawyers may take relatively low-paying work— criminal prosecution or real estate title searches, for example—because it is the only type of work open to them. Nonetheless, some lawyers no doubt choose to take the types of cases that will earn them only small fees (or a small salary) or no fee at all. And it may well be, to pursue our examples, that decisions to go into criminal prosecution are more likely to reflect such a choice than are decisions to do real estate title searches.

24. See Edwin M. Lemert, *Human Deviance, Social Problem, and Social Control* (Englewood Cliffs, N.J.: Prentice-Hall, 1967), pp. 40–64, on "secondary deviation."

25. Cf. Benjamin S. DuVal, Jr., "The Class Action as an Antitrust Enforcement Device: The Chicago Experience (I)," 1976 *American Bar Foundation Research Journal* (Summer): 1021, 1032.

26. The analyses discussed here differ in minor respects from those reported in chapter 3. These differences arise because we employed different rules in assigning particular persons to fields of law and because the prestige analysis used a somewhat different list of fields.

27. Though all respondents were asked their religious preferences and their ethnic or national origins, only the percentage of Jewish practitioners in each field is reported here because the "percentage Jewish" had a stronger negative correlation with prestige than did any of the other religious and ethnic categories, and it is, in our opinion, the most interesting and important of those variables. There is considerable literature on anti-Semitism within the bar; see especially, Jerold S. Auerbach, *Unequal Justice:*

Lawyers and Social Change in Modern America (New York: Oxford University Press, 1976). "Percentage Catholic" was also negatively correlated with prestige, though not to a statistically significant degree, and "percentage Protestant" had a strong positive correlation with the prestige of the fields (.67, even stronger than the negative correlation of "percentage Jewish"). Too few nonwhites appear in our sample to permit separate statistical analysis of that category.

28. Cf. Nathan Glazer and Daniel Patrick Moynihan, *Beyond the Melting Pot: The Negroes, Puerto Ricans, Jews, Italians and Irish of New York City* (Cambridge: MIT Press, 1963); Laumann, *supra* note 18.

29. E. Digby Baltzell, *Philadelphia Gentlemen: The Making of a National Upper Class* (Glencoe, Ill.: Free Press, 1958).

30. The other three client categories that we analyzed and their correlations with prestige are "mean percentage of law practice income derived from personal (versus business) clients" (-.71); "mean percentage of personal clients who have professional, technical, or managerial occupations" (.79); and "mean percentage of income from business clients that is derived from 'small businesses,' e.g., neighborhood stores, local restaurants, local real estate brokers, etc.—less than $250,000 in sales per year" (-.71).

31. Because an individual's income tends to increase with age, and because higher prestige fields tend to have disproportionately younger lawyers, we were concerned to eliminate the confounding influence of age on income and prestige. To do so, we projected incomes of persons active in a particular field as if all the fields had the same age distribution. When the income distribution is thus standardized by age, its correlation with field prestige (.40) just fails to achieve statistical significance.

32. But see chapter 2, note 15.

33. See Allan M. Schwartzbaum, John H. McGrath, and Robert A. Rothman, "The Perception of Prestige Differences Among Medical Subspecialties," *Social Science and Medicine* 7(1973): 365, 370. See also S. M. Shortell, "Occupational Prestige Difference Within the Medical and Allied Health Professions," *Social Science and Medicine* 8(1974): 1.

34. For a good, brief introduction to this mode of statistical analysis, see Hubert M. Blalock, Jr., *Social Statistics* (New York: McGraw-Hill, 1960), pp. 326–58.

35. See Goldthorpe and Hope, *supra* note 3.

36. Indeed, if the general good or bad repute of the fields had substantial impact on the ratings of these characteristics made by our panel of scholars, then these imputed characteristics would, to that extent, not be "independent variables"—i.e., they would not be independent of the general prestige of the fields. But the correlations of the individual imputed characteristics with the prestige judgments are relatively modest and thus suggest that this is not the case. (Three of the five correlations are about .5; one, rapidity of change, is .08; and the fifth, intellectual challenge, is .65)

37. Cf. Paul M. Siegel and Robert W. Hodge, "A Causal Approach to the Study of Measurement Error," in Hubert M. Blalock, Jr., and Ann B. Blalock, eds., *Methodology in Social Research* (New York: McGraw-Hill, 1968), p. 28; Robert A. Gordon, "Issues in Multiple Regression," *American Journal of Sociology* 73 (1968): 592.

38. "The Jewish Law Student and New York Jobs—Discriminatory Effects in Law Firm Hiring Practices," *Yale Law Journal* 73 (1964): 625–60; Jerold S. Auerbach, *Unequal Justice: Lawyers and Social Change in Modern America* (New York: Oxford University Press, 1976); Jack Ladinsky, "Careers of Lawyers, Law Practice, and Legal Institutions," *American Sociological Review* 28 (1963): 52–54; idem., "The Impact of Social Backgrounds of Lawyers on Law Practice and the Law," *Journal of Legal*

Education 16 (1963): 137–38; idem., "The Social Profile of a Metropolitan Bar: A Statistical Survey in Detroit," *Michigan State Bar Journal* 43 (1964): 19–20.

39. Though no amount of cross-sectional analysis can fully substitute for the absence of longitudinal data, it may be instructive to examine the types of practice engaged in by Jewish respondents of differing ages. Thus, if prestigious areas of practice were formerly closed to Jews but more recently have become open to them, we would expect to find that the observed tendency for Jewish lawyers to be overrepresented in the less prestigious jobs differs with the age of our respondents, the effect being much stronger among older lawyers than among younger ones.

A superficial look at some of our data might suggest strong support for this hypothesis. Thus, the percentage of Jewish respondents who are solo practitioners (a reasonably good proxy variable to use as a summary indicator of lower status practice) declines markedly with age. If we divide our respondents into three age categories that produce approximately equal numbers of Jews in each age range—age 46 and older (includes 78 Jewish respondents), age 34 to 45 (includes 74), and age 33 and younger (also 74)—we find that 42 percent of the Jewish respondents in the oldest group are solo practitioners, as compared to 26 percent of those in the middle group and only 12 percent in the youngest group. Similarly, if we use employment in a large law firm (30 or more lawyers) as a proxy for a high status position, we find that only 5 percent of the Jewish respondents in the oldest group are in such firms, but that this increases to 10 percent in the middle group and 19 percent in the youngest group. This would appear, then, to be evidence of a substantial improvement in the position of Jews in the Chicago bar in recent years.

On the other hand, if we look somewhat more closely at the data, we find that these trends are very substantially due to decreases and increases, respectively, in those types of practice generally—that is, the trends reflect an overall growth in the share of the profession that practices in firms of 30 or more lawyers and precipitous decline in the solo practice. The proportion of solos decreases from 33 percent of the oldest group to 19 percent of the middle group and only 8 percent of the youngest lawyers, while the large firm share of the total bar increases from 12 percent of the oldest group to 18 percent of the middle group and 26 percent of the youngest.

If we examine instead, then, the enthnoreligious composition of the total number of lawyers in each of the practice settings by age, we find that the percentage of Jews in the large firm category does not yet come close to equaling the percentage in the total profession, even in the youngest age group. The Jewish share of the total Chicago bar increases steadily across the three age groups, from 30 percent of the oldest group to 33 percent of the middle group and 38 percent of the youngest, while the comparable percentages of Jews in the large firm category are 13, 18, and 28. The degree of underrepresentation thus decreases from 17 percentage points in the oldest group to 15 points in the middle group and 10 percentage points in the youngest group. While the gap narrows appreciably in the youngest group, then, even in that age category Jewish respondents are still substantially underrepresented in the large firms. At the other end of the status hierarchy, the picture is even less supportive of the hypothesis that opportunities have equalized—the percentage of solo practitioners who are Jewish actually increases in the younger age categories, from 39 percent in the oldest group to 43 percent in the middle group and 53 percent in the youngest. One should exercise great caution in giving weight to this finding, however, because the decline in the solo practitioners' share of the total profession means that there are few respondents in the younger categories. In absolute numbers, there are 33 Jewish solo practitioners in the oldest age category and only 9 in the youngest.

In sum, while there appears to have been some improvement in the position of Jews within the Chicago bar, that improvement has not been as great as one might have expected. Even in the youngest age group, Jewish respondents exceed their percentage of the total profession only in the solo practice and in the small and medium-sized firm categories and exceed it most among the solos and small firm practitioners. The greatest improvement in the access of Jews appears to have come in the medium-sized firm—from 17 percent among the oldest group to 46 percent in the youngest. While the percentage of Jewish respondents in the large firms increases in the younger groups, Jews are still underrepresented—by a full 10 percentage points, even in the youngest age group. The increase among house counsel has been less steady, but is quite substantial in the youngest group. Even there, however, Jewish respondents remain underrepresented by 11 percentage points. From these data, it would be hard to argue that the vestiges of anti-Semitism have disappeared.

40. The differences between the intellectual challenge scores of each of these pairs are, in fact, very small, ranging from 0 to 3 points. In the five comparisons in which there is a difference in the intellectual challenge scores of the two sides of the case (in environmental law, the scores are identical), however, the difference is always in the same direction—the higher score is given to the "nonestablishment" side of the field. Thus, the direction of the differences suggests that the scholars who served as our judges of intellectual challenge were not biased by the "establishment" view of the prestige of the fields. The tendency in their ratings could, of course, indicate some bias in the opposite direction, but it also might reflect a perception that differences in the resources available to the two sides make the tasks of the lawyers for the nonestablishment side systematically more demanding. See note 41.

41. Differences in the burden of proof or extralegal differences in the resources available to the lawyers might make it consistently easier to try one side of the case than the other, but the direction of these differences, if any, will usually tend to make the jobs of the lawyers on the establishment side less demanding. That is, the greater resources are likely to be on the establishment side. In criminal cases, the burden of proof will be favorable to the defense rather than to the establishment (government) side, but in all of the other pairs of fields, which are civil, the establishment sides, as the defense, will usually have the benefit of the burden of proof. Insofar as these differences exist between the two sides of the fields, therefore, the higher prestige of the establishment sides is not explained by a greater degree of intellectual challenge. Rather, if anything, the differences will usually cut in the opposite direction.

42. Cf. Robert E. Blauner, *Alienation and Freedom: The Factory Worker and His Industry* (Chicago: University of Chicago Press, 1964).

43. Note, however, that personal injury plaintiffs' work also received one of the lowest public service scores, even though it is disproportionately likely to serve lower-status clients. The service to impecunious clients in that field is not usually done on a no-fee or reduced-fee basis, but rather on a contingent fee that is intended to be highly profitable to the lawyer. The prestige of the field, however, corresponds not to its public service score but to the social status of its clients—it serves persons of low status and it has low prestige within the profession.

44. Karl N. Llewellyn, "The Bar Specializes—With What Results?" *Annals of American Academy of Social and Political Sciences* 167(1933): 177.

45. Cf, Francis X. Sutton et al., *The American Business Creed* (Cambridge: Harvard University Press, 1956).

46. Andrew Abbott, "Status and Status Strain in the Professions," *American Journal of Sociology* 86 (1981): 819.

47. Ibid., pp. 823–24.

48. Ibid., pp. 825–26.

49. Ibid.

50. Barlow F. Christensen, *Lawyers for People of Moderate Means: Some Problems of Availability of Legal Services* (Chicago: American Bar Foundation, 1970), pp. 92–97.

51. See Charles D. Kelso, "Adding up the Law Schools," *Learning and the Law,* Summer 1975, p. 38.

Chapter 5

1. The list was not intended to include all of the most noteworthy lawyers in Chicago—and it surely did not. Rather, the list sought to represent notable lawyers with a variety of social and professional backgrounds, as described in the text below, and prominent lawyers of a type that was well represented on the list were, therefore, excluded. It is surely the case that many Chicago lawyers who were not included on our list are more prominent or well known than some of those who were listed.

2. For an account of this counter-bar organization, see Michael Powell, "Anatomy of a Counter-Bar Association: The Chicago Council of Lawyers," 1979 *American Bar Foundation Research Journal* 501–41 (summer).

3. See Jeffrey S. Slovak, "Working for Corporate Actors: Social Change and Elite Attorneys in Chicago," 1979 *American Bar Foundation Research Journal* 465–500 (summer).

4. Some persons included on the list had held public office in the past, and one private practitioner currently held the part-time elective post of trustee of the University of Illinois. We do not believe that that position was likely to be the source of any great power or influence within the profession.

5. Six of the 43 lawyers included on the final list were in their mid-30s (including the 4 presidents of the CCL) and 3 were in their early 70s. The distribution of the remaining 34 lawyers was skewed toward the high end—7 were in their 40s, 11 in their 50s, and 16 in their 60s.

6. The list of notable lawyers that we used in our interviews included 49 names. Six of those have been dropped from the analysis as it is presented here—2 because they were "ringers" in the first place, relatively unknown lawyers included as a validity check and to establish the baseline probability of acquaintance, 1 (a tax lawyer from a small firm) because he died between the printing of the interview instrument and the administration of the survey and we were uncertain about the effect of this on the results, and 3 because they were elderly and known by relatively few respondents.

7. Chi square significant at $< .01$; $r = .17$.

8. See chapter 1 for definitions of the categories of law schools.

9. Chi square significant at $< .01$; $r = .34$.

10. The simple Pearson's correlation between age and the number of notables known is .3.

11. F significant at $< .01$; $r = .25$.

12. The partial correlation is .29, significant at $< .01$.

13. That is, the chi squares do not achieve the .05 level of significance.

14. F significant at $< .01$; eta $= .20$.

15. Since many of these notable lawyers will be readily identifiable by persons familiar with the Chicago bar or by others who take the trouble to inquire, the use of pseudonyms will not be adequate to preserve the anonymity of many of the notables. But the real names would mean little or nothing to most of the readers of this book, and for those readers there would thus be no advantage in use of those names. The pseudonyms, however, do provide an advantage—they permit us to use the initial letters of the names to identify the major category of notability that caused the lawyer to be included in the list. This makes figure 9.1 easier to comprehend. When data are as complex as these, a device that organizes the data and aids comprehension is surely welcome.

As to the matter of anonymity, we should note that none of the biographical information presented was obtained from confidential sources. We did not seek to interview the notables. In some instances, however, notables were interviewed as respondents included in one or another of our samples. Two happened to come up in our random sample for the cross-sectional survey. Twelve were included in one or more of the samples of elites, identified positionally, that were used in other surveys conducted by our associates. (See, e.g., Slovak, *supra* note 3.) Even for those notables who were interviewed, however, no use has been made in these biographies of information obtained during the interviews. The information presented here on the subjects' practice and personal characteristics was gathered from published sources or from persons who are well informed about the Chicago bar. Many of the notables are included in standard biographical reference works; newspaper accounts have also been used. In several cases, our biographical sketches do not include information on a notable's political party preference, ethnicity or religion. These are cases where the information was not available from published sources nor from persons knowledgeable about the Chicago bar. If these facts were unknown to our informants, it may be reasonable to assume that the characteristics are not an important part of the roles of those notables in the profession.

16. The reader will, by now, be familiar with the essentials of the smallest space technique and with the general mode of its interpretation (see chap. 4).

17. In two dimensions, Kruskal's stress was .19; in the three-dimensional solution it declines to .148. An alternative measure of fit, the Guttman-Lingoes coefficient of alienation, produces similar results—for the two-dimensional solution it was .21; using three dimensions, it declines to .162. Both of these measures indicate that the representation of the relationships among the points includes a good deal of stress, even in three dimensions, but it is minimally satisfactory. See J. B. Kruskal, "Multi-dimensional Sealing by Optimizing Goodness of Fit to a Nonmetric Hypothesis." *Psychometrika* 29 (March 1964): 3; and Louis Guttman, "A General Nonmetric Technique for Finding the Smallest Coordinate Space for a Configuration of Points," *Psychometrika* 33 (December 1968): 486.

18. The average number of respondents knowing each of these 4 persons is 27.5, compared to an average of 51.7 for the 43 notables overall.

19. Their age also sets these 4 apart from most of the other notables, but we doubt that youth is their most salient common characteristic. Drootin, the dean of the DePaul Law School, is the same age, for example, but he is found on the opposite side of the top of the space, at the far upper right. One of the distinctive characteristics of the CCL is the relative youth of its members and leaders, however, and age may well be a part of the ties that unite the CCL constituency. The age and CCL variables are, thus, confounded in a manner that has substantive significance. This illustrates the point that, because each notable has multiple characteristics, they can be classified

in a number of alternative ways, and we certainly make no claim that the interpretations that we have made are the only possible ones.

20. It is more important to note that, in any event, the less clear cases of classification occur near the margins of the categories that are in question.

21. It is quite unlikely that a given respondent will know both of 2 notables who are located on opposite sides of the space. Thus, of 70 respondents who know either Lynch or Trumbauer, for example, only 1 knows both of them. This is the case in spite of the systematic bias in the set of respondents who are likely to know any of the notables and in spite of the fact that both Lynch and Trumbauer are litigators who represent major corporations. Their other characteristics obviously serve to assign them to two, separate, largely segregated circles of acquaintance.

22. See Howard S. Becker, *Outsiders: Studies in the Sociology of Deviance* (New York: Free Press, 1973). The youth of the CCL presidents probably largely accounts for the fact that they were less widely known than most of the notables (see *supra* note 19). The careers of these persons have progressed since the time our data was gathered, and they would probably be substantially better known today.

23. Mingus is a member of a socially elite Jewish family and is a patron of the arts; Barents, a past president of the CBA, is a partner in an old, conservative firm. Though both surely qualify as notable lawyers, neither is so close to the power centers of the profession (quite apart from his position in the figure) as to be generally thought of as a member of the profession's establishment. Neither represents major corporations in his law practice or is an influential figure in the world of business and finance.

24. All 777 respondents were asked whether they had held office in a bar association. The variable used here includes the respondents who reported that they had served as a committee chairman, as a member of the board, or as an officer (president, secretary, etc.) of either the Chicago Bar Association or the Illinois State Bar Association.

25. Herman Kogan, *The First Century: The Chicago Bar Association 1874–1974* (Chicago: Rand McNally, 1974), pp. 202–4.

26. The American Trial Lawyers Association includes primarily personal injury lawyers and criminal defense lawyers. The Chicago Council of Lawyers is an organization of younger, reform-oriented lawyers; see Powell, *supra* note 2.

27. For a full discussion of the economic liberalism scale, see chapter 5 in the original edition of *Chicago Lawyers* (1982).

28. The correlations among these three variables all range between .75 and .78, ignoring the signs; $p = < .0001$.

29. Catholics are disproportionately represented among the graduates of Loyola and DePaul law schools.

30. These are Protestants of generally higher social status (see chap. 1).

31. Mancur Olson refers to the modern proponents of this view as "analytical pluralists"; see Mancur Olson, Jr., *The Logic of Collective Action* (Cambridge: Harvard University Press, 1965), p. 118.

32. David B. Truman, *The Governmental Process* (New York: Alfred Knopf, 1951), pp. 508–9. The other conceptual element that he views as "of crucial significance" is "the function of unorganized interests, or potential interest groups" (p. 508).

33. The earlier chapters of this book argued that the principal division within the bar is that between lawyers who represent corporations or large organizations and those who represent individuals or small businesses, while in this portion of our analysis we find the bar to be divided not into two principal parts, but three. This

is not an inconsistency but rather a consequence of the difference in the subjects of the analyses.

34. Clyde Nunn, Harry Crockett, and Allen Williams, *Tolerance and Nonconformity* (San Francisco: Jossey-Bass, 1978).

35. The correlation between religion and Chicago political preference is very strong; $x^2 = 125.9$, p = < .00001. While 32 percent of the type I Protestants in our total sample express a preference for the Republicans, only 6 percent of the Catholics and 3 percent of the Jews share that preference. Forty-eight percent of the Jews call themselves Independent Democrats, while 34 percent of the Catholics and 27 percent of the type I Protestants choose the label. Though Regular Democrats are only 16 percent of our total sample, 26 percent of the Catholics express that preference, compared to 16 percent of the Jews and only 6 percent of the type I Protestants.

36. Arthur F. Bentley, *The Process of Government* (1908; reprint Evanston, Ill.: Principia Press, 1949), pp. 208–9.

Chapter 6

1. See Dietrich Rueschemeyer, *Lawyers and Their Society: A Comparative Study of the Legal Profession in Germany and the United States* (Cambridge: Harvard University Press, 1973), pp. 13–30; Erwin O. Smigel, *The Wall Street Lawyer: Professional Organization Man?* 2d ed. (Bloomington: Indiana University Press, 1969), pp. 171–204.

2. One might even wonder whether these two categories of clients are really served by different lawyers. That is, will not the same law firms who handle the legal work of corporations owned or controlled by wealthy individuals also look after the personal legal affairs of those individuals? Perhaps, and perhaps not, but even if the same *firm* handles both sorts of work we find that the two are unlikely to be done by the same *lawyers* within the firm. A few large law firms have added divorce lawyers to their staffs to help the corporate executives disentangle their marital difficulties, several large corporate firms have probate departments, and many of the firms will accommodate corporate executives by handling the purchase or sale of their residences. But the lawyers who do the corporate work within the firm may have little in common with, and relatively little contact with, their partners or associates who do the divorce work and who draft the wills or do the estate tax planning. And if the residential real estate closing or title search is handled by the same real estate department within the firm that does real estate development work, syndications, and acquisitions of real estate for the corporate clients, the residential work is likely to be done by the most junior members of that department. See Robert L. Nelson, "Practice and Privilege: Social Change and the Structure of Large Law Firms," 1981 *American Bar Foundation Research Journal* 112–17. See also *infra* note 8.

3. See E. Digby Baltzell, "The Protestant Establishment Revisited," *The American Scholar* 45 (1976): 499–518; idem., *Philadelphia Gentlemen: The Making of a National Upper Class* (New York: Free Press, 1966): idem., *The Protestant Establishment: Aristocracy and Caste in America* (New York: Random House, 1964).

4. James S. Coleman, "Loss of Power," *American Sociological Review* 38 (1973): 1–17.

5. The greater financial resources of corporations also permit their lawyers to go into their legal problems in greater depth, exploring the full complexity of the issues. Indeed, the more complex the issues can be made, the better the corporation often

likes it. The complexity prolongs the litigation and thus puts off the day of reckoning, which is often to the advantage of the corporation.

The greater depth and complexity of analysis that the corporate assets make possible may enhance the sense of professional accomplishment of corporate lawyers. It is not so necessary for them to deal "superficially" with a high volume of cases.

6. See, e.g., Wilbert E. Moore, *The Professions: Roles and Rules* (New York: Russell Sage, 1970), pp. 15–16. See also Ernest Greenwood, "Attributes of a Profession," *Social Work* 2 (1957): 45–55.

7. See chapter 2 at table 2.1.

8. On the other hand, corporate officers do get divorced with some regularity, and, as noted in footnote 2 of this chapter, a few of the large, corporate law firms have therefore added small divorce departments as an accommodation to these clients. The more usual pattern, however, is to refer the divorce cases of corporate officers to small firms specializing in divorce work, who present no threat of taking over any portion of the corporation's legal work. In such referrals, the divorce specialist handles the divorce itself and related questions of child custody or visitation rights, but the large firm may often retain control of the financial settlement.

9. For this reason, we have in recent years begun to see the emergence of some quite small, very highly specialized firms that are self-consciously organized to handle only a clearly restricted range of corporate law problems so that they may more "safely" be referred the specialized work, the specialty firms being unlikely to pose a competitive threat to the large firms that practice corporate law generally. Those new firms, which have been called "boutique specialty firms," deal with areas such as bankruptcy and corporate takeover bids. See Nelson, *supra* note 2.

10. Durkheim, among others, noted that specialization creates interdependence among the specialized parts and thus a pressure toward coordinating or integrating the parts so that they are in some sort of adjustment. Emile Durkheim, *The Division of Labor in Society*, trans. George Simpson (New York: Free Press, 1964), pp. 62, 200, 301–2, 353, 364, 406 passim. But the simultaneous existence of substantial numbers of both specialists and generalists may lead to conflict. Inherent antagonisms arise between the interests of specialists and the interests of part-timers. Because the specialists are wholly devoted to a narrowly circumscribed field of activity, their standing among their peers rests on their unremitting service to their chosen field. They tend to be acutely aware of the variable levels of competence, performance, and knowledgeability of practitioners, and they have a strong interest in raising standards of performance by eliminating the "unqualified" who grab the occasional case and bungle it, thus threatening the reputation of the field. The part-timer, by contrast, has an interest in maintaining ease of entry into a field of practice; he will thus oppose formal certification procedures and other barriers to entry, such as specialized referral schemes. The specialist's interest in standardizing entry and practitioner performance will be viewed by the part-timer (and perhaps others) as a tactic for securing a monopoly position; see, generally, Jerold S. Auerbach, *Unequal Justice: Lawyers and Social Change in Modern America* (New York: Oxford University Press, 1976); Eliot Friedson, *Profession of Medicine: A Study of the Sociology of Applied Knowledge* (New York: Dodd, Mead, 1970); idem., *Professional Dominance: The Social Structure of Medical Care* (New York: Atherton Press, 1970); Magali Sarfatti Larson, *The Rise of Professionalism. A Sociological Analysis* (Berkeley: University of California Press, 1977).

The history of the emergence of medical specialty boards is replete with examples of these confrontations between specialists and generalists (see Glenn Greenwood and Robert F. Frederickson, *Specialization in the Medical and Legal Professions* [Chicago: Callaghan, 1964], pp. 15–24; Rosemary Stevens, *American Medicine and the Public Interest* [New Haven: Yale Unversity Press, 1971]), and history appears to be repeating itself in the more recent controversies in the legal profession over specialty certification (see Barlow F. Christensen, *Specialization* [Chicago: American Bar Foundation, 1967]; Richard Zehnle, "Specialization in the Legal Profession," in *Legal Specialization*, American Bar Association, Specialization Monograph no. 2 (Chicago, 1976); Jerome A. Hochberg, "The Drive to Specialization," in Ralph Nader and Mark Green, eds., *Verdicts on Lawyers* [New York: Thomas Y. Crowell, 1977], p. 118). Our findings suggest that the balance of power among lawyers on the issue of specialization is now heavily weighted in favor of the generalists in most fields of practice, but the increasingly successful prosecution of malpractice suits against lawyers could produce growing pressures toward certification of specialties. (Insurance companies already require specialty certification as a prerequisite to the issuance of certain kinds of medical malpractice policies.) Note, however, that such pressure for change would not be endogenously generated but rather would be a lagged response to extra-professional demands for accountability.

11. Howard S. Becker, *Outsiders: Studies in the Sociology of Deviance* (New York: Free Press, 1973), pp. 147–63.

12. Jerome E. Carlin, *Lawyers on Their Own: A Study of Individual Practitioners in Chicago* (New Brunswick, N.J.: Rutgers University Press, 1962), pp. 175–84.

13. Max Weber, *Economy and Sociology: An Outline of Interpretive Sociology*, ed. Guenther Roth and Claus Wittich (Berkeley: University of California Press, 1978), pp. 775–76.

14. Within the corporate hemisphere, we find no significant differences between litigators and office lawyers in the percentage of their practice income that they receive from major corporations or from smaller businesses. In the personal client hemisphere, however, litigators receive far more of their income from blue-collar workers than do office lawyers (17 percent for the office lawyers and 30 percent for the litigators; this difference is significant at the .001 level). Personal client litigators also receive significantly more of their income from unemployed persons and from sales and clerical workers than do office lawyers practicing in the personal client hemisphere.

15. Talcott Parsons, "Professions" in David L. Sills, ed., *International Encyclopedia of the Social Sciences* (New York: Free Press, 1968), p. 539; Talcott Parsons, "The Professions and Social Structure," in *Essays in Sociological Theory* rev. ed. (Glencoe, Ill.: Free Press, 1954), pp. 34–49.

16. Terence Johnson, *Professions and Power* (London: Macmillan, 1972), pp. 56–57.

17. See Friedson, *supra* note 10, *Profession of Medicine*, pp. 203–331; idem., *Professional Dominance*, p. 6; Barbara Wootton, *Social Science and Social Pathology* (London: Allen and Unwin, 1959); and Kingsley Davis, "Mental Hygiene and the Class Structure," *Psychiatry* 1 (1938): 55–65.

18. Talcott Parsons observed that the professional role emphasizes "affective neutrality"; see his *The Social System* (Glencoe, Ill.: Free Press, 1951), chap. 10.

19. In addition to the works of Eliot Freidson, *supra* note 10, see, e.g., Jeffrey L. Berlant, *Profession and Monopoly: A Study of Medicine in the United States and Great Britain* (Berkeley: University of California Press, 1975); Larson, *supra* note 10, Robert Stevens and Rosemary Stevens, *Welfare Medicine in America* (New York: Free Press, 1974); Rosemary Stevens, *supra* note 10. Dietrich Rueschemeyer has explicitly compared the legal and medical professions; see his "Doctors and Lawyers: A Com-

ment on the Theory of the Professions," *Canadian Review of Sociology and Anthropology* 1 (1964): 17. His perspective differs from ours, but he covers some of the same points and we have benefited from his analysis.

20. See Greenwood, *supra* note 6; Douglas Rosenthal, *Lawyer and Client: Who's in Charge?* (New York: Russell Sage, 1976).

21. Other factors possibly contributing to this autonomy are, e.g., social class differences between professional and client, or mystification that sets apart the role of the professional regardless of any real difference in knowledge.

22. Hospitals are, of course, large organizations, and they do exercise several forms of control over both physicians and patients. But it is important to note that hospitals of any size or consequence are not owned by individual doctors, nor even by groups of doctors, but are responsible in form at least to boards of trustees, usually composed in substantial part of laypeople representing interests external to the profession. In terms of their regulatory effects upon the structure of the profession—as institutions that touch and in part control the profession, institutions that are partly within the profession but also partly controlled from outside—hospitals are probably more closely analogous to the courts than they are to the large law firms. See Charles Perrow, "Hospitals: Technology, Structure and Goals," in James G. March, ed., *Handbook of Organizations* (Chicago: Rand McNally, 1965), pp. 910–971.

23. We are, of course, aware of the growth of HMOs and other group health plans. Even by the most optimistic of estimates, however, these plans in 1981 served no more than 5 percent of the nation's population, and most HMOs are operated by insurance companies or by Independent Physicians Associations (IPAs), not by consumers. See *Group Health News*, 22 (May 1981): 2. See also Jeffrey C. Goldsmith, *Can Hospitals Survive?* (Homewood, Ill.: Dow Jones-Irwin, 1981), pp. 93–95, esp. at fig. 4–2, p. 94.

24. For a study that did deal with the individual lawyer-client relationship, see Rosenthal, *supra* note 20.

25. Dietrich Rueschemeyer, "Doctors and Lawyers," *supra* note 19, pp. 17, 19.

26. The adversary nature of the litigation process, as well as the clients' differing social types, make some conflict inevitable—e.g., labor unions versus management, criminal defendants versus prosecutors, taxpayers versus tax consumers.

27. The fact that both the doctrines and the lawyers' practices tend to be bounded by clients' social types is surely not coincidental but a result of interrelated, mutually dependent processes. That is, the doctrinal limits may be defined in part by client type (perhaps through client influence on the curricula of law schools), and the boundaries between doctrines may in turn define the literature that a given practitioner will read, the literature in which he will attempt to "keep up with developments."

28. William Prosser argued that the right to privacy, the creation of which owed much to the noted article by Samuel Warren and Louis D. Brandeis, "The Right to Privacy" (4 *Harvard Law Review* 193 [1890]) referred to "not one tort, but a complex of four." Prosser continued, "The law of privacy comprises four distinct kinds of invasion of four different interests of the plaintiff, which are tied together by the common name, but otherwise have almost nothing in common except that each represents an interference with the right of the plaintiff, in the phrase coined by Judge Cooley, 'to be let alone.'" William Prosser, "Privacy," 48 *California Law Review* 383, 389 (1960). For a historical account of the Warren and Brandeis collaboration and contribution, see Dorothy Glancy, "The Invention of the Right to Privacy," 21 *Arizona Law Review* 1 (1979); for the view that Prosser's own influence on the law of privacy

rivals that of Warren and Brandeis, see Edward Bloustein, "Privacy as an Aspect of Human Dignity: An Answer to Dean Prosser," 39 *NYU Law Review* 962, 964 (1964).

Leon Green wrote often on the limits of doctrine and on the extent to which the content of doctrine is determined by the contexts of the cases; see his *Judge and Jury* (Kansas City: Vernon Law Book Co., 1930), pp. 2–3, 16, and 19–20; idem., "The Study and Teaching of Tort Law," 34 *Texas Law Review* 1, 18 (1955); idem., "Tort Law: Public Law in Disguise (pt. 2)," 38 *Texas Law Review* 257, 266 (1960); idem., "Protection of Trade Relations Under Tort Law," 47 *Virginia Law Review* 559, 560 (1961). See also Clarence Morris, *How Lawyers Think* (Cambridge: Harvard University Press, 1937).

29. Maitland's famous metaphor, commenting on history rather than law, was first published in his "Prologue to a History of English Law," 14 *Law Quarterly Review* 13 (1898). It is also found in the first sentence of the second and subsequent editions of Frederick Pollock and Frederic William Maitland, *The History of English Law*, Vol. 1, 2d ed.; reissue (Cambridge: Cambridge University Press, 1968).

30. Though we did not attempt it, one approach toward assessing the relative importance to a profession of internal and external interests might be to examine the frequency with which the professionals advocate each sort of interest, but this assumes that these interests could be clearly distinguished. They may, in fact, often be inseparable.

31. Some of our colleagues, however, have examined the bar associations in detail; see Terence C. Haliday and Charles L. Cappell, "Indicators of Democracy in Professional Associations: Elite Recruitment, Turnover, and Decision-Making in a Metropolitan Bar Association," 1979 *American Bar Foundation Research Journal* 697–767 (fall); Michael Powell, "Anatomy of a Counter-Bar Association: The Chicago Council of Lawyers," 1979 *American Bar Foundation Research Journal* 501–41 (fall); Charles L. Cappell, "A Legal Elite: Investigations into the Structure of Decision-Making and the Production of Law" (Ph.D. diss., University of Chicago, 1982); Terence C. Halliday, "Parameters of Professional Influence: Policies and Politics of the Chicago Bar Association, 1945–70" (Ph.D. diss., University of Chicago, 1979); Michael Powell, "The Politics, Policies and Influence of a Legal Elite: The Association of the Bar of the City of New York" (Ph.D. diss., University of Chicago, 1982).

32. These institutions are either within the profession or ancillary to it, depending upon how one defines the scope of the profession, an issue that does not concern us here.

33. Michael Powell, "Professional Self-Regulation: The Transfer of Control from a Professional Association to an Independent Commission" (Paper read at the American Sociological Association's Annual Meeting, New York, 1976).

34. Michael Powell, "Developments in the Regulation of Lawyers: Intra- and Extra-Professional Controls" (Paper read at the American Sociological Association's Annual Meeting, Toronto, 1981).

35. Albert P. Blaustein and Charles O. Porter, *The American Lawyer* (Chicago: University of Chicago Press, 1954), p. 253, assert that "the power of the courts to investigate and to control the membership of the bar through disciplinary proceedings is as old as the profession itself."

The courts might be thought of as a part of the legal profession and, if so, the transfer of power from the bar associations to the courts might be seen not as taking the control away from the profession but as transferring it from one of the profession's institutions to another. Note that the law is the only profession about which such a contention might plausibly be made—the transfer of any part of another profession's governance from an association of the professionals to a governmental agency would constitute a clear loss of power by the profession. But, because the courts and the agencies under their control are staffed largely by a "special sort of lawyer," it can be argued that court control of the profession is *intra*-professional control. (And lawyers are, of course, said to be "officers of the court.") The courts are, however, just as clearly also agencies of government, and it is not at all clear that the primary loyalty of judges is to the profession from which they came to the bench. Judges may well feel bound by standards and principles that are independent of the profession and that may conflict with those of the profession. There is certainly no guarantee, nor perhaps even a likelihood, that the judges' decisions on these matters will be representative of the collective views of the bar.

36. David B. Truman, *The Governmental Process* (New York: Alfred Knopf, 1951), pp. 202 and 96. See also, Rue Bucher and Anselm Strauss, "Professions in Process," *American Journal of Sociology* 66 (1961): 325–34.

37. That occurred in the Chicago Bar Association, for example, when it delegated the drafting of a new criminal code to a committee composed almost exclusively of criminal lawyers. See John P. Heinz, Robert W. Gettleman, and Morris A. Seeskin, "Legislative Politics and the Criminal Law," 64 *Northwestern University Law Review* 277, 317–25 (1969).

38. David B. Truman, *The Governmental Process*, 2d ed. (New York: Alfred Knopf, 1971), p. 200.

39. It may be unnecessary in some forms of public health medicine, but it is essential even for those doing most forms of medical research.

40. See Brian Abel-Smith and Robert B. Stevens, *Lawyers and the Courts: A Sociological Study of the English Legal System, 1750–1965* (Cambridge: Harvard University Press, 1967); Michael Zander, *Lawyers and the Public Interest: A Study in Restrictive Practices* (London: Weidenfeld and Nicolson, 1968), p. 2, observes:

> The regulation of the Bar, its practices, and rules has never yet been the subject of legislative interference. Every barrister has to belong to one of the four ancient Inns of Court which, since their foundation, probably in the fourteenth century, have had control over the admission of students, the examination required before Call to the Bar, and the discipline of students and barristers. The government of the Inns, and thus of the profession, was in the hands of the Benchers of the Inns, a self-perpetuating body of elders including, since 1875, judges. Many of the powers of the Inns, including examinations and discipline, have recently been delegated to the Senate of the Four Inns of Court established in 1966, two-thirds of whose members are practising barristers, the remainder being judges. The General Council of the Bar, or Bar Council, by contrast, is a voluntary association, founded as late as 1895, whose function it is to look after and promote the interests of practitioners. It is the Bar Council, rather than the Inns, which has promulgated the Bar's rules of etiquette and practice.... About ninety percent of the 2,200 or so practising barristers subscribe to the Bar Council.

Unlike barristers, however, solicitors are regulated by the English courts.

41. See Alfred Z. Reed, *Training for the Public Profession of the Law* (New York: Carnegie Foundation for the Advancement of Teaching, 1921), pp. 35–40. See also Martin Garbus and Joel Seligman, "Sanctions and Disbarment: They Sit in Judgment," in Ralph Nader and Mark Green, eds., *Verdicts and Lawyers* (New York: Thomas Y. Crowell, 1976), pp. 47–60; Ronald L. Akers, "The Professional Association and the Legal Regulation of Practice," 2 *Law and Society Review* 463–82 (May 1968);

"Disbarment in the Federal Courts," 85 *Yale Law Journal* 975–89 (June 1976); Comment "Controlling Lawyers by Bar Associations and Courts," 5 *Harvard Civil Rights-Civil Liberties Law Review* 301–92 (April 1970).

42. In most jurisdictions, the only required course has been "professional ethics." The limited number of courses available in the curricula of many law schools may result in de facto course requirements, however—that is, the students may not have a wide range of choice. Because the bar exams cover specified lists of subjects, students may also feel pressure to take courses in those areas.

43. See Warren Burger, "The Special Skills of Advocacy: Are Specialized Training and Certification of Advocates Essential to Our System of Justice?," 42 *Fordham Law Review* 227–242 (December 1973). See also Judge Irving Kaufman, "The Court Needs a Friend in Court," 60 *American Bar Association Journal* 175–78 (February 1974). While Burger and Kaufman have argued that as many of one-half of trial attorneys are "incompetent," research on the subject has indicated that the majority of federal judges view the figure as much lower; see Dorothy Maddi, "Trial Advocacy Competence: The Judicial Perspective," 1978 *American Bar Foundation Research Journal* 105–51 (winter); Roger C. Cramton and Erik M. Jensen, "The State of Trial Advocacy and Legal Education: Three New Studies," 30 *Journal of Legal Education* 253–69 (November 1979).

44. In 1973, for example, the Indiana Supreme Court adopted Admission and Discipline Rule 13, which mandated certain law school courses as a prerequisite to taking the bar examination. See Frances X. Beytagh, "Prescribed Courses as Prerequisites for Taking Bar Examinations: Indiana's Experiment in Controlling Legal Education," 26 *Journal of Legal Education* 449–66 (November 1974). At least one state supreme court has followed Indiana's example (see the Rules of Admission to the Bar of South Carolina, 5A, 5B, 16). For background, see Bruce Littlejohn, "Ensuring Lawyer Competency: The South Carolina Approach," *Judicature*, 64 (1980): 109–13.

45. The primary impetus for such requirements was the "Devitt Report," the result of a commission chaired by Federal District Judge Edward J. Devitt; see Final Report to the Judicial Conference of the United States of the Committee to Consider Standards for Admission to Practice in the Federal Courts (September 19–20, 1979). See also Edward J. Devitt, "The Search for Improved Advocacy in the Federal Courts," 13 *Gonzaga Law Review* 897–933 (November 1978).

46. See Frances Kahn Zemans and Victor G. Rosenblum, *The Making of a Public Profession* (Chicago: American Bar Foundation, 1981).

47. See John J. Osborn, Jr., *The Paper Chase* (Boston: Houghton Mifflin, 1971).

48. See Duncan Kennedy, "How the Law School Fails: A Polemic," 1 *Yale Review of Law and Social Action* 71 (1970).

49. On the development and structure of legal education in the United States, see two works by Robert B. Stevens, "Two Cheers for 1870: The American Law School," in Donald Fleming and Bernard Bailyn, eds., *Perspective in American History* (Cambridge: Harvard University Press, 1971), vol. 5, *Law in American History* pp. 405–58; and "Law Schools and Legal Education, 1879–1979," in 14 *Valparaiso University Law Review* 179–259 (winter 1980).

50. Professor William Carey, a former chairman of the S.E.C., said of Francis T. P. Plimpton that he "can write an indenture in iambic pentameter"; see Geoffrey Helman, "Period Piece Fellow," *The New Yorker*, December 4, 1971, p. 103.

51. Abraham Flexner, *Medical Education in the United States and Canada. A Report by the Carnegie Foundation for the Advancement of Teaching* (New York, 1910). For

a discussion of the effects of the Flexner report, see Rosemary Stevens, *supra* note 10, pp. 66–73.

52. Reed, *supra* note 41, pp. 237–39.

53. Ibid., p. 419. Our notion that the legal profession might be separated into hemispheres, one corporate and one personal, thus has a precursor that is sixty years old. (The old ideas are always best.) The unpalatability of Reed's observation helps to account for the hostile reception given his report. We are resigned.

54. Jerold S. Auerbach, *Unequal Justice: Lawyers and Social Change in Modern America* (New York: Oxford University Press, 1976), pp. 98–100, 106–9.

55. Arthur L. Corbin, "Democracy and Education for the Bar," 4 *The American Law School Review* 731 (1922).

56. See Donna Fossum, "Law School Accreditation Standards and the Structure of American Legal Education," 1978 *American Bar Foundation Research Journal* 515–43 (summer 1978).

57. The medical schools may have overdone their exclusivity; the restrictions on the number of places available in American medical schools resulted in increased pressure to supply the domestic market with physicians trained abroad. Recently, the medical profession has begun to sound the alarm once again, claiming that the United States now has an oversupply of doctors. (U.S. Department of Health and Human Services, Report of the Graduate Medical Education National Advisory Committee to the Secretary, 7 vols. [Washington D.C.: Government Printing Office, 1980] vol. 1, pp. 3, 21–22.)

58. Talcott Parsons, *The Social System* (Glencoe, Ill.: Free Press, 1951) pp. 434–73.

59. Doctors probably feel even more confident about assuming that the health of their individual patients is entirely consistent with the general interest; there are few institutional mechanisms that confront them with the proposition that the common interest might be anything other than the sum of the individual interests of each patient. See Rene Dubos, *The Mirage of Health: Utopias, Progress, and Biological Change* (New York: Harper and Row, 1959).

60. See, e.g., *Time*, April 10, 1978, pp. 56, 66.

61. Abraham S. Blumberg, "The Practice of Law as a Confidence Game: Organizational Cooptation of a Profession," 1 *Law and Society Review* 15–39 (June 1967).

62. New York: Russell Sage, 1976.

63. That is, the lawyer will be paid from the client's award of damages only if the lawyer wins the case. The fee is usually a percentage of the award or settlement—typically, as much as a third.

64. James S. Eisenstein and Herbert Jacob, *Felony Justice: An Organizational Analysis of Criminal Courts* (Boston: Little, Brown, 1977), p. 50; Blumberg, *supra* note 68; idem., *Criminal Justice* (Chicago: Quadrangle, 1967), p. 47.

65. One of the forms of expansion in large law firms has been the growth of "specialty firms," which formerly had relatively few lawyers, into organizations that rival in size the largest of the general corporate law firms. An example in Chicago is Seyfarth, Shaw, Fairweather and Geraldson, a firm specializing in labor law work on the management side. Other specialties where such growth has occurred are litigation and tax, specialties for which there is an especially broad market. Because the flow of work to these firms is less dependent upon a few large clients than upon their reputation for their specialty, they may enjoy greater autonomy. Another type of firm that has grown in recent years is the "boutique specialty firm"—a firm with an even more intense specialization in an even narrower area of corporate law, such as takeover bids or bankruptcies. These firms are usually still relatively small (though

a few of them are now quite large) and most of them are new firms, having been organized within the last few decades. See *supra* note 9.

66. For a thoughtful and systematic consideration of the sociology of the large law firm, see Robert Nelson, *supra* note 2.

67. In his survey of practitioners in large Chicago law firms, Robert Nelson asked, "Have you ever refused an assignment or potential work because it was contrary to your personal values?" Of 222 respondents, only 36 had ever done so and only 12 of these had done so as often as twice.

68. A. J. Liebling, *The Sweet Science* (New York: Viking Press, 1956), pp. 68–71.

69. Harold D. Lasswell and Abraham Kaplan, *Power and Society* (New Haven: Yale University Press, 1950).

70. Johnson, *supra* note 16, pp. 45–46.

71. Ibid, p. 66.

72. See U.S., Congress, Senate, Committee on Government Operations, staff study prepared by the Subcommittee on Reports, Accounting, and Management, "The Accounting Establishment," Doc. 95–34, March 31, 1977. 95th Cong., 1st sess.

73. Johnson, *supra* note 16, p. 46.

74. Jerome E. Carlin, *Lawyers' Ethics: A Survey of the New York City Bar* (New York: Russell Sage, 1966), pp. 176–82; Auerbach, *supra* note 54., pp. 4–7.

75. American Bar Association, Special Committee on Evaluation of Ethical Standards, *Code of Professional Responsibility,* Final Draft, July 1, 1969. Thus, Disciplinary Rule 2–104(A) forbids in-person solicitation of clients who have not requested legal advice. This "ambulance chasing" restriction was upheld against a First Amendment challenge in Ohralik v. Ohio State Bar Association, 436 U.S. 447 (1978). See Andrew Kaufman, *Problems in Professional Responsibility* (Boston: Little, Brown, 1976), pp. 445–63.

76. Carlin, *Lawyers' Ethics, supra* note 74, pp. 66–83. It may be, however, that the potential consumers of legal services who are solicited at the country club are, as a class, more sophisticated than are those solicited in the emergency room, and that only the latter are in need of protection by the machinery of the bar.

77. Carlin, *supra* note 74, pp. 160–61; American Bar Association Special Committee on Evaluation of Disciplinary Enforcement, *Problems and Recommendations in Disciplinary Enforcement* (Chicago: American Bar Association, 1970), pp. 1–9; F. Raymond Marks and Darlene Cathcart, "Discipline Within the Legal Profession: Is It Self-Regulation?," 1974 *University of Illinous Law Forum,* 193–236.

78. The study was conducted by Daniel Cantor and Co., Inc., of Philadelphia; see Doug Lavine, "Corporate Legal Units Moving Up," *The National Law Journal,* October 9, 1978, pp. 1, 11. The same article also notes that 60 corporations responding to a survey by the *New York Law Journal* reported that their in-house legal staffs had grown by an average of 62.5 percent in the preceding five years (i.e., 1973 to 1978); nearly a quarter of the respondents said that their staffs had doubled during that period.

79. Johnson, *supra* note 16, p. 68.

80. Such reasoning assumes, of course, that the corporation will be able to do the work as efficiently and competently as would the law firm.

81. In relatively rare cases, house counsel may even induce a dispute where none existed before. By noting the existence of a potential legal claim that its corporation might make against another business enterprise, counsel may create litigation that otherwise would not have been brought. As we argue below, however, this is unlikely to occur unless it is consistent with business purposes.

82. The status of house counsel appears to have improved recently, consistent with this speculation; see Morris I. Leibman, "The Change in Client Relationships—The Interface with General Counsel," *The Business Lawyer* 34 (1979); 957–62.

83. One of the troubling issues that we raised at the beginning of this consideration of the roles of lawyers and clients in the corporate sector was the ambiguity concerning whether house counsel were to be regarded as lawyers or clients, as a part of their corporations or a part of the bar. When house counsel are not engaged in servicing the legal problems of the corporation but are choosing outside counsel and negotiating with them the fees that they will be paid by the corporation, they are essentially performing the role of the client—acting for the client as its agent, not as its counsel. (To make a legal distinction, house counsel is then acting more as an "attorney-in-fact" than as an "attorney-at-law.") Though house counsel may use different criteria of judgment or different types of expertise than would other corporate officers in making these decisions about the use of outside counsel, the role would nonetheless be the same. Someone would still need to select the lawyers and to scrutinize the fees. House counsel are, in a very real sense, the *consumers* of the services of the corporate law firms.

One part of the legal profession thus regularly performs the role of client of another part of the profession. To what extent does this occur in other professions? Employed engineers probably play a similar role with respect to independent, consulting engineers, but to what extent are consulting engineers regularly or often retained by corporations that already have engineers as employees? The referral from one doctor to another is not analogous—just as referrals among lawyers are not—because in that situation the referring professional is not in any sense the consumer of the services.

84. The source of this information for 1960 and 1970 is *Martindale-Hubbell Lawyer's Directory;* the 1980 information is from the "national law firm survey" of the *National Law Journal,* October 6, 1980, pp. 32–37, and October 13, 1980, pp. 34–39. For the purposes of this analysis, we excluded the firm of Baker and McKenzie, which is conceived as a multicity and, indeed, multinational enterprise.

Much of the growth has occurred in branches in Washington, D.C. A survey in 1980 found that 178 out-of-town firms had branches in Washington, employing nearly 1,800 attorneys; of the 25 largest Washington firms, 7 were branches. In contrast, there were virtually no branches in the early 1970s. "Out-of-Towners Muscle In," *Legal Times of Washington,* June 9, 1980, pp. 26–29, 32.

85. We have interviewed several lawyers, both in Chicago and in Washington, D.C., who have acknowledged that many branch offices do not cover their own costs. (They were understandably reluctant to discuss their own firms' finances on the record, however, and we are therefore not at liberty to cite examples.) See also Orville N. Schell, "The Development of National Law Firms," *The Business Lawyer* 34 (1979): 963–68.

86. See "Crowell & Moring Debuts Friday," *Legal Times of Washington,* May 28, 1979, p. 7. In addition to these management problems, branch offices also increase the likelihood that the firm will become involved in formal conflicts of interest. It constitutes a conflict of interest if lawyers from the same firm represent opposing parties or parties whose interests are likely to be in conflict. Given the number of corporations that come and go as clients and the number of potential relationships and transactions among these corporations, it is quite difficult to monitor the firm's work for the existence of possible conflicts. That difficulty is compounded by branch

offices, where supervision is more difficult. See Westinghouse Electric Corp. v. Kerr-McGee Corp., 580 F. 2d 1311 (7th Cir. 1978), cert. denied, 439 U.S. 955 (1978).

Branch offices also raise issues about the manner in which the income of the firm will be divided. Will income from the main office and all of the branches be pooled, the less profitable branches sharing in the income produced by the more profitable ones, or will the partners who work in a particular branch share only in the revenue generated locally? Put another way, what portion of the profit of a successful branch will be taken by the main office? Such issues can be quite divisive.

87. A senior partner of a major, highly prestigious Chicago law firm told us that one of the firm's most important clients had said to the firm, "Do you want to go to New York with us, or don't you?" He also told us, "Another client took the position that it wasn't a first rate law firm if it wasn't in Washington." The firm went both places. See also Schell, *supra* note 85.

88. As divorce has become more common in polite society, however, matrimonial work has become more acceptable in the large firms, and more now do some of it as an accommodation to the personal needs of corporate executives. But the increasing use of criminal charges in antitrust cases does not yet seem to have resulted in much increase in the criminal work done by large, corporate law firms, apart from the large firms that began as litigation specialty firms. The defense of corporate executives charged with price-fixing is still usually referred to trial lawyers experienced in "white-collar crime" cases.

89. Some litigation specialty firms represented both plaintiffs and defendants in antitrust cases, but those firms were the exception. Litigation specialty firms do most of their work on referral. They thus have few regular clients to whom loyalty might be expected and by whom it might be demanded.

The reason that was often given by the defense firms for avoiding plaintiffs' work was that they did not wish to be in the position of "making law against themselves"—that is, they expressed concern that their work on behalf of an antitrust plaintiff might create a legal precedent that they would then, later, have to overcome in their role as defense counsel in another case. Though this could happen, it is not really very likely. The rationale assumes, first, that the firm's work for the plaintiff would be so ingenious that it would create a legal theory that would not be constructed by other counsel who might represent the plaintiff nor by those who will represent other plaintiffs in similar cases, and thus the law on the subject would in fact be appreciably different than it would have been but for their participation; and, second, that some lawyer from the firm will then have a subsequent case that raises, from the opposing side, exactly that same point of law. The latter of the two necessary assumptions is much more plausible than the former—which is not very plausible at all.

90. See Durkheim, *supra* note 10.

91. John Thibaut and Laurens Walker, *Procedural Justice* (New York: Halsted Press, 1975), chaps. 8 and 12, esp. pp. 78–80, table 8.5; see also Steven LaTour, Pauline Houlden, Laurens Walker, and John Thibaut, "Procedure: Transnational Perspectives and Preferences," 86 *Yale Law Journal* 258 (1976).

92. See Eisenstein and Jacob, *supra* note 64, pp. 19–39.

93. See Moore, *supra* note 6, pp. 28–36; Bronislaw Malinowski, "Magic, Science and Religion," in Malinowski, ed., *Magic, Science and Religion, and Other Essays* (New York: Free Press, 1948), pp. 17–92.

94. Smigel, *supra* note 1, p. 314.

95. Edward Shils, *Center and Periphery* (Chicago: University of Chicago Press, 1975), pp. 4–6, 267–71, 279.

96. Ibid., pp. 301–3.

Name Index

Name Index

Name Index

Weber, Max, 133, 156, 202 n. 13
Williams, Allen, 200 n. 34
Williams, E. Douglass, 177 n. 6, 178 n. 28
Wittich, Claus, 202 n. 13

Wood, Arthur L., 17, 178 n. 1, 184 n. 57
Wootton, Barbara, 202 n. 17

Zander, Michael, 183 n. 48, 205 n. 40

Zehnle, Richard, 182 n. 29, 182 n. 30, 202 n. 10
Zemans, Frances Kahn, 17, 183 n. 48, 184 n. 54, 206 n. 46

Subject Index

Subject Index

Loyola University Law School, 10

Macrostructural theories of prestige generation, 56–57
Martindale-Hubbell Law Directory, 6, 180 n. 10, 209 n. 84
Marxian approach to social organization of legal profession, 16
Matrimonial law. *See also* Divorce law; Family law
  devotion of lawyers to emotional needs of client in, 39
Mediative occupation, 158, 168
Medical profession
  comparison of legal profession with, 137–39
  conceptual framework in, 142–44
  defining work in, 139–42
  co-specialization in, 30
Mergers, handling of, in corporate law, 168–69
Metropolitan origin of lawyer, correlation between prestige and, 74
Michigan, University of, Law School, 10
Minorities, recruitment of for law school, xviii–xix, 7
Moonlighting, 187 n. 15, 188 n. 7
Multicollinearity, 45
Multidimensional scalogram analysis, 49–51, 188 n. 11
  on social structure, 134–35
Multiple regression analysis, 81–84
Municipal law
  distribution of legal effort in, 24, 29
  imputed characteristics of, 68
  prestige ranking of, 58
Mutual interdependence, task specialization associated with, 132

National Science Foundation, xxii
Neighborhood lawyer. *See also* Practice setting(s)/type
  attempts by to handle all legal problems of client, 30
  stability of clientele, 78
  workload of, 131
Networks
  among Chicago lawyers, 4, 28
  of notable Chicago lawyers, 105–13
New York City bar, analysis of, xxi, 18
New York University Law School, 11
No-fault issue, 124, 133
Northwestern University Law School, 10
Notable Chicago lawyers
  characteristics of, 96–105
  defining social organization of by respondent characteristics, 113–21
  gender distribution, 94

likelihood of knowing, 94–96
networks of, 105
racial distribution, 94, 115
smallest space analysis of, 105–13
spheres of influence of, 121–26
Not-for-profit organizations, xix
Notre Dame University Law School, 11

Office practice, distinction between litigation and, 51, 134–36, 202 n. 14
Organic solidarity, 167

Partnership(s)
  clientele of, 2
  growth of large, 11, 12
Patent law
  background of, 2
  distribution of legal effort in, 24, 29
  imputed characteristics of, 68
  origins, 189 n. 16
  practitioner characteristics of, 74, 79
  prestige ranking of, 58
  referral system in, 37–38
  relationship between antitrust law and, 31, 52–53
  as specialty, 12, 22, 26, 27
Patronage occupations, as distinguished from collegiate occupations, 156–58
Pennsylvania, University of, Law School, 11
People persuasion, 38
Personal characteristics, as measure of social differentiation, 41, 42
Personal client sector
  amount of overlap between personal and corporate sectors, 25–26, 200 n. 2
  client relationships in, 171–72
  distinction between litigation and office practice in, 134–36, 202 n. 14
  distribution of legal effort in, 24, 29
  size, separation, and social differentiation of lawyers and clients in, 46
  social differentiation of lawyers and clients in, 134
  specialization within, 33, 130–33
  total legal effort in, 25
Personal injury law, 133
  client status in, 2, 54, 196 n. 43
  client volume, 41
  distribution of legal effort in, 24, 29
  imputed characteristics of, 68, 70, 71
  income derived from, 190 n. 20, 196 n. 43
  practitioner characteristics of, 74, 75, 77, 78
  prestige ranking of, 58, 59–60, 84, 85
  social differentiation within, 53

220

Subject Index

Regular Democratic Organization, 7. *See also* Political affiliation

Regulatory cluster
distribution of legal effort in, 24, 29
innovation in, 39
social differentiation in, 46

Religious affiliation. *See also* Ethno-religious affiliation
of Chicago lawyers, 10
correlation with knowing Chicago notables, 96, 117–18
correlation with prestige, 193 n. 27
as measure of social differentiation, 41, 42, 49

Republican party. *See* Political affiliation

Residential real estate law, 185 n. 11. *See also* Personal real estate law; Real estate law

Response rate, 5–6

Securities law
distribution of legal effort in, 24, 29
imputed characteristics of, 68, 69, 70, 71
practitioner characteristics of, 74, 75, 77, 78, 79
prestige ranking of, 58, 59
relationship with general corporate cluster, 31
social differentiation in, 42

Self-regulation, lawyers support for, 146

Seyfarth, Shaw, Fairweather and Geraldson, 207 n. 65

Smallest space analysis
of Chicago notable networks, 105–13
of occupational prestige, 61–65

Social bonds, kinds and degree of, among lawyers, 4–5

Social differentiation
conclusions on, 52–54
degree of, 40–48
dimensions of, 48–52
effect on legal profession, 37–54
patterns of in legal practice, 22

Social distance, types of, 187 n. 1

Social integration, and division of labor among lawyers, 3–4

Social power, types of, mobilized in corporate sector, 172–74

Socratic method, 149

Solo practice, 76. *See also* General practitioners; Practice setting(s)/type
in criminal defense work, 72
decline of, 11, 14
diversification in, 2
effect of franchised firms on, xx
income levels in, xvii–xviii
loss of power of, xvi

percentage of lawyers in, xvii
prestige of, 74
representation in bar associations, 11

Specialist(s)
distribution of legal work, 28, 29
as function of supply and demand, 27
legal fields dominated by, 22
number of lawyers who consider themselves as, 33–34

Specialization
acceptance of, 12
meaning of, among lawyers, 131–32
measurement of, in legal fields, 22, 26–28

Stanford University Law School, 10

State practice, distinction between federal practice and, 39

Sullivan's Law Directory for the State of Illinois, 6, 180 n. 10

Supporting personnel, size and range of, 186 n. 13

Symbol manipulation, 38

Task specialization, as associated with mutual interdependence, 132

Tax law, 22. *See also* Business tax law; Personal tax law
imputed characteristics of, 68, 69
prestige ranking of, 58, 60

Telephone Secretaries Unlimited, 180 n. 11

Trademark law, as specialty, 12

Treble damage actions, 72–73, 189 n. 16

Trial lawyers, representation of, in Chicago notables, 103–5, 124, 125

Unethical conduct, power to investigate, 146

Union law. *See* Labor union law

United States, number of lawyers in, 13

Urban lawyer(s)
characteristics of, 13
community involvement by, 14

U-shaped distribution of legal work, 50–52, 134

Washington, George, University of, Law School, 11, 12

Watergate, 7

Westinghouse Electric Corp. v. *Kerr-McGee Corp.* (1978), 210 n. 86

White-collar crime, 210 n. 88

Wisconsin, University of, Law School, 10

Women
as Chicago lawyers, xviii–xix, 6–7
as Chicago notables, 94
in large law firms, xix

Yale University Law School, 10

222